Severe intellectual disability can lead to challenging behaviour which may encompass aggression, self-injury, destructiveness, hyperactivity, inappropriate sexual or social conduct and bizarre mannerisms. Such behaviour adversely affects the health and safety of both the person with intellectual disabilities and those who care for them.

In this thoroughly revised and updated new edition, Eric Emerson provides a comprehensive overview of the current findings about the nature, epidemiology, causes and treatment outcomes of challenging behaviour. The material about motivational factors and the relationship between challenging behaviour and psychiatric disorder has been considerably expanded, and the book combines evidence and research drawn from the fields of psychology, psychiatry and medicine. It will be essential reading for clinicians and all health care professionals involved in the assessment and treatment of challenging behaviour.

### From a review of the first edition:

'In *Challenging Behaviour* Emerson carefully defines his terms, sets the problem in the social context, and demonstrates a systematic approach to the analysis and treatment of behavioural pathology in this little understood aspect of learning difficulties . . . and it has the great merit of being set against issues of quality of life.'
    *British Medical Journal*

**Eric Emerson** is Professor of Clinical Psychology at the Institute for Health Research at Lancaster University.

# Challenging behaviour

## Analysis and intervention in people with severe intellectual disabilities

Second edition

Eric Emerson

Institute for Health Research, Lancaster University

CAMBRIDGE
UNIVERSITY PRESS

PUBLISHED BY THE PRESS SYNDICATE OF THE UNIVERSITY OF CAMBRIDGE
The Pitt Building, Trumpington Street, Cambridge, United Kingdom

CAMBRIDGE UNIVERSITY PRESS
The Edinburgh Building, Cambridge CB2 2RU, UK
40 West 20th Street, New York, NY 10011-4211, USA
10 Stamford Road, Oakleigh, VIC 3166, Australia
Ruiz do Alarcón 13, 28014 Madrid, Spain
Dock House, The Waterfront, Cape Town 8001, South Africa

http://www.cambridge.org

First edition published 1995
Second edition published 2001

Printed in the United Kingdom at the University Press, Cambridge

*Typeface* Minion 10.5/14pt    *System* Poltype® [vn]

*A catalogue record for this book is available from the British Library*

*Library of Congress Cataloguing in Publication data*

Emerson, Eric, 1953–
Challenging behaviour: analysis and intervention in people with severe learning
disabilities/Eric Emerson – 2nd ed.
    p.   cm.
Includes bibliographical references and index.
ISBN 0 521 79444 7 (pbk.)
1. Mentally handicapped – Mental health.   2. Mentally handicapped – Behavior
modification.    I. Title.
RC451.4 M47 E44 2000
362.2'7 – dc21    00-058518

ISBN 0 521 79444 7 paperback

---

---

# Contents

# 1

# Introduction

Over one million people across Europe, North America and Australasia have a severe intellectual disability and also show additional problematic or challenging behaviours. These include such behaviours as aggression, self-injury, destructiveness, overactivity, inappropriate social or sexual conduct, bizarre mannerisms and the eating of inappropriate objects. The combination of intellectual and behavioural disabilities can blight the lives of those affected and place the health, safety and welfare of those who care for them in jeopardy. They also represent a significant challenge to agencies involved in the purchase or provision of educational, health and welfare services.

Over the past three decades, behavioural psychology has been particularly influential in shaping the way we think about challenging behaviours. Behaviourally based approaches to intervention have been shown to be effective in bringing about rapid and socially significant reductions in challenging behaviour. They have also, however, attracted considerable controversy.

The goals of this book are twofold: first and foremost, to provide a relatively concise introduction to the area; secondly, to draw attention to some of the more recent developments in the area of applied behaviour analysis and related fields which will need to be incorporated into practice if behavioural approaches are to continue to contribute to the struggle to help people with severe disabilities overcome their challenging behaviours and become more fully participating members of our communities.

This is not, however, a 'how-to-do-it' book. Rather, it will focus on describing those developments in basic and applied research which are likely to have important implications for practice. Those with more pressing practical needs are referred to any one of the number of excellent books and guides which are currently available (e.g. Carr et al., 1994; McBrien & Felce, 1994; Zarkowska & Clements, 1994).

## Terms and definitions

The terminology used to identify and describe people with severe disabilities has undergone numerous changes over the last century. Scientific and lay terminologies also vary between English-speaking countries. Lay and technical terms themselves reflect cultural beliefs and, as they enter the common vocabulary, quickly acquire disparaging connotations. Today's scientific terminology quickly becomes tomorrow's terms of abuse. 'Idiots', 'imbeciles', 'morons', 'subnormals' and 'retards' are, nowadays, nothing more than terms of denigration.

### Intellectual disability

Throughout this book, the term 'intellectual disability' will be used in preference to the UK terms 'learning disability' and 'learning difficulty' and the North American term 'mental retardation'. This choice reflects the emergence of intellectual disability as the preferred terminology within the international scientific community. It avoids the confusion arising from terms which have very different meanings in different countries (e.g. learning disability) and also avoids the use of terms which in many countries have acquired highly disparaging connotations (e.g. mental handicap, mental retardation).

The use of the term intellectual disability should, however, be regarded as being synonymous with the UK term learning disability and the North American term mental retardation. Mental retardation has been defined as referring to

significantly subaverage general intellectual functioning [IQ <70] resulting in or associated with concurrent impairments in adaptive behaviour and manifested during the developmental period (Grossman et al., 1983).

More recently, this definition has been amended to

substantial limitations in present functioning. It is characterised by significantly subaverage intellectual functioning [IQ <75], existing concurrently with related limitations in two or more of the following applicable adaptive skill areas: communication, self-care, home living, social skills, community use, self-direction, health and safety, functional academics, leisure and work. Mental retardation manifests itself before age 18. (Luckasson et al., 1992, p. 5).

People with a *severe* intellectual disability (severe learning disability or severe mental retardation) will, in addition to the above general characteristics, score below 50 on standardized tests of intelligence, show clear signs of significant disabilities in the acquisition of adaptive behaviours from early in life and will need considerably more support than their peers to participate successfully in everyday activities. Most of them will show some evidence of damage to their central nervous system; many of them will have additional physical or sensory handicaps (Hatton, 1998).

**Challenging behaviour**

Over the past decade, the term 'challenging behaviour', initially promoted in North America by The Association for People with Severe Handicaps, has come to replace a number of related terms including abnormal, aberrant, disordered, disturbed, dysfunctional, maladaptive and problem behaviours. These terms have previously been used to describe a broad class of unusual behaviours shown by people with severe intellectual disabilities. They include aggression, destructiveness, self-injury, stereotyped mannerisms and a range of other behaviours which may be either harmful to the individual (e.g. eating inedible objects), challenging for carers and care staff (e.g. noncompliance, persistent screaming, disturbed sleep patterns, overactivity) and/or objectionable to members of the public (e.g. regurgitation of food, the smearing of faeces over the body).

The term challenging behaviour has been defined as

culturally abnormal behaviour(s) of such an intensity, frequency or duration that the physical safety of the person or others is likely to be placed in serious jeopardy, or behaviour which is likely to seriously limit use of, or result in the person being denied access to, ordinary community facilities. (Emerson, 1995).

The term challenging behaviour will be used throughout the remainder of the book for a number of reasons. Firstly, it is free from implicit assumptions regarding the psychological characteristics of the behaviour in question. A number of alternative terms have unhelpful connotations regarding either the organisation of behaviour (e.g. disordered behaviour) or the nature of the relationship between the behaviour and ongoing events (e.g. dysfunctional or maladaptive behaviour). As we shall see, considerable evidence suggests that 'challenging' behaviours may be both orderly, in being integrated within an individual's behavioural repertoire in a coherent fashion, and adaptive, in that they may be functionally related to important events occurring in the person's social environment. Indeed, many challenging behaviours can be construed as (at least in the short term) coherently organized adaptive responses to 'challenging' situations.

Secondly, the term is specific to a socially significant subclass of abnormal, odd or unusual behaviours. Challenging behaviour only refers to behaviours which involve significant risks to people's physical well-being or act to reduce markedly access to community settings. This consequently excludes behaviours which may be either statistically or culturally infrequent but have a less pronounced physical or social impact. Culturally abnormal behaviours shown by people with severe intellectual disabilities which are likely to place the physical safety of the person or others in serious jeopardy include serious physical aggression, destructiveness and self-injury as well as such health-threatening behaviours as the smearing of faeces over the body and the eating of inedible objects. Behaviours which are likely to limit seriously the use of, or result in the person being denied access to, ordinary community facilities include, in addition to all the behaviours listed above, behaviours such as less serious forms of physical and verbal aggression and, perhaps, minor self-injury and stereotypy, i.e. behaviours which may lead to significant levels of avoidance by members of the public (e.g. Jones, Wint & Ellis, 1990). In the main, however, the focus throughout this book will be on more seriously challenging behaviours.

It should be noted that challenging behaviour is not synonymous with psychiatric disturbance. Not all psychiatric disorders (e.g. anxiety, mild depression) place the safety of the person or others in jeopardy, or lead to the person being denied access to community settings. On the other hand, many challenging behaviours appear to be functional adaptive responses to particular environments rather than the manifestations of any underlying psychiatric impairment.

Finally, the use of the term 'challenge' may help to focus our attention on the process by which social problems are defined; that is, it may help to broaden the focus of enquiry by placing individual 'pathology' in the social and interpersonal context in which certain acts are deemed problematic. As Blunden and Allen (1987) point out, the term challenging behaviour

emphasises that such behaviours represent challenges to services rather than problems which individuals with intellectual disabilities in some way carry around with them. (Blunden & Allen, 1987, p. 14).

To construe a situation as a challenge rather than a problem may encourage more constructive responses, although it would, of course, be mistaken to believe that minor changes in terminology are capable of bringing about major changes in practice.

## An overview

Much has been written over recent years on some of the general issues involved in providing community-based services for people with challenging behaviours. The purpose of this book, however, is to address more technical or clinical issues relating to the analysis of, and intervention in, challenging behaviours.

Clinical activities do not, of course, exist in a vacuum. Rather, they need to be seen as an important component of a comprehensive strategy for supporting people with challenging behaviours. Such a strategy can be seen as comprising of four overlapping components (see also Department of Health, 1993; Mansell, McGill & Emerson, 1994b).

- The *prevention* of challenging behaviour through, for example, targeting resources at those considered at greatest risk and ensuring that people with severe intellectual disabilities live, learn and work in enriched environments in which they receive appropriate help and encouragement to develop adaptive and socially appropriate behaviours.

- *Early detection and intervention* to ensure that potential challenges are identified and responded to as they arise. This applies equally to the emergence of challenging behaviour in young children and the identification of signs of potential breakdown in families, residential settings and day services.
- The provision of *practical, emotional and technical support* to people in the places in which they normally live, learn, work and enjoy their leisure to help them overcome their challenging behaviours. This will also require effective approaches for the management of crises.
- For a few people, the *development and support of new places for them to live, learn or work* which will maximise their quality of life while continuing to strive (possibly over many years) to understand and respond appropriately to their challenging behaviour. Such specialized community-based services are likely to require very high levels of practical, emotional and technical support over extended periods of time.

In the remainder of this book the focus, in the terms of the above framework, will be on the content of the types of *technical support* which should be available to people with severe intellectual disabilities. Before that, however, it will be necessary to provide a context within which to place such discussion.

In Chapter 2, 'The social context of challenging behaviour', some of the social processes which are involved in defining behaviour as challenging will be highlighted and some of the personal and social consequences which arise from having a severe intellectual disability and challenging behaviour will be examined. Throughout these discussions it will be argued that challenging behaviour must be seen as a social construction. The implications of this perspective will then be explored in relation to approaches to assessing the social validity of behavioural interventions. Chapter 3, 'Epidemiology', will look at the available evidence regarding the prevalence, incidence and natural history of challenging behaviours. This information will add to our understanding of the social significance of challenging behaviour and will also provide a backdrop against which the successes and failures of intervention may be judged. In addition, the research which has attempted to identify factors which place people at risk of developing challenging behaviour will be reviewed. Such information is important if approaches to the prevention of challenging behaviour are to be efficiently targeted and may give some insight into the types of processes which might underlie challenging behaviours.

In Chapter 4, 'Models and theories', the models and concepts which underlie behavioural approaches to analysis and intervention will be discussed. Attention will be drawn to some of the more recent developments in behavioural theory and practice which are likely to strengthen significantly the effectiveness of behavioural approaches. In addition, the more prominent neurobiological models of challenging behaviour will be briefly reviewed prior to discussion of the possibilities for the integration of behavioural, neurobiological and psychiatric approaches. The discussion of the concepts which underlie behavioural approaches will be continued in Chapter 5, 'The bases of intervention'. Here consideration will be given to some of the broad perspectives and issues which should guide behavioural (and other) approaches to intervention.

In Chapter 6, 'Assessment and analysis', the aims of a behavioural assessment will be discussed in terms of identifying the social impact of the person's challenging behaviour and understanding its behavioural function. This will involve an evaluation of informant-based, descriptive and experimental approaches to assessment.

In Chapter 7, 'Behavioural approaches', behavioural approaches to reducing challenging behaviour will be examined. In doing so, particular attention will be paid to some of the more recent developments in the emerging technology of positive behavioural support (Carr et al., 1999a). These include the modification of 'setting events' or 'establishing operations' to alter the motivational bases of challenging behaviour and the use of functional displacement and skill building to provide the person with more socially appropriate alternatives to challenging behaviour. In Chapter 8, 'Psychopharmacology', the evidence in support of psychopharmacological approaches to reducing challenging behaviour will be briefly reviewed.

In Chapter 9, 'Community-based supports', some of the issues involved in providing effective support to enable people with severe intellectual disability and severe challenging behaviour to be included in their local communities will be highlighted. Finally, Chapter 10, 'Challenges ahead', will summarize and draw together the conclusions arising from the previous chapters. In addition, consideration will be given to the implications of these conclusions for behavioural practice in the twenty-first century.

# 2

# The social context of challenging behaviour

In the first edition of this book, challenging behaviour was defined as culturally abnormal behaviour of such an intensity, frequency or duration that the physical safety of the person or others is likely to be placed in serious jeopardy, or behaviour which is likely to limit seriously use of, or result in the person being denied access to, ordinary community facilities (Emerson, 1995).

This amendment to the definition made by Emerson et al. (1988) made explicit the importance of social and cultural expectations and contextual factors in defining behaviour as challenging. Indeed, the phenomenon of challenging behaviour can only be fully understood when viewed as a social construction, a position which is highly consistent with the 'contextualist' world view of behaviour analysis (Morris & Midgley, 1990).

Whether a behaviour is defined as challenging in a particular context will be dependent on such factors as:

- social rules regarding what constitutes appropriate behaviour in that setting;
- the ability of the person to give a plausible account for their behaviour;
- the beliefs held by other participants in the setting about the nature of intellectual disabilities and the causes of the person's 'challenging' behaviour; and
- the capacity of the setting to manage any disruption caused by the person's behaviour.

Behaviour in social settings is, at least in part, governed by implicit and explicit rules and expectations regarding what constitutes appropriate conduct. In general, the more formal the setting, the more explicit the rules. Indeed, context is essential in giving meaning to any behaviour. Behaviour can only be defined as challenging in particular contexts. For example, loud shouting and the use of 'offensive' language is likely to be tolerated (if not actually condoned) on the factory floor or at a football match; the same behaviour would certainly be 'challenging' during a church service. Physical aggression is positively valued in the boxing ring. Severe self-directed aggression, however, is likely to be seen as challenging when shown by a person with intellectual disabilities, although it may be viewed as a mark of religious piety when shown by a flagellant. At a more mundane level, stereotypic rocking is less likely to be tolerated in public places than in an institution for people with intellectual disabilities or at a nightclub.

Expectations concerning the appropriateness of particular behaviours are also determined by cultural beliefs and general role expectations. Supporting a young man to enjoy an alcoholic drink in the local pub may be seen as a positive achievement by young white staff in a residential service for people with intellectual disabilities, as unremarkable by other customers in the local pub and as highly problematic by the young man's devout Muslim family. Similarly, physical aggression may be seen as being more deviant (in terms of involving a greater discrepancy between performance and cultural expectations) when shown by a woman with intellectual disabilities than when shown by a man.

As well as transgressing social conventions, people with disabilities are also likely to be cast in deviant or abnormal social roles. These roles may serve to modify the operation of contextual rules which ascribe meaning to behaviour. Thus, for example, viewing people with intellectual disabilities as 'eternal children' (Wolfensberger, 1972, 1975) may be associated with a tendency to fail to attribute personal responsibility to challenging behaviour shown by people with intellectual disabilities. In a similar vein, if a person is labelled 'mentally retarded', observers will tend to ascribe their success on a task to external factors such as the ease or simplicity of the task, while ascribing failure to internal factors such as the person's cognitive impairments (Severence & Gastrom, 1977).

These processes may have a number of consequences, including increased tolerance for deviant behaviour, as long as the person is clearly identified as belonging to a defined deviant group. Indeed, the expectations surrounding group membership may include a positive expectation that the person will behave in unusual or odd ways. So, for example, members of the public may show greater tolerance for stereotypic rocking when shown by a person whom they can clearly label as having a intellectual disability than they would of an 'ordinary' member of the public.

The capacity of a setting to cope with any disruption caused by a person's challenging behaviour is also likely to contribute to determining whether they will be excluded. So, for example, the increased pressure in the UK on mainstream schools to demonstrate academic achievement is likely to increase the pressure to exclude pupils with intellectual disabilities who show challenging behaviour (Mental Health Foundation, 1997). Similarly, fluctuations in the levels of experience, competence, stress, stability and fatigue among members of a staff team are likely to determine their capacity to cope with the disruption caused by someone who shows severe self-injury.

Of course, none of these factors is static. The social acceptability of particular behaviours changes over time within and across cultures (e.g. the reduced toler-ance of smoking in public places in the UK and North America). Expectations and norms governing behaviour within settings vary over time and across locations. The meaning of having an intellectual disability is currently undergoing some potentially significant changes. As has been discussed above, the capacity of settings to manage the social disruption caused by challenging behaviour is likely to be influenced by factors ranging from public policy to local fluctuations in staff sickness.

While contextual factors are crucial to defining behaviour as challenging, it would be surprising if there were no commonalities between people and settings in their tendency to perceive particular behaviours as more or less challenging. Emerson et al. (1988) asked service agencies in the south-east of England to identify the two or three individuals with an intellectual disability who presented the greatest challenge to services in their area. Of the 31 people identified, 25 (81%) showed aggressive behaviour, 16 (52%) showed destructive behaviour and eight (26%) showed self-injurious behaviour. More recently, Lowe and Felce (1995a,b) summarized the results of two studies which suggested that the level of social disruption caused by a behaviour was integral to its definition as 'challeng-ing' by carers and care staff. In the first study, analysis of carer and staff ratings collected over a 4-year period on 92 people with intellectual disabilities indicated that behaviours which caused the greatest social disruption (e.g. aggression) or had significant implications for the duty of care exercised by carers or care staff (e.g. running away) were rated as creating the most severe management problems. In the second study, they reported that the probability of referral to specialized challenging behaviour services was significantly increased if the person showed high levels of behaviours which were likely to be socially disruptive (e.g. aggres-sion, noncompliance).

Similarly, Kiernan and Kiernan (1994) employed discriminant function analy-sis to identify factors which distinguished 'more difficult' from 'less difficult' pupils with severe intellectual disabilities in a survey of segregated special schools in England and Wales. The first ten factors, in order of significance for mobile pupils, identified in this analysis were: physical aggression involving significant risk to others; persistent interruption of activities of other pupils; social disruption (e.g. screaming); violent temper tantrums occurring weekly; unpredictability of challenging behaviour; breakage of windows, fixtures and fittings; aggression towards other pupils; lack of understanding of emotions of others; and noncom-pliance.

Consideration of the range of social issues involved in defining behaviour as challenging is important for a number of reasons. Firstly, it highlights the import-ance of acknowledging explicitly the operation of such factors in the definition of challenging behaviour, including operational definitions of challenging behaviour employed in epidemiological research. Many existing definitions (e.g. of self-injurious behaviour: Fee & Matson, 1992) are clearly incomplete, in that socially normative behaviours which do meet the formal properties of the definition are nevertheless excluded from consideration in the resulting literature. Unless we acknowledge the importance of social and cultural factors in defining challenging behaviour, we may be tempted to search for ever more refined mechanical and physical definitions of an inherently social process. Such a course of action would, of course, be doomed to failure.

Secondly, viewing challenging behaviour as a social construction illustrates the complexity of the phenomenon and helps us to begin to identify some possible approaches to intervention. Thus, for example, if a person's minor stereotypy has been defined as challenging primarily due to the avoidance behaviours it elicits in others, intervention in some situations may be most appropriately aimed at reducing such avoidance, rather than eliminating stereotypy.

Finally, there has been considerable concern expressed over recent years regarding the *social validity* of behavioural interventions. An intervention which is socially valid should (a) address a socially significant problem, (b) be undertaken in a manner which is acceptable to the main constituencies involved and (c) result in socially important outcomes or effects (Kazdin & Matson, 1981; Schwartz & Baer, 1991; Wolf, 1978). Re-conceptualizing challenging behaviour as a complex social phenomenon, rather than simply as a problem of aberrant behaviour, has considerable implications for evaluating the social significance of the outcomes of intervention. Prior to discussing this point in more detail, it will be necessary to examine the social impact of challenging behaviours.

## The impact of challenging behaviours

The social significance of challenging behaviours is determined by the interaction of two factors. Firstly, as we shall see in Chapter 4, a significant minority of people with intellectual disabilities show challenging behaviours. Secondly, such behaviours are often associated with a range of negative personal and social consequences.

By definition, seriously challenging behaviours may significantly impair the health and/or quality of life of the person themselves, those who care for them and those who live or work in close proximity. Thus, for example, self-injurious behaviours can result in damage to the person's health. Repeated self-injury may lead to secondary infections, permanent malformation of the sites of repeated injury through the development of calcified haematomas, loss of sight or hearing, additional neurological impairments and even death (cf. Borthwick-Duffy, 1994;

Nissen & Haveman, 1997). Similarly, serious aggression may result in significant injury to others as well as to the person themselves as a result of the defensive or restraining action of others (cf. Konarski, Sutton, & Huffman, 1997; Spreat et al., 1986).

However, the consequences of challenging behaviours go far beyond their immediate physical impact. Indeed, the combined responses of the community, carers, care staff and service agencies to people who show challenging behaviours may prove significantly more detrimental to their quality of life than the immediate physical consequences of the challenging behaviours themselves. These social responses may include abuse, inappropriate treatment, exclusion, deprivation and systematic neglect.

## Abuse

It is, perhaps, not surprising that the difficulties involved in caring for people with challenging behaviours and, in particular, the management of episodes of challenging behaviour, may, at times, lead to inappropriate reactions from carers and care staff. Some of these reactions include physical abuse. Thus, for example, Rusch, Hall and Griffin (1986), in an analysis of documented instances of abuse in a North American institution, identified challenging behaviour as the major predictor of who was likely to be abused. Similarly, Maurice and Trudel (1982) reported that one in 40 ward staff in Montreal institutions for people with intellectual disabilities indicated that their *typical* response to an episode of self-injury was to hit the resident.

## Inappropriate treatment

The challenge posed by severe problem behaviours has, not unnaturally, led services to develop methods of control, not all of which can be considered beneficial to the person themselves. Studies undertaken in North America and the UK suggest that, in many localities, approximately one in two people with severe intellectual disabilities who show challenging behaviours are prescribed neuroleptic (anti-psychotic) medication (Davidson et al., 1994; Emerson et al., in press a; Kiernan, Reeves & Alborz, 1995; Meador & Osborn, 1992; Oliver, Murphy & Corbett, 1987; Robertson et al., in press a).

The widespread use of such powerful psychopharmacological agents raises a number of concerns as: (1) there is little evidence that neuroleptics have any specific effect in reducing challenging behaviours (see Chapter 8); (2) such medication has a number of well-documented serious side-effects including sedation, blurred vision, nausea, dizziness, weight gain, opacities of the cornea, grand mal seizures and a range of extrapyramidal syndromes including parkinsonian syndrome, akathisia, acute dystonic reaction and tardive dyskinesia (Baumeister,

Sevin & King, 1998; Thompson, Hackenberg & Schaal, 1991); (3) prescription practices for people with intellectual disabilities and a clearly diagnosed psychiatric illness have been judged to be inappropriate in many instances (Davis et al., 1998); and (4) the prevalence of prescribing of neuroleptics has been substantially reduced through peer review processes with no apparent negative effects for the majority of participants (Ahmed et al., 2000; Davis et al., 1998). As Singh and Repp (1989) point out, while the results of drug reduction programmes 'are heartening, they suggest that much of the medication was unnecessary when either originally prescribed or by the time the reduction programme was instituted' (Singh & Repp, 1989, pp. 273–4).

Similarly, the use of mechanical restraints and protective devices to manage self-injury gives cause for serious concern. Such procedures can lead to muscular atrophy, demineralization of bones and shortening of tendons as well as resulting in other injuries during the process of the restraints being applied (Griffin, Ricketts & Williams, 1986; Luiselli, 1992a; Richmond, Schroeder & Bickel, 1986; Spreat et al., 1986). Finally, people with severe intellectual disabilities may be at risk of exposure to unnecessarily degrading or abusive psychological treatments (e.g. Altmeyer, Williams & Sams, 1985; G. Allan Roeher Institute, 1988).

## Exclusion, deprivation and systematic neglect

People with challenging behaviours are significantly more likely to be excluded from community-based services and to be admitted, re-admitted to or retained in institutional settings (Borthwick-Duffy, Eyman & White, 1987; Eyman & Call, 1977; Hill & Bruininks, 1984; Intagliata & Willer, 1982; Lakin et al., 1983; Schalock, Harper & Genung, 1981). Once admitted to institutional care they are likely to spend most of their time in materially deprived surroundings (cf. Emerson & Hatton, 1994), disengaged from their world and avoided by staff (Emerson et al., 1992; Mansell, 1994, 1995). They are also at risk of having their needs neglected. Most episodes of inappropriate client behaviours occurring in institutions are ignored by staff (Cullen et al., 1983; Felce et al., 1987) and the low levels of attention which are provided are likely to be disproportionately negative in character (Grant & Moores, 1977).

People with challenging behaviours are also likely to be excluded from services provided *within* institutional settings. Oliver et al. (1987), for example, reported that nearly half of institutional residents with self-injury in the south-east Thames region of England received no programmed day activity. Some of the *socially* undesirable effects of medication and restraint procedures include the general sedative effects of neuroleptic medication (Baumeister et al., 1998), the impact of mechanical restraints in precluding the person's participation in many everyday activities and the effect of restraints in setting the occasion for reduced levels of interaction with carers (Luiselli, 1992a). The little evidence that is available also suggests that, at least for frequent or severe self-injury, the psychological interventions which are provided are more likely to be of a punitive nature (Altmeyer et al., 1987).

Within the community, challenging behaviours may serve to limit the development of social relationships (Anderson et al., 1992), reduce opportunities to participate in community-based activities (Hill & Bruininks, 1984) and prevent access to health and social services (Jacobsen, Silver & Schwartz, 1984). They are also, of course, a major cause of stress experienced by carers (Quine & Pahl, 1985, 1991; Qureshi, 1992; Saxby & Morgan, 1993; Sloper et al., 1991; Stores et al., 1998) and care staff (Bersani & Heifetz, 1985; Hatton et al., 1995; Jenkins, Rose & Lovell, 1997).

Care staff also report that they and significant numbers of their colleagues experience strong emotional reactions such as anger, despair, sadness, fear and disgust in response to episodes of challenging behaviour (Bromley & Emerson, 1995; Harris, Cook & Upton, 1996). Given that services provided to young adults with challenging behaviours living at home with their parents are often insufficient, especially in the area of providing advice or assistance within the parental home to manage effectively episodes of challenging behaviour (Kiernan & Alborz, 1994, 1996; Qureshi, 1992), it is hardly surprising to find that the presence of challenging behaviours is one of the main predictors of whether parents will seek a residential placement for their son or daughter (e.g. Tausig, 1985).

People who show challenging behaviours are unlikely to receive effective psychological support for their challenging behaviours (Emerson et al., in press a; Griffin et al., 1986; Oliver et al., 1987; Qureshi, 1994). Thus, for example, Emerson et al. (in press a) investigated treatment and management practices among 265 people with challenging behaviours who were receiving some form of residential support in 1998. Only 15% of participants had a written behaviourally orientated treatment programme. Given the extensive evidence which now exists in support of the use of such treatment approaches (see Chapters 4 and 7), these data highlight a glaring failure in the extent to which current services for people with severe intellectual disability in the UK embody the principle of 'evidence-based practice'.

## Summary

The above sections illustrate some of the negative ways in which challenging behaviours can shape the lives of people with severe intellectual disability and those who support them. It is important to keep in mind, however, that these are not inevitable consequences which are inherent to the phenomena of challenging behaviour. Rather, they are associations which have arisen in particular service systems located in particular cultures at particular points in time. While, as mentioned in the previous chapter, it would be surprising if there were no commonalities between social responses to challenging behaviour in English-speaking countries, it is important that we keep in mind that these consequences result from the ways in which service systems support (or fail) people with challenging behaviour.

For example, Emerson et al. (1999a) undertook a series of multivariate analyses to identify those personal and environmental characteristics which were associated with variation in a range of aspects of the quality of life among 281 people receiving community-based residential supports from agencies nominated as providing examples of better practice (see also Robertson et al., in press a,b,c). This series of analyses failed to identify any significant relationship between the severity of challenging behaviour shown by participants and their quality of life in areas such as self-determination, contact with members of their family, social inclusion, employment, physical activity, risk and community participation.

## The social validity of intervention outcomes

So far, this chapter has highlighted some of the social processes involved in establishing behaviour as challenging and, in the section above, has drawn attention to aspects of the potential impact of challenging behaviours. In addition, the notion of social validity has been introduced. To recap, it has been proposed that an intervention which is socially valid should (a) address a socially significant problem, (b) be undertaken in a manner which is acceptable to the main constituencies involved and (c) result in socially important outcomes or effects.

The concept of social validity was introduced into behavioural practice in order to address two issues that were considered to underlie the apparent failure of services to implement behavioural procedures which had been 'demonstrated' to be effective (Wolf, 1978). These were:

- conflict between applied behaviour analysts and other stakeholders in the intervention process (e.g. the person with disabilities, their families, staff in service settings, the general public) regarding the appropriateness or acceptability of the intervention procedures themselves; and
- differences between stakeholders regarding the perceived significance of any changes brought about through intervention.

It is clear from the discussion so far in this chapter that challenging behaviour needs to be considered as a complex social phenomenon, both in terms of the processes which lead to particular behaviours being defined as challenging and in terms of the social consequences of people displaying challenging behaviour. This suggests that any attempt to evaluate the successes and failures of behavioural, or any other, approaches to intervention will need to take into account the full range of outcomes which are of significance to the major stakeholders in the intervention process.

Unfortunately, both behavioural research (Meyer & Evans, 1993a,b; Meyer & Janney, 1989; Schwartz & Baer, 1991; Symons, Koppekin & Wehby, 1999a) and psychopharmacological research (Poling & Ehrhardt, 1999; Poling & LeSage, 1995; Symons et al., 1999a) have largely failed to live up to this task. Applied behavioural research has tended to focus solely on demonstrating functional relationships between intervention processes and changes in the rate (or occasionally duration) of challenging behaviours. Thus, for example, Symons et al. (1999a) reviewed the type of outcomes included in studies of self-injurious behaviour published in peer-reviewed journals between 1978 and 1996. Of the 89 behavioural studies identified, only 20 (22%) included information on the impact of the intervention on any aspects of the participants' 'quality of life' other than changes in the severity or frequency of self-injury (see also, Dunlap, Clarke & Steiner, 1999). The vast majority of these studies relied exclusively on anecdotal reports.

Evans and Meyer (1985) have argued the case for expanding current practice to include the assessment of the 'meaningful outcomes' of intervention (see also, Emerson et al., 1991; Horner, 1991; Meyer & Evans, 1989, 1993a,b; Meyer & Janney, 1989). These include the assessment of change in:

- the targeted challenging behaviour and other challenging behaviours shown by the person;
- replacement skills and behaviours, including, for example, the development of self-control strategies to support behaviour change and the development of alternative communicative responses;
- procedures for managing the person's challenging behaviour including use of medication, restraint and crisis management techniques;
- health-related consequences of the person's challenging behaviour such as trauma and skin irritations;
- the restrictiveness of the person's residential and vocational placement;
- broader aspects of the person's quality of life including physical and social integration, personal life satisfaction, affect and the range of choices available to the individual; and
- the perceived significance of the person's challenging behaviour by others (e.g. family, staff, public).

The importance of such a multifaceted approach to evaluating the impact of intervention is, in many ways, self-evident once the significance of social processes in the definition and response to challenging behaviour has been recognized. Thus, for example, a reduction in the rate of a person's self-injury by 75% is unlikely to be of social significance if they remain at risk of losing their sight, continue to be mechanically and psychopharmacologically restrained, and are still avoided by most people and excluded from community settings and activities.

More recently, Fox and Emerson (in press) attempted to identify the outcomes of intervention which were considered particularly salient by a number of stakeholder groups, including people with intellectual disability, parents of people with intellectual disability, clinical psychologists, psychiatrists, nurses, managers and direct support workers. Their results indicated that reduction in the severity of challenging behaviour was considered to be the most important outcome of intervention by approximately half of the stakeholder groups. Other outcomes considered to be the *most* important by stakeholder groups included increased friendships and relationships, changes in the perceptions of individuals by others, the person learning alternative ways of ensuring that their needs are met, and increased control and empowerment. Further, they reported that, while there were high levels of agreement on the relative importance of outcomes between stakeholder groups who did not have an intellectual disability, levels of agreement between people with intellectual disability and all other stakeholder groups did not reach the level of statistical significance.

In adopting broader criteria against which to judge the impact of intervention, however, it is important to ensure that a plausible association exists between the person's challenging behaviour and these wider dimensions of outcome. Thus, for example, it would be inappropriate to assess the effectiveness of an intervention to reduce challenging behaviour in terms of changes in the person's participation in community-based activities unless evidence existed to suggest that their behaviour did, in fact, act as a significant barrier to such participation. While such a relationship may be assumed to operate in general, other factors (e.g. physical isolation of the setting; service policies, resources and orientation) may be much more important in specific situations.

This points to the importance of tailoring the measurement of 'meaningful outcomes' to particular social contexts and, by implication, for conducting an evaluation of the social significance of a person's challenging behaviour prior to intervention. These two issues will be discussed further in Chapter 6.

# 3

# Epidemiology

In this chapter, a number of issues will be addressed which relate to the epidemiology of challenging behaviour. These include:

- the number of people with intellectual disabilities who show challenging behaviour;
- the prevalence of particular forms or topographies of challenging behaviour;
- the co-occurrence of different forms of challenging behaviour;
- personal and environmental 'risk factors' associated with showing challenging behaviour; and
- the emergence and persistence of challenging behaviour.

Epidemiological studies of challenging behaviours have focussed, almost exclusively, on attempting both to identify the *prevalence* of particular behaviours and investigate the relationship between prevalence and personal or environmental risk factors. In other words, they have attempted to identify the number of individuals in the population under study (e.g. total population of Lancaster) who, at a given point in time, show challenging behaviour and, through the use of correlational methods, to identify those personal and environmental characteristics associated with people being at increased risk of exhibiting these behaviours.

Prevalence rates vary as a function of the incidence and duration (or persistence) of a particular disorder (Kiely & Lubin, 1991). Incidence is a measure of the number of new 'cases' appearing within a given population within a specified period of time (e.g. number of live births per year of children with Down's syndrome in Lancaster, number of people *developing* self-injurious behaviour per year in Cardiff). Duration or persistence is a measure of the length of time a condition is present (e.g. life expectancy of people with Down's syndrome, mean number of years a person will show self-injurious behaviour). As Kiely and Lubin point out, in the hypothetical case in which neither incidence nor duration vary, prevalence may be calculated as the product of incidence and duration (i.e. $P = I \times D$).

Unfortunately, there are few, if any, studies which directly address the issue of the incidence of challenging behaviours among people with intellectual disabilities (see, for example, the review of the incidence and prevalence of self-injurious behaviour provided by Johnson & Day, 1992) and only a limited number of studies which address the issue of the duration or persistence of challenging behaviour (see below).

## The prevalence of challenging behaviours

In Chapter 2, stress was placed on the importance of social processes in leading to particular behaviours being seen as challenging. One implication of this approach is that attempts to measure the prevalence of challenging behaviour are themselves bound by the constraints and expectations of particular contexts and cultures. Estimates of the prevalence of challenging behaviour will also, of course, be influenced by such methodological factors as the selection of operational definitions, methods of case identification (e.g. review of case notes vs. interview with care staff) and the overall sampling strategy adopted within the study (e.g. total administratively defined population of people with intellectual disabilities, children with intellectual disabilities at school).

Relatively few studies have attempted to identify the prevalence of multiple forms of challenging behaviour among all people with intellectual disabilities in the total population living in a defined geographical area. More commonly, studies have focussed on determining the prevalence of specific forms of challenging behaviour (e.g. self-injurious behaviour: Hillery & Mulcahy, 1997; Oliver et al., 1987; aggression: Harris, 1993) or have restricted sampling to specific subpopulations of people with intellectual disabilities; for example, those living in institutional settings (e.g. Griffin et al., 1987; Maurice & Trudel, 1982), community settings (e.g. Rojahn, 1986) or children attending schools (e.g. Kiernan & Kiernan, 1994).

The results of two relatively large-scale studies, both of which were undertaken in 1987, will be used in order to illustrate some of the issues involved in the epidemiological study of challenging behaviour; one of these studies was undertaken in the north-west of England (Kiernan & Qureshi, 1993; Qureshi, 1994; Qureshi & Alborz, 1992), the other in California (Borthwick-Duffy, 1994). Both studies sought to identify the prevalence of various forms of challenging behaviour among the total population of people with intellectual disabilities in a defined geographical area. In both studies, 'people with intellectual disabilities' were operationally defined as people receiving services for people with intellectual disabilities.

Qureshi, Kiernan and colleagues conducted their survey in seven administrative areas in the north-west of England with a total (general) population of 1.54

million. They screened approximately 4200 people with intellectual disability and identified people as showing serious challenging behaviours if they had either:

- at some time caused more than minor injury to themselves or others, or destroyed their immediate living or working environment;
- shown behaviours at least once a week that required the intervention of more than one member of staff to control, or placed them in danger, or caused damage which could not be rectified by care staff or caused more than one hour's disruption; or
- shown behaviours at least daily that caused more than a few minutes' disruption.

Using this definition, 1.91 people per 10 000 of the general population (range 1.41–2.55 per 10 000 across the seven areas) were identified as having an intellectual disability and serious challenging behaviour. This translates to an estimated prevalence rate of 7% of all people within these areas who had been administratively defined as having an intellectual disability. Two recent studies have employed very similar methods, again in north-west England. Emerson and Bromley (1995) identified 3.33 people per 10 000 of the general population as having an intellectual disability and serious challenging behaviour (equivalent to 8% of the people with intellectual disabilities who were screened) in an additional administrative area with a general population of 0.21 million.

Emerson et al. (in press b) repeated the procedures used in the 1987 study in two of the original areas (total population, 0.47 million). Using a slightly amended definition of 'serious', they reported overall prevalence rates of 3.62 people per 10 000 of the general population as having an intellectual disability and serious challenging behaviour (equivalent to 8% of the people with intellectual disabilities who were screened). Combining the results of these three studies gives an overall prevalence for serious challenging behaviour of 2.40 per 10 000 of the general population or 7.3% of people administratively defined as having an intellectual disability.

Borthwick-Duffy (1994) examined the prevalence of challenging behaviours among 91 164 people with intellectual disabilities served by the California Department of Developmental Services. People were identified as showing one or more of four possible types of challenging behaviour on the basis of data derived from their annual Client Development Evaluation Report. These were:

- *aggressive behaviour*, defined as one or more violent episodes causing serious physical injury (requiring immediate medical attention) to others within the last year;
- *frequent and severe self-injurious behaviour*, defined as behaviour causing severe self-injury and requiring a physician's immediate attention at least once

**Table 3.1.** Prevalence of different forms of challenging behaviours

| | Kiernan & Qureshi, 1993; Qureshi, 1994; Qureshi & Alborz, 1992; Emerson & Bromley, 1995; Emerson et al., in press b (base $n = 7286$) | Borthwick-Duffy, 1994 (base $n = 91164$) |
|---|---|---|
| | Behaviour rated as | |
| | Present and serious management problem (%) | Present (%) |
| Physical aggression | 2.1 | 2.1 |
| Self-injury (frequent and severe) | 1.3 | 2.2 |
| Self-injury (frequent) | — | 9.3 |
| Property destruction | 1.3 | 7.1 |
| Other | 3.4 | — |

a month and/or behaviour causing minor self-injury and requiring first aid at least once per week;

- *frequent self-injurious behaviour*, defined as self-injurious behaviour occurring at least once per week; and
- *property destruction*, defined as serious property destruction within the past year and/or minor property damage on six or more occasions within the past year (Borthwick-Duffy, 1994, p. 9).

On the basis of this exercise, 18 826 people were identified as showing challenging behaviour. This is equivalent to 14% of the population of people with intellectual disabilities who were screened or 6.33 per 10 000 of the general population.

The discrepancy in overall prevalence rates between these two studies may be due to a number of factors including differences in the operational definitions employed to identify people as showing challenging behaviour and differences in the populations studied. In particular, the inclusion of the category 'frequent self-injurious behaviour' in the Californian study is likely to have led to people being identified in that study who may not have been identified in the UK study. While behaviours in this category were markedly more prevalent than behaviours in other categories (see Table 3.1), the data do not allow for the identification of those people who only showed frequent self-injury (see discussion below on the co-occurrence of different forms of challenging behaviour).

## Types of challenging behaviours

Table 3.1 summarizes the data from these two studies, providing general prevalence estimates for physical aggression, self-injury, property destruction and, for the Kiernan, Qureshi, Alborz, Emerson and Bromley series of studies, other forms of challenging behaviour.

Of course, each of these broad groups of challenging behaviours is likely to contain a range of specific behavioural topographies. Studies which have focussed on the prevalence of particular forms of challenging behaviour provide a more detailed breakdown of the topographical variants contained in general classes of challenging behaviours. Harris (1993), for example, reported that the most prevalent forms of aggression shown in the previous month by 168 people with intellectual disabilities identified in one administratively defined area were: punching, slapping, pushing or pulling (51% of people showing aggression); kicking (24%); pinching (21%); scratching (20%); pulling hair (13%); biting (13%); head-butting (7%); using weapons (7%); and choking, throttling (4%). Similarly, Emerson et al. (in press b) reported that the most prevalent behaviours shown by 153 people with intellectual disabilities who showed aggression were: hitting others with their hands (75% of people showing aggression); verbal aggression (60%); hitting others with objects (41%); meanness or cruelty (34%); scratching (27%); pulling hair (23%); pinching (20%); and biting (16%).

Oliver et al. (1987) reported that the most common topographies of self-injurious behaviour shown by 596 people with intellectual disabilities identified through a total population survey carried out in south-east England were: skin picking (39%); self-biting (38%); head punching/slapping (36%); head-to-object banging (28%); body-to-object banging (10%); other (10%); hair removal (8%); body punching or slapping (7%); eye poking (6%); skin pinching (4%); cutting with tools (2%); anal poking (2%); other poking (2%); banging with tools (2%); lip chewing (1%); nail removal (1%); and teeth banging (1%). It should be noted that, in both studies, the totals add up to more than 100% due to the co-occurrence of different forms of challenging behaviour in the same individual, an issue which will be discussed in more detail below.

An illustration of the range of behaviours which may be defined as challenging in a particular type of setting is provided by Kiernan and Kiernan (1994). In a postal survey of a sample of day schools for children with severe intellectual disabilities in England and Wales, they identified 22% of the school population as presenting some degree of challenge, including 8% of the school population who were identified as presenting a significant challenge. The forms of challenging behaviour shown by the 'more' and 'less' challenging groups are presented in Table 3.2.

**Table 3.2.** Challenging behaviours shown by 'more' and 'less' challenging pupils of segregated day schools for children with **severe intellectual disabilities** in England and Wales

|  | 'More' challenging $n = 367$ (%) | 'Less' challenging $n = 662$ (%) |
|---|---|---|
| Aggression | 42 | 17 |
| Social disruption | 36 | 12 |
| Temper tantrums | 34 | 10 |
| Self injurious behaviour | 33 | 15 |
| Physical disruption | 31 | 8 |
| Destructive behaviours | 27 | 7 |
| Noncompliance | 27 | 10 |
| Rituals | 24 | 14 |
| Stereotypy | 19 | 15 |
| Wandering | 18 | 6 |
| Masturbation in public | 13 | 8 |
| *Average number of behaviours shown per child* | *4.1* | *1.7* |

## The co-occurrence of challenging behaviours

As has been indicated, people may show more than one form of challenging behaviour. Thus, in the Kiernan, Qureshi, Alborz, Emerson and Bromley series of studies, between one-half and two-thirds of people identified as showing challenging behaviour did so in two or more of the four possible areas of aggression, self-injury, property destruction and 'other' behaviour (Emerson et al., in press b; Emerson & Bromley, 1995; Qureshi, 1994).

Similarly, analysis of the Californian data indicated that, once the two categories of self-injurious behaviour were collapsed, 11% of the population sampled showed just one form of challenging behaviour, 3% two forms and 1% all three forms (Borthwick-Duffy, 1994). Thus, of those identified as showing challenging behaviour, 25% did so in more than one of the three possible areas (aggression, self-injury, property destruction). Murphy et al. (1993) report that, of the people with self-injurious behaviour identified in south-east England who wore protective devices, 40% also showed physical aggression and 36% property destruction. Indeed, the occurrence of self-injury appears to be the single most important predictor of whether people with intellectual disabilities will show aggressive behaviours (Davidson et al., 1996).

In addition to the co-occurrence of challenging behaviour across broadly defined categories, people are also likely to show multiple forms of challenging behaviour within categories. Thus, for example, Oliver et al. (1987) report that 54% of the people identified as showing self-injurious behaviour engaged in more than one form of self-injury. Indeed, 3% (20 of the 596) engaged in five or more different forms of self-injury, which rose to 7% for people whose self-injury was sufficiently severe to justify the use of protective devices (Murphy et al., 1993). Emerson et al. (in press b) used the Behavior Problems Inventory to provide a more detailed breakdown of the co-occurrence of challenging behaviours among all people with intellectual disabilities in two localities ($n = 264$). Overall, 79% of the participants who showed serious or controlled aggression showed two or more forms of aggressive behaviours, while 19% showed five or more forms. Similarly, 72% of participants who showed serious or controlled self-injury showed two or more self-injurious behaviours, while 26% showed five or more forms.

## Personal and environmental risk factors

One of the more potentially significant contributions of epidemiological research is to identify those personal and environmental factors which are associated with variation in the prevalence of a particular disorder. The identification of such 'risk factors' is obviously important if preventative interventions are to be targeted appropriately. It may also point to possible social and/or biological causal mechanisms. Provided below is a brief summary of the evidence regarding some of the better established correlates of challenging behaviour among people with intellectual disabilities.

### Gender

In general, boys and men are more likely to be identified as showing challenging behaviour than girls and women (Di Terlizzi, Cambridge & Maras, 1999). This relationship appears to be more pronounced:

- for aggression and property destruction than for self-injury (Borthwick-Duffy, 1994; Johnson & Day, 1992; Oliver et al., 1987; Rojahn, 1994);
- in institutional settings (Qureshi, 1994); and
- for more severe challenging behaviour (Kiernan & Kiernan, 1994).

Thus, for example, 73% of the people identified as showing both property destruction and aggression in the Californian survey were men, compared with 53% of people who showed frequent self-injury and 49% of those who showed no challenging behaviour. There is, however, some evidence to suggest that women may be more likely to show multiple topographies of self-injurious behaviour (Maurice & Trudel, 1982; Maisto, Baumeister & Maisto, 1978).

## Age

The overall prevalence of challenging behaviours appears to increase with age during childhood, reach a peak during the age range 15–34 and then decline (e.g. Borthwick-Duffy, 1994; Kiernan & Kiernan, 1994; Oliver et al., 1987; Rojahn, 1994). When comparisons are made with the age structure of the total population of people with intellectual disabilities, it is apparent that challenging behaviours appear to be particularly over-represented in the 15–24 age group (Kiernan & Qureshi, 1993). However, when comparisons are made with the predicted age structure of the population of people with *severe* intellectual disabilities, it appears that age-specific prevalence rates may not decline until late middle age (Emerson et al., in press b). These patterns are more complicated, however, when the prevalence of particular forms of challenging behaviour are examined. Oliver et al. (1987), for example, report that while multiple topographies, head-to-object banging, head punching and finger chewing are significantly more prevalent in younger people with self-injurious behaviour, skin picking and cutting with tools are more prevalent among older people.

## Specific syndromes and disorders

An increase in the prevalence of some particular forms of challenging behaviour has been reported to occur in association with specific syndromes associated with intellectual disabilities. These include:

- occurrence of self-injurious behaviour, specifically hand and lip biting, among *all* people who have Lesch–Nyhan syndrome (Anderson & Ernst, 1994; Harris, 1992; Nyhan, 1994);
- very high prevalence of self-injurious hand-wringing in Rett syndrome (Harris, 1992);
- greater than expected prevalence of various forms of self-injurious behaviour in the Cornelia de Lange, Riley–Day and Fragile-X syndromes (Harris, 1992);
- greater than expected prevalence of hyperkinesis, attention deficits and stereotypy in Fragile-X syndrome (Borghgraef et al., 1990; Einfeld et al., 1999; Lachiewicz et al., 1994; Turk, 1998);
- greater than expected prevalence of self-injury among people with autism spectrum disorders (Ando & Yoshimura, 1978; Lewis & Bodfish, 1998);
- high prevalence of challenging behaviours in Prader–Willi syndrome (Clarke & Boer, 1998; Clarke et al., 1996; Dykens, Cassidy & King, 1999; Dykens & Kasari, 1997; Einfeld et al., 1999; Holland, 1999; Murphy, 1994; Symons et al., 1999b).

In addition, an increased prevalence of challenging behaviour has been reported among people with epilepsy, both in general (cf. Kiernan & Kiernan, 1994) and in relation to specific forms of epilepsy (e.g. Gedye, 1989a,b).

### Level of intellectual impairment

In general, the prevalences of aggression, property destruction, self-injurious behaviour and other forms of challenging behaviours are positively correlated with degree of intellectual impairment (e.g. Borthwick-Duffy, 1994; Hillery & Mulcahy, 1997; Johnson & Day, 1992; Kiernan & Kiernan, 1994; Kiernan & Qureshi, 1993; Oliver et al., 1987; Oliver, 1993; Qureshi, 1994; Rojahn, 1994). Thus, for example, in the Californian survey, 7% of people with mild mental retardation, 14% of people with moderate mental retardation, 22% of people with severe mental retardation and 33% of people with profound mental retardation showed one or more forms of challenging behaviour (Borthwick-Duffy, 1994). People with more severe intellectual impairment are also likely to show multiple forms of challenging behaviour (Borthwick-Duffy, 1994; Oliver et al., 1987; Rojahn, 1986, 1994) and, if self-injurious, are more likely to be restrained (Oliver et al., 1987).

### Additional disabilities

In addition to the overriding effects of level of intellectual impairment, challenging behaviours are more likely to be seen in people who:

*   have additional impairments of vision or hearing (e.g. Kiernan & Kiernan, 1994; Maisto, Baumeister & Maisto, 1978; Schroeder et al., 1978);
*   are non-verbal or who have particular difficulty with receptive or expressive communication (e.g. Bott, Farmer & Rhode, 1997; Borthwick-Duffy, 1994; Dura, 1997; Emerson et al., in press b; Kiernan & Kiernan, 1994; Schroeder et al., 1978; Sigafoos, in press);
*   have poorer social skills (Duncan et al., 1999);
*   are reported to have periods of disturbed sleep (Kiernan & Kiernan, 1994);
*   have mental health problems (e.g. Borthwick-Duffy, 1994).

Self-injury, in particular, is markedly more prevalent among people with severe intellectual disabilities who have significant impairments of mobility (Kiernan & Kiernan, 1994; Kiernan & Qureshi, 1993).

### Setting

The prevalence of challenging behaviour is also positively related to the level of restrictiveness in the person's residential placement (Borthwick-Duffy, 1994; Bruininks et al., 1994; Emerson, 1992; Johnson & Day, 1992; Harris, 1993). Again, data from the Californian survey indicate that 3% of people living independently, 8% of people living with their families, 9% of people living in smaller (1–6 place) community facilities, 24% of people living in larger community-based facilities and 49% of people living in institutions show one or more forms of challenging behaviour (Borthwick-Duffy, 1994).

The interpretation of the relationship between setting and challenging behaviour is problematic due to the important role played by severity of intellectual disability and challenging behaviour in increasing the risk of admission and re-admission to more restrictive settings (Borthwick-Duffy et al., 1987; Eyman & Call, 1977; Hill & Bruininks, 1984; Intagliata & Willer, 1982; Lakin et al., 1983; Schalock et al., 1981). Indeed, since studies of deinstitutionalization have failed to identify any consistent effects on challenging behaviour reported by key informants (Emerson & Hatton, 1994; Larson & Lakin, 1989; Young et al., 1998), it would appear that such behaviours lead to institutionalization, and not that institutional environments lead to challenging behaviour.

## Summary

A number of interlinked personal and environmental characteristics have been associated with variations in the prevalence of challenging behaviour. Unfortunately, due to methodological limitations and the use of relatively simplistic approaches to analysis, it is not possible to identify the unique contribution made by individual factors. For example, such factors as increased mortality among people with challenging behaviour (Borthwick-Duffy, 1994; although also see Nissen & Haveman, 1997; Wieseler, Hanson & Nord, 1995) and among people with more severe intellectual disabilities may account, in part, for the noted decline in the prevalence of challenging behaviour during adulthood. It is to be hoped that future research will help untangle this and other issues. Nevertheless, the existing data do provide a basis for identifying those populations most at risk and are suggestive of some possible underlying mechanisms, an issue to which we shall turn in Chapter 4.

## The natural history of challenging behaviours

As noted above, little is known about the natural history of challenging behaviours. The information which is available, however, suggests that seriously challenging behaviours are likely to have their onset in childhood (Guess & Carr, 1991; Murphy et al., 1999) and may be highly persistent over time.

## Onset

A number of retrospective studies have reported that seriously challenging behaviours are likely to have their onset in childhood. Murphy et al. (1993), for example, report that the mean age of onset for people whose severe self-injurious behaviour was managed by protective devices was 7 years of age. Similarly, Emerson et al. (1988) reported that, of the 29 individuals (mean age 28 years) identified by service agencies as being the 'most challenging', 27 had entered some form of institutional care. The average age of admission for this group was 9.6 years, admissions often being for the same challenging behaviours they were displaying nearly two decades later. Schneider et al. (1995) reported that approximately two-thirds of a group of people with self-injurious behaviour were reported by their parents to have commenced self-injuring by the time they were 5 years old.

More recently, Murphy et al. (1999) followed up for 18 months a cohort of 17 young children (mean age at recruitment to the study, 5 years 7 months) who had been identified by teachers as *beginning* to show self-injury *in the previous 3 months*. While, as a group, participants showed evidence of increased duration of self-injury over the study period, considerable variation was shown by individual participants. The only factor identified as being associated with the trajectory of the children's self-injury over time was the level of concern expressed by teachers at the onset of the study.

## Persistence

Very few studies have examined the course of challenging behaviour over time. Kiernan et al. (1997) reported that 63% of 179 people identified as showing 'more demanding' challenging behaviour in a total population survey under- taken in 1987 were still showing 'more demanding' challenging behaviour when followed up 7 years later. Turner and Sloper (1996) reported persistence rates of over 80% over a 10-year period for many categories of challenging behaviour shown by children with Down's syndrome. On a more modest scale, Stenfert Kroese and Fleming (1993) reported that only one of a group of 17 children with challenging behaviour showed no challenging behaviour over each of the following 3 years.

A number of studies have examined the persistence of specific forms of chal- lenging behaviour. Schroeder et al. (1978), for example, reported that 54 of 101 people with self-injury in a large institutional setting showed no change or deterioration in their self-injury over a 3-year period. More dramatically, Windahl (1988) reported that, of people identified in a Swedish special hospital in 1975 as showing self-injurious behaviour, 87% of those who remained in the institution and 97% of those who had been relocated to another provision were still showing self-injurious behaviour 10 years later. Similarly, Murphy et al. (1993) reported that 52 out of 54 people who showed severe self-injurious behaviour were still injuring themselves at a similar level 2 years later. Kiernan & Alborz (1996) reported persistence rates for severe self-injurious behaviour of 75% over a 5-year period for a cohort of 44 young adults with intellectual disabilities living with their families. Emerson et al. (1996a) reported persistence rates for severe self-injurious behaviour of 72% over a mean $8\frac{1}{2}$-year follow up of a cohort of 55 children who attended a behaviourally orientated residential special school. Finally, Emerson et al. (in press c) reported persistence rates for severe self-injurious behaviour of 71% over a 7-year follow-up period among a total population sample of 95 people with severe self-injurious behaviour.

Leudar, Fraser and Jeeves (1984) in a 2-year follow up of 118 adults with intellectual disabilities reported extremely high levels of persistence of aggression (see also Eyman, Borthwick & Miller, 1981). Kiernan and Alborz (1996) reported persistence rates of 83% for aggression and of 70% for destructive behaviour over a 5-year period for a cohort of 44 young adults living with their families. Reid and Ballinger (1995) reported that behaviours such as social withdrawal and stereotypies were highly stable over a 16–18 year period among a group of 67 people with severe intellectual disabilities.

Evidence from the long-term follow up of intervention studies provides a similarly bleak picture. Schroeder, Bickel and Richmond (1986) report that *all* of the 52 individuals who had received treatment in a specialized facility for people with severe self-injurious behaviour (Schroeder et al., 1982) still required 'high level behavior management programs' 8 years later.

While there is ample evidence that behavioural interventions may bring about significant reductions in challenging behaviour over the short to medium term (see Chapters 4 and 7), evidence from long-term follow-up studies indicates that such gains rarely involve the elimination of challenging behaviour and may be difficult to sustain. Schroeder and MacLean (1987), for example, report that only 4% of individuals receiving treatment in a specialized facility (Schroeder et al., 1982) remained free from self-injurious behaviour after 2 or more years of discharge. Indeed, it is notable that, even in celebrated cases of long-term successes, the individuals concerned were reported to continue to exhibit low-level challenging behaviour, at least on a periodic basis.

Foxx (1990), for example, reported a 10-year follow up of Harry, a man with severe intellectual disabilities and severe self-injurious behaviour. At the time of the initial intervention, Harry was 22 years old. His self-injury, which had started in infancy, was managed through the use of hinged arm splints and a face mask. Assessment suggested that self-injury was negatively reinforced by escape from social demands and positively reinforced by access to restraints. Intervention focussed on: (1) the fading of restraints from arm splints and a face mask to spectacles and, later, a baseball cap; (2) reinforcing compliance during high-demand situations with praise, physical contact, drinks and access to restraints; and (3) punishing self-injury through the implementation of a brief 5-minute time-out period, without restraints. These procedures rapidly reduced Harry's self-injury to very low levels, made use of mechanical restraint unnecessary and enabled him to participate in a much wider range of community-based activities The achievements were all maintained over the following 10 years (Foxx, 1990; Foxx & Dufrense, 1984). However, the data presented also indicated that Harry's self-injury and need to self-restrain still persisted, albeit at a very low level, and that his self-injury partially re-emerged after 7 years in response to him commencing a supported employment programme.

Jensen and Heidorn (1993) also reported a 10-year follow up of the treatment of severe self-injurious behaviour shown by a 27-year-old man with severe intellectual disabilities. By the time of the initial intervention, he had blinded himself through his self-injurious eye poking which appeared to have emerged in response to an untreated eye infection. He also rubbed his head on walls, floors and other objects, and dug his nails into his forehead and nose; these behaviours resulted in him losing cartilage from his nose and developing a large lesion above his eye. His self-injury was (ineffectively) managed by the use of physical restraints for up to 17 hours per day. Assessment indicated that his self-injury was multiply controlled; in low-demand situations it appeared to be maintained by socially mediated positive reinforcement while in high-demand situations it appeared to be maintained by escape from demands. Intervention, therefore, combined differential reinforcement of other behaviour (DRO), escape extinction and stimulus fading (Heidorn & Jensen, 1984). Ten-year follow-up data indicated significant reductions in actual injury, minimal rate of self-injury, discontinuation of the use of restraint and reduction in medication. Again, however, his self-injury did persist, albeit in a different form and at a much lower rate. As Jensen and Heidorn state, 'in recent years he is reported to pick at his skin and then pick or scratch at the scabs. He reportedly can pick at one scab for several months at a time . . . occasionally he will become agitated and put his thumb in his eye, make loud vocalisations, and drop to the floor on his knees' (Jensen & Heidorn, 1993).

Very few studies have attempted to identify personal or environmental characteristics associated with variations in the persistence of challenging behaviours. Kiernan et al. (1997) reported that persistence of 'more demanding' challenging behaviour among 179 people between 1988 and 1995 was associated with participants in 1988 showing: more severe challenging behaviour; more severe self-injurious behaviour (and specific topographies of self-injury); more frequent stereotypy; more severe intellectual disability; poorer communication skills, self-care skills and lower ability to use money; and lower ability to occupy themselves constructively or to behave appropriately in social situations. Emerson et al. (in press c) examined the persistence of self-injurious behaviour in a subsample of 95 people taken from the Kiernan et al. study. They reported that self-injury status at follow up was predicted with 76% accuracy by a logistic regression model containing three variables: site of injury (higher persistence being shown by people exhibiting head-directed self-injury); reported (greater) stability of self-injury when first identified; and (younger) age. Finally, Shoham-Vardi et al. (1996) examined the personal and environmental characteristics associated with people being re-referred to a crisis intervention service. They reported that, among younger participants, not living with their family and exhibiting self-injurious behaviour were the strongest predictors of re-referral. Among older participants, aggression was the strongest predictor of re-referral.

While caution must be taken in extrapolating from such a restricted database, the available evidence does suggest that severe challenging behaviours may be highly persistent *despite* discharge from specialized congregate care settings or significant changes in staffing resources and the quality of the physical environment (Emerson & Hatton, 1994; Larson & Lakin, 1989; Young et al., 1998). The possible chronicity of challenging behaviours points to the need for services to develop the capacity to manage effectively the physical, personal and social consequences of severe self-injurious behaviours over considerable periods of time, an issue which will be discussed in more detail in Chapter 9.

## 4

# Models and theories

The previous chapters have concentrated on defining the social significance of challenging behaviour on the basis of its prevalence, persistence and the impact such behaviours may have on the person themselves and those who support them. Attention was also drawn to some of the personal and environmental 'risk factors' which are associated with variation in the prevalence and, to a lesser extent, persistence of challenging behaviour. In this chapter, we will turn our attention to trying to understand why a substantial minority of people with severe intellectual disability show challenging behaviour.

Behavioural and neurobiological/psychiatric traditions have dominated applied research within the field of intellectual disabilities. These approaches have generated voluminous amounts of basic and applied research and have lead directly to the development of approaches to intervention, many of which have been empirically validated. This is not to say that other approaches – other 'ways of knowing' – have no contribution to make to furthering our understanding of challenging behaviour (see, for example, Meyer & Evans, 1993b; and commentaries by Baer, 1993; Evans & Meyer, 1993; Ferguson & Ferguson, 1993; Kaiser, 1993; Morris, 1993). Rather, it would appear that research within alternative paradigms has either been largely unproductive (e.g. psychoanalytic interpretations of challenging behaviour: see Carr, 1977) or is still in its relative infancy.

As a result, this chapter will first summarize the results of research undertaken within these two traditions before exploring possible interconnections between them.

## Applied behaviour analysis

Since the late 1940s, psychologists have sought to apply principles derived from learning theory to the solution of social problems, including the performance deficits and challenging behaviours shown by people with intellectual disabilities. These attempts have been accompanied by, and have themselves made a significant contribution to, a revolution in our understanding of the nature of severe intellectual disabilities.

Early demonstrations of the power of simple behavioural techniques played an important role in challenging the idea that people with severe disabilities have little potential for change (e.g. Azrin & Foxx, 1971; Bailey & Meyerson, 1969; Lovaas et al., 1965; Tate & Baroff, 1966; Ullman & Krasner, 1965). Tate and Baroff (1966), for example, describe the use of brief time-out from social contact to reduce the severe self-injurious behaviour of a 9-year-old boy with intellectual disabilities. His self-injury, which consisted of 'banging his head forcefully against floors, walls, and other hard objects, slapping his face with his hands, punching his face with his fists, hitting his shoulder with his chin, and kicking himself', had resulted in partial detachment of his right retina and the development of a 7 cm haematoma on his forehead. His self-injury had been treated, without success, for the previous 4 years by individual and group psychotherapy, and drugs. Intervention (in the first phase of the study) consisted of the withdrawal of all social contact for 3 seconds following each self-injurious act, which resulted in his self-injurious behaviour rapidly reducing from an average of one hit every 9 seconds to one hit every 10 minutes.

The explicit focus of the early behavioural approaches on the *environmental* determinants of behaviour stood in stark contrast to prevailing conceptions which were based on the notion that challenging behaviours were most appropriately viewed as being the external manifestations of internal pathology. The growing influence of the behavioural model drew attention to the impact of the environment on the behaviour of people with severe disabilities, including the types of environments provided within institutional services (e.g. Bijou, 1966).

Initial successes in the use of behavioural approaches led to their increasing use. In 1968, the emergence of the discipline of applied behaviour analysis was marked by the launch of the *Journal of Applied Behaviour Analysis*. In its first issue, Baer, Wolf and Risley (1968) described the basic nature of applied behaviour analysis as it *ought* to be practised. They suggested, and reiterated 20 years later (Baer, Wolf & Risley, 1987), that applied behaviour analytic studies should be:

- *applied* – in that the behaviours and events studied should be of importance to society;
- *behavioural* – in that studies should be concerned with what people actually do;
- *analytic* – in that studies should provide a 'believable demonstration', usually through demonstrating experimental control, that changes in behaviour are linked to the environmental events postulated;
- *technological* – in that the techniques used to change behaviour are identified and described in a manner that allows their replication;

- *conceptually systematic* – in that the procedures used are shown to be related to basic behavioural principles;
- *effective* – in that socially significant changes in behaviour are achieved; and
- *general* – in that the behavioural change achieved 'proves durable over time . . . appears in a wide variety of possible environments or . . . spreads to a wide variety of related behaviours'.

Since then, the practice of applied behaviour analysis has steadily advanced both in its traditional areas of application and in many new fields. The application of applied behaviour analysis to the field of severe intellectual disabilities has primarily focussed on two related areas: enhancing people's competence and reducing challenging behaviours (cf. Bailey et al., 1987; Carr et al., 1999a; Dunlap, Clarke & Steiner, 1999; Matson et al., 1996; Remington, 1991). Many studies have demonstrated the success of behavioural approaches in teaching skilled behaviour and in motivating people's participation (e.g. Bellamy, Horner & Inman, 1979; Gold, 1980). Increasingly, these techniques are being used to support people's active participation in integrated settings (e.g. Scotti & Meyer, 1999).

More importantly, in the context of the present book, applied behavioural analysis has revolutionized thinking about the causes and management of seriously challenging behaviours (Carr, 1977). The dominant approach within applied behaviour analysis has been to view challenging behaviours as examples of *operant behaviour*: that is, they are seen as forms of behaviour which are shaped and maintained by their environmental consequences. In this sense, challenging behaviours are seen as functional and adaptive; they are behaviours which have been 'selected' or shaped through the person's interaction with their physical and, more importantly, social world. In lay terms, they can be thought of as behaviours through which the person exercises control over key aspects of their environment.

The consequences which shape or maintain behaviour are termed reinforcers. Two types of contingent relationship between behaviour and reinforcers are important in establishing and maintaining operant behaviour.

- *Positive reinforcement* refers to an increase in the rate of a behaviour as a result of the contingent *presentation* of a reinforcing stimulus (positive reinforcer). Illustrative examples of positive reinforcement include pressing a light switch to switch on the lights in a room (operant behaviour: pressing switch; positive reinforcer: light going on), smiling and saying hello to a colleague to initiate further conversation (operant behaviour: smiling and saying 'hello'; positive reinforcer: conversation), and requesting a drink when thirsty (operant behaviour: asking for drink; positive reinforcer: being given a drink).
- *Negative reinforcement* refers to an increase in the rate of a behaviour as a result of the contingent *withdrawal* (or prevention of occurrence) of a reinforcing stimulus (negative reinforcer). Illustrative examples of negative reinforcement

include completion of a piece of work in order to escape hassle from your manager (operant behaviour: completion of work; negative reinforcer: withdrawal of/escape from demands) and the *avoidance* of potential crashes and fines by stopping at red traffic lights when driving (operant behaviour: stopping at red lights; negative reinforcer: avoidance of fines and/or crashes).

The operant approach to understanding behaviour has three important characteristics. Firstly, it is concerned with the discovery of *functional relationships* between behaviours and environmental factors. Secondly, it places a strong emphasis on the importance of the *context* in which behaviour occurs. Finally, it views the behaviours shown by a person as the product of a *dynamic system*.

## The importance of function

Applied behaviour analysis focusses on the discovery of functional relationships between events. This is illustrated in the definitions of reinforcing and punishing stimuli, response classes and in the nature of credible evidence within behaviour analysis.

In behavioural theory, reinforcing stimuli are defined functionally, solely in terms of the impact which their withdrawal or presentation has upon subsequent behaviour. Positive reinforcers, for example, are those stimuli which increase the rate of a behaviour when presented contingently. They cannot be defined or identified independently of their function; that is, no a priori assumptions are made regarding whether particular types or classes of stimuli are reinforcing. Instead, the capacity of a particular stimulus or event to act as a reinforcer in a particular context must be demonstrated.

This reliance on functional definitions leads to behavioural theory appearing highly circular or tautological: behaviour changes being due to the contingent presentation or withdrawal of reinforcers; reinforcers being those events which, when presented or withdrawn contingent upon behaviour, bring about change. One way round this problem has been provided by the notion of response deprivation which conceptualizes reinforcement contingencies as constraints imposed on the preferred distribution of behaviour in a particular context (Konarski et al., 1981; Realon & Konarski, 1993; Remington, 1991). Imagine you were locked in a room with this book and with nothing else to do but pace up and down. If you were free to do as you wished (technically, under conditions of a free operant baseline), you may choose to read for 80% of your time and pace for the remaining 20% (for the sake of simplicity we will ignore all the other creative activities you could invent in such a situation). Theoretically, it would be possible to introduce constraining relationships which would lead to either reading or pacing to act as reinforcers for each other. For example, pacing could be used to reinforce reading if you had to read for 90 minutes before being allowed to pace for 10 minutes.

Alternatively, reading could be used to reinforce pacing if you had to pace for 30 minutes before being allowed to read for 70 minutes.

The key here is that the constraining relationship will act as a reinforcer if it results in an imbalance in your preferred or optimal distribution of activities. Specifically, a reinforcing contingency will exist if the ratio of reinforcer to response in the constrained condition is less than the ratio of reinforcer to response under free operant baseline. In the first example, above, 10/90 is less than 20/80; in the second, 70/30 is less than 80/20. Similarly, punishment contingencies through 'response satiation' could be implemented by ensuring that the ratio of reinforcer to response in the constrained condition is *greater* than the ratio of reinforcer to response under free operant baseline.

The concern within applied behaviour analysis with the analysis of functional relationships also extends to the way in which behaviour is classified. So far we have used the term operant behaviour; it would be more accurate, from the perspective of behavioural theory, however, to talk about behaviours which are members of an operant *response class.* In a behavioural analysis, attention is normally directed to determining the effect (or function) that a person's behaviour may have on their environment, rather than the particular form (or topography) of behaviour. For example, a behaviour analyst would be interested in understanding the conditions under which you pressed a light switch rather than on how you pressed it (e.g. with your fingers, elbow or arm). Behaviours which result in the same environmental effects are classified as members of the same response class. In most experimental research, the focus of attention lies on the environmental determinants or control of response classes (e.g. lever pressing). Little attention has been paid to examining the inter-relationships between the actual behaviours which may be members of a particular response class (Mace, 1994a).

Finally, the concern of behaviour analysts with the study of functional relationships and their reliance on functional definitions has implications with regard to what is seen as 'credible evidence' in behavioural studies. As we have seen, one implication of defining reinforcement contingencies functionally is that such relationships need to be demonstrated. The notion that credible evidence requires experimental manipulation is reflected in the suggestion that applied behaviour analysis should provide a 'believable demonstration', *through demonstrating experimental control,* that observed changes in behaviour are linked to the suggested environmental events (Baer et al., 1968, 1987). We shall see below that this reliance in the behavioural community on the use of experimental control to provide 'believable demonstrations' has (at times quite unhelpfully) focussed attention almost exclusively on the relationship between challenging behaviour and a limited range of proximal environmental factors.

### The contextual control of behaviour

Analysis of the context in which behaviour occurs is fundamental to the behaviour analytic perspective. Contextual factors influence behaviour in two ways. Firstly, they establish the motivational base which underlies behaviour. Secondly, aspects of the context in which behaviour occurs may provide important information or cues to the individual concerning the probability of particular behaviours being reinforced.

As we have seen, the behavioural approach makes no assumptions regarding the capacity of particular stimuli or events to function as reinforcers. Indeed, behavioural theory suggests that the reinforcing power of stimuli needs to be *established* by contextual relations (Bijou & Baer, 1978; Kantor, 1959; McGill, 1999; Michael, 1982, 1993; Wahler & Fox, 1981).

For example, food is only likely to operate as a positive reinforcer if the person is denied free access to it and also if, among other things, they have not recently eaten. Indeed, food could in other contexts (e.g. immediately after a very large meal or during a stomach upset) operate as a negative reinforcer (increasing behaviours which lead to the withdrawal or postponement of the presentation of food) or a positive punisher (decreasing behaviours which are 'rewarded' by the presentation of food). Similarly, a particular classroom task may only become aversive (and consequently become established as a negative reinforcer) for a child when repeated over a short period, when presented in a noisy or stressful setting, or when the child is ill. Social contact with adults may become aversive (and hence act as a negative reinforcer) after the experience of sexual abuse.

Thus, personal, biological, historical and environmental contexts influence the motivational basis of behaviour by determining or establishing the reinforcing and punishing potential of otherwise neutral stimuli. Michael (1982) introduced the term *establishing operation* to describe such relationships. He defined this as 'any change in the environment which alters the effectiveness of some object or event as reinforcement and simultaneously alters the momentary frequency of the behavior that has been followed by that reinforcement' (Michael, 1982, pp. 150–1).

In addition to this motivational influence, aspects of the contexts in which behaviour occurs may gain 'informational value' as a result of their previous association with variations in the probability with which particular behaviours have been reinforced, i.e. contextual *discriminative stimuli* distinguish between situations in which specific consequences for a given behaviour are more or less likely. So, for example, an 'out of order' notice on a lift provides information regarding the operation (or not) of a particular contingency (the probability of button pressing being followed by the appearance of a lift). An oncoming driver flashing their lights may have informational value in signifying the operation of a police speed trap (contingency – behaviour: speeding; consequence: fine). The difference between these two general classes of antecedent or contextual stimuli is crucial. In lay terms, establishing operations and stimuli change 'people's behaviour by changing what they want . . . [as opposed to discriminative or conditional stimuli, which change] . . . their chances of getting something that they already want' (Michael, 1982, p. 154).

These basic arrangements between A(ntecedent) : B(ehaviour) : C(onsequence) comprise what is commonly described as the *three-term contingency* which defines *discriminated operant behaviour*; that is, operant or 'voluntary' behaviour which shows contextual sensitivity to informational as well as motivational factors.

In recent years, experimental analyses of human behaviour have lead to an expansion of interest in the informational value of stimuli in order to encompass the area of conditional relations (the contextual control over the 'meaning' of discriminative stimuli: Sidman, 1986), and the role of verbal rules in regulating human behaviour (Hayes, 1989). The latter issue is crucial to our understanding of much human behaviour. Skinner (1966) suggested that, while the operant behaviour of nonhumans is directly shaped by reinforcement contingencies, much human behaviour is *rule governed*; that is, he suggested that verbal rules (instructions and self-instructions) play an important role in mediating between environmental contingencies and our behaviour.

An example of the importance of verbal rules is provided by the comparison of the performance of people and nonhumans on a simple experimental task. On a fixed-interval schedule of reinforcement, the reinforcer (e.g. food, money, points) becomes available after a *fixed* period of time has elapsed since it was last presented (e.g. 30 seconds). Thus, the next appropriate response (e.g. bar press, button push) after the reinforcer becomes available will be reinforced. In this situation it does not matter at all what the person does in the intervening period. The most cost-efficient strategy would be to simply wait for the fixed period of time to finish, respond in order to access the reinforcer and then start waiting again. Nonhumans rarely do this. Typically, their rate of responding (e.g. lever pressing) will increasingly accelerate during the interval. Adults who are not briefed regarding the nature of the task, however, usually do one of two things: either they show the type of efficient pattern of responding described above (wait–respond–wait–respond), or they show a consistently high rate of responding throughout, which is a remarkably inefficient strategy. The most plausible explanation of these differences lies in the types of verbal rules people have formulated about the task (Lowe, 1979). People who show the (efficient) low rate of responding will, when debriefed, tend to describe the nature of the task reasonably accurately (e.g. being able to earn points after waiting for a while). People who show the (inefficient) high rate of responding, however, tend to describe the task (inaccurately) as one in which points are earned on the basis of *how many times* they respond.

While trivial in itself, this example does illustrate two important points. Firstly, verbal rules (or self-instructions) formulated by people mediate between the actual contingency and performance. Secondly, such rules may lead to inefficient (or inaccurate) performance. Indeed, one of the characteristics of rule-governed behaviour is its tendency to make people insensitive to changes in the actual contingencies operating on behaviour (Hayes, 1989).

A key question, given our current interests in accounting for the behaviour of people with severe intellectual disabilities, concerns the conditions under which rule-governed behaviour is likely to emerge. Unfortunately, there are no clear answers to this issue. Some evidence suggested that, on the type of simple experimental task described above, the performance of preverbal infants showed no evidence of rule governance, the performance of children over 5 years of age appeared to be predominantly rule governed, and the performance of children in an intermediate age range of $2\frac{1}{2}$–4 years showed a mixed and confusing pattern of responding (Bentall, Lowe & Beasty, 1985). More recent evidence, however, has described performance assumed to be characteristic of rule governance in preverbal infants (Darcheville, Rivière & Wearden, 1993). The only safe assumption, it would appear, is that the concept of rule-governed behaviour *may* have some relevance to the explanation of the challenging behaviours shown by people with severe intellectual disabilities. As Hastings and Remington (1994a) point out, however, it is likely to be highly relevant to understanding the behaviour of carers and staff towards people with challenging behaviour. This latter point will be discussed in more detail in Chapter 9.

## A systems approach

In the real world, we live, work and play in settings in which we could potentially engage in an enormous range of behaviours, *all* of which will be under the control of different reinforcement contingencies. As a result, what we actually do needs to be seen as the product of a complex and dynamic behavioural system, rather than reflecting the operation of one discrete contingency on a particular behaviour (Schroeder & MacLean, 1987; Scotti et al., 1991a; Voeltz & Evans, 1982; Willems, 1974). The study of variables influencing choice between competing alternative behaviours has been at the forefront of experimental research for many years (Davison & McCarthy, 1988; Fisher & Mazur, 1997; Mace, 1994a). In addition, there has been a long-standing interest within both experimental and applied research on the 'side-effects' of particular contingencies of reinforcement or approaches to intervention (e.g. Balsam & Bondy, 1983; Hutchinson, 1977; Newsom, Favell & Rincover, 1983; Staddon, 1977). These issues will be given further consideration at a number of points in the following chapters.

## Applied behaviour analysis and challenging behaviour

Viewing challenging behaviours shown by people with intellectual disabilities as examples of operant behaviour has opened up two avenues of approach. Firstly, in primarily analytic studies, it led to the search for the contextual factors and environmental consequences responsible for maintaining challenging behaviours. Secondly, it opened up the possibility of developing intervention or treatment techniques based on either the modification of naturally occurring contingencies or the introduction of new contingencies in order to reduce the rate of the challenging behaviours or increase the rate of competing behaviours.

In the sections below, evidence relevant to the idea that challenging behaviours shown by people with severe intellectual disabilities may be maintained by their environmental consequences will be reviewed. Following this, a parallel notion, that challenging behaviours may be maintained by their *internal* consequences, by processes of automatic or perceptual reinforcement, will be discussed (Carr, 1977; Kennedy, 1994a; Lovaas, Newsom & Hickman, 1987; Vollmer, 1994). Finally, two alternative behavioural approaches to understanding challenging behaviour will be mentioned. In these approaches, challenging behaviours are seen as examples of respondent behaviour (learned reflexive behaviour which is elicited by environmental stimuli) or as schedule-induced behaviour (behaviour which occurs as the 'side-effect' of other behaviour–environment relationships).

### The positive and negative reinforcement hypotheses

These complementary approaches suggest that challenging behaviour may be maintained by a process of either positive or negative reinforcement. This idea is represented schematically (and simplistically) in Figure 4.1.

Firstly, aspects of the personal and environmental context interact to produce a particular motivational state. This, in effect, establishes the reinforcing potential of previously neutral stimuli. It is also, when matched with a particular learning history and the presence of discriminative stimuli which signal the availability of reinforcement, likely to precipitate an episode of challenging behaviour. Reinforcement of the challenging behaviour will contribute to the person's learning history by increasing the probability that such behaviour is likely to occur in the future in response to similar motivational and environmental conditions.

For example, let us assume that a young man with severe intellectual disabilities has not eaten for a number of hours and is hungry (biological state). He is sitting in the lounge of a small community residence with little to do, but with no obvious threats to his immediate safety (environmental context). He would quite like something to eat (motivational state: food becomes established as a potential positive reinforcer). He does not have the skills (personal context: current

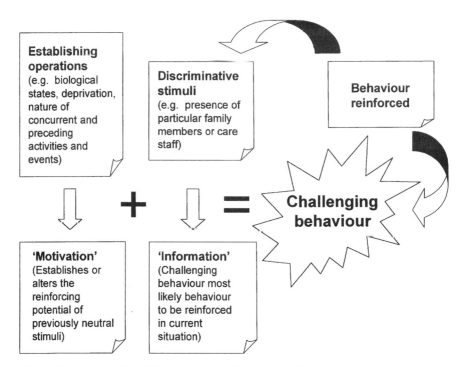

Figure 4.1.   Schematic representation of the operant model of challenging behaviour.

behavioural repertoire) or opportunity (environmental context) to prepare his own food. A member of staff wanders in with a hamburger (environmental context: discriminative stimulus indicating presence of food and presence of someone capable of providing food). As a result of previous learning (personal context: learning history), he begins to moan, cry and bite his hand. The member of staff, who is trying to eat his hamburger, correctly guesses that he is 'communicating' his desire to have something to eat and yells to a colleague in the kitchen to bring the young man a biscuit (positive reinforcement: delivery of food).

In another scenario, a young woman with severe intellectual disabilities is feeling irritable and jumpy. She is about to start her period (personal context: biological state). She is being asked to complete a complex task in her noisy and hot supported work placement (environmental context). The combination of these factors makes her feel very stressed indeed (motivational state: work tasks become established as a negative reinforcer). She does not have the negotiating skills (personal context: current behavioural repertoire) or opportunity (environmental context) to postpone the task to another day. A sympathetic work colleague comes over (environmental context: discriminative stimuli indicating possibility of escape). As a result of her previous experience (personal context: learning history), she begins to moan, cry and bite her hand. The sympathetic colleague notices her distress, feels upset at the sight of it and persuades her job coach to let her have a break (negative reinforcement: escape from work task).

Each of these examples has three common themes.

- Firstly, a motivational state is established by the interaction of personal (biological) and environmental conditions (hunger plus few competing activities; menstrual state plus noise/heat). This motivational set establishes the reinforcing potential of otherwise neutral stimuli (food; work tasks).
- Secondly, through previous experience, the person has learned that specific 'challenging' behaviours are more likely to be reinforced by the presentation/ withdrawal of these reinforcers under certain conditions (presence of particular discriminative stimuli: members of staff).
- Finally, the *co-occurrence* of the motivation state and discriminative stimuli evokes an episode of challenging behaviour which is subsequently reinforced by contingent presentation (or withdrawal) of the pertinent reinforcer.

Four sources of evidence indicate that some examples of challenging behaviours shown by people with severe intellectual disabilities may be maintained by their environmental consequences. These are: (1) descriptive studies which have examined the context in which challenging behaviours occur; (2) experimental studies which have demonstrated the contextual control of challenging behaviour; (3) experimental studies which have directly manipulated the contingencies hypothesized to maintain challenging behaviour; and (4) experimental studies which have directly manipulated the contingencies operating on competing members of the response class containing challenging behaviour.

## Descriptive studies

At the simplest level, a number of descriptive studies have examined aspects of the social context in which challenging behaviours occur. Edelson, Taubman and Lovaas (1983), for example, observed 20 young people with intellectual disabilities residing in a state institution in North America. They recorded, for approximately 5 hours for each participant, occurrences of self-injurious behaviour and various staff behaviours directed towards the young person (e.g. demands, denial, punishment, praise). Their results indicated that, for 19 of the 20 participants, rates of self-injury escalated markedly in the period immediately following staff demands, denials or punishment. While other explanations cannot be ruled out, such results are certainly consistent with the notion that the participants' self-injury may have been maintained by a process of negative reinforcement; that is, the presentation of a potential negative reinforcer (staff contact) may have elicited the behaviour (self-injury) which may have been reinforced in the past by the subsequent withdrawal of staff contact.

More recently, Emerson et al. (1995, 1996b) employed the statistical technique of lag sequential analysis to examine the relationship between staff behaviour and the severe challenging behaviours shown by five children and one young adult with severe intellectual disabilities. Analysis of 8 hours of observation per participant undertaken in their everyday settings indicated that 28 of the 34 separate forms of challenging behaviour shown by the participants occurred in situations which were consistent with them being maintained by a process of either positive or negative reinforcement.

Additional data from descriptive studies, which are consistent with the notion that challenging behaviours may be maintained by processes of positive or negative reinforcement, are provided by Hall and Oliver (1992, 2000), Maurice and Trudel (1982), and Toogood and Timlin (1996).

### Experimental demonstrations of the contextual control of challenging behaviour

More convincing evidence in support of the operant hypothesis is provided by experimental demonstrations of the contextual control of challenging behaviour. Two types of studies are relevant here. Firstly, numerous studies have demonstrated that challenging behaviour is reliably more likely to occur under the types of environmental conditions which are consistent with the behaviour being maintained by a process of positive or negative reinforcement (e.g. Iwata et al., 1982, 1994a). Secondly, a growing number of studies have demonstrated the contextual control of such (apparently) functional relationships (e.g. Carr, Newsom & Binkoff, 1976).

Iwata et al. (1982), in a classic study, used an alternating treatment design to examine the effect of context on the self-injurious behaviour of nine children with intellectual disabilities. They recorded the rates of self-injury shown under four different conditions, selected as representing three general cases of contexts under which self-injury maintained by operant processes may occur, and one control condition.

In the *social disapproval* condition, an adult was present throughout, but did not interact with the child except to express concern or mild disapproval (e.g. 'don't do that') on the occurrence of self-injury. This condition was assumed to be discriminative for the occurrence of self-injury maintained by positive social reinforcement. In the *academic demand* condition, an adult was present throughout and encouraged the child to complete an educational task using a graduated (ask–show–guide) prompting procedure. However, the adult withdrew their attention for 30 seconds contingent on any self-injury shown by the child. Such a condition was assumed to be discriminative for self-injury maintained by negative social reinforcement (i.e. escape from demands). In the *alone* condition, no adults or materials were present, a condition assumed to be discriminative for behaviours maintained by automatic or perceptual reinforcement (see below). The *control* condition consisted of a stimulating environment in which social attention is delivered contingent upon the nonoccurrence of self-injury.

Each child was observed under each condition for 15 minutes on at least four occasions. The order of presentation of the conditions was random. Of the nine children, two showed their highest rates of self-injury under conditions of academic demand, one under conditions of social disapproval and three while alone. The remaining three children showed undifferentiated responding across conditions. Thus, one-third of the children showed patterns of self-injury which were consistent with their behaviour being maintained by environmental consequences.

Recently, Iwata et al. (1994a) have summarized the results of such *experimental functional analyses* for 152 people with intellectual disabilities who showed self-injurious behaviour, 93% (142) of whom had a severe intellectual disability. Of the 152 people, 38% showed patterns of responding consistent with their self-injury being maintained by negative reinforcement, 26% showed patterns of responding consistent with their self-injury being maintained by positive reinforcement, 21% showed patterns of responding consistent with their self-injury being maintained by internal or automatic reinforcement, 5% showed patterns of responding consistent with their self-injury being maintained by multiple controlling variables (e.g. positive and negative reinforcement), and 10% showed undifferentiated or unpredictable patterns of responding.

Similarly, Derby et al. (1992) reported the cumulative results of similar brief analytic procedures conducted on various forms of challenging behaviour shown by 79 people with intellectual disabilities. Their data were consistent with the notion that, of these different forms of challenging behaviour, 29% were maintained by negative reinforcement, 22% by positive reinforcement and 15% by automatic reinforcement. The controlling variables for the remaining 34% were unclear.

Similar approaches have been used to demonstrate the contextual control of aggression (Derby et al., 1992; Emerson, 1990; Hall, Neuharth-Pritchett & Belfiore, 1997; Mace et al., 1986; Paisey, Whitney & Hislop, 1991), destructive behaviours (Bowman et al., 1997; Fisher et al., 1998a), running away (Piazza et al., 1997a), inappropriate social behaviour (Frea & Hughes, 1997), pica (Goh, Iwata & Kahng, 1999; Piazza, Hanley & Fisher, 1996; Piazza et al., 1998a), breath holding (Kern et al., 1995) and hand mouthing (Goh et al., 1995). Other types of experimental conditions (and hence types of potential reinforcers) employed in these studies have included continuous social attention (Oliver, 1991), delayed access to food (Durand & Crimmins, 1988), noise (Iwata et al., 1994a), contingent access to individually defined reinforcers (Day et al., 1988), medical examination

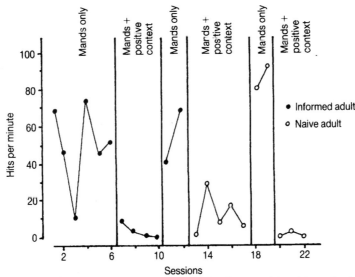

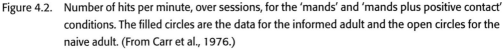

Figure 4.2.   Number of hits per minute, over sessions, for the 'mands' and 'mands plus positive contact' conditions. The filled circles are the data for the informed adult and the open circles for the naive adult. (From Carr et al., 1976.)

(Iwata et al., 1990a), adults talking to each other (Mace et al., 1986), response cost (Steege et al., 1989) and differing forms of instructional demands (Fisher et al., 1998a).

These experimental functional analyses have provided 'believable demonstrations' that, for many participants, challenging behaviour is reliably more likely to occur under the types of environmental conditions which are consistent with the behaviour being maintained by a process of positive or negative reinforcement; that is, they have demonstrated a form of contextual control over challenging behaviour which is consistent with the operant hypothesis.

A growing number of studies have taken this issue further by demonstrating the contextual control of the types of (apparently) functional relationships demonstrated by experimental functional analyses, providing data which are consistent with the role played by contextually specific *establishing operations* in creating the conditions under which processes of positive or negative reinforcement may or may not occur (McGill, 1999; Smith & Iwata, 1997).

In one of the earliest of such studies, Carr, Newsom and Binkoff (1976) demonstrated that the self-injurious head hitting shown by Tim, an 8-year-old boy with intellectual disabilities and autism, was reliably elicited by adult requests (compared with other types of interaction and free time). They then went on to show that changing the context in which the requests were made brought about dramatic changes in Tim's behaviour (see Figure 4.2). When interaction consisted solely of requests ('mands' in behavioural terminology), his self-injury occurred, as previously, at very high rates. However, when the time between making the same requests was filled with telling Tim a story, his self-injury immediately dropped to near-zero levels. Perhaps the most plausible explanation of these results is that adult requests functioned, in certain contexts, as a negative re-inforcer for Tim's self-injury (i.e. he had in the past learned that his self-injury would lead to the withdrawal of requests). What is particularly interesting in this study, however, is the dramatic demonstration of the contextual control of this functional relationship and that relatively small changes in the situation (telling a story) appeared to be capable of totally disrupting this powerful relationship (see also Kennedy, Itkonen & Lindquist, 1995).

More recent studies have identified a wide range of variables which, for particular individuals, appear to determine whether challenging behaviours are likely to occur under the types of environmental conditions which are consistent with the behaviour being maintained by a process of positive or negative re-inforcement. These have included: location (Adelinis et al., 1997); music (Durand & Mapstone, 1998); illness or pain (Carr, Reeve & Magito-McLaughlin, 1996; Carr & Smith, 1995; Kennedy & Meyer, 1996; O'Reilly, 1997); sleep deprivation (Horner, Day & Day, 1997; Kennedy & Meyer, 1996; O'Reilly, 1995); prior activity (Kennedy & Itkonen, 1993; O'Reilly, 1999; O'Reilly & Carey, 1996; O'Reilly, Lancioni & Emerson, in press); food deprivation (Wacker et al., 1996a); delay in or cancelling of previous activities; mood (Carr et al., 1996); and the presence of idiosyncratic variables such as small balls, puzzles and magazines (Carr, Yarbrough & Langdon, 1997).

### Experimental manipulations of the reinforcing contingencies hypothesized to be maintaining challenging behaviour

The strongest evidence in support of the operant model is provided by those studies which have demonstrated control over challenging behaviours by manipu-lating the contingencies of reinforcement which are hypothesized to maintain them. If a behaviour is maintained by a process of positive reinforcement, preventing the reinforcer occurring contingent on the behaviour should lead to the *extinction* of the behaviour. Similarly, if a behaviour is maintained by a process of negative reinforcement, preventing the withdrawal of the reinforcer contingent on the behaviour should lead to the extinction of the behaviour (the latter technique is referred to as negative or escape extinction).

Some of the earliest evidence supporting the operant model used this approach (Lerman & Iwata, 1996). Lovaas and Simmons (1969), for example, demonstrated that withholding adult attention led to the extinction of the severe self-injurious behaviours shown by two boys with severe intellectual disabilities. They then went on to reinstate, before finally eliminating, the self-injury shown by one of the boys by providing 'comforting' attention contingent on his self-injury. The 'comforting' attention which led to a rapid *worsening* of his self-injury consisted of such natural responses as holding his hand and reassuring him that everything was 'OK'. Lovaas has subsequently referred to such 'humane' reactions as an example of 'benevolent enslavement', in that the good intentions of carers in comforting the child appeared themselves primarily responsible for maintaining the self-injury (Lovaas, 1982). More recently, Zarcone et al. (1993) demonstrated the use of escape extinction to reduce the self-injurious behaviours of three women with severe intellectual disabilities which appeared to be maintained by a process of negative reinforcement.

### Experimental manipulations of the reinforcing contingencies hypothesized to be maintaining other behaviours belonging to the same response class as the person's challenging behaviour

Finally, a number of studies have provided strong evidence in support of the operant model by demonstrating functional control over challenging behaviour by *differentially reinforcing* a more socially appropriate member of the same response class. In other words, they have identified the behavioural function of the person's challenging behaviour (e.g. to escape from teacher demands, to elicit teacher attention) and have then taught and systematically reinforced a *functionally equivalent* response (e.g. to request a break as an alternative to escape motivated challenging behaviour). Under conditions which are themselves predictable from behavioural theory, this approach can lead to rapid and significant reductions in the person's challenging behaviour (e.g. Carr & Durand, 1985a; Durand, Berotti & Weiner, 1993).

### Summary

These studies, in combination, provide strong evidence to support the proposition that some examples of challenging behaviours shown by people with severe intellectual disabilities may be maintained by processes of either positive or negative reinforcement.

All the examples of negative reinforcement which have been discussed have involved the person's challenging behaviour acting as an *escape* behaviour (i.e. leading to escape from, or withdrawal of, the negative reinforcer). Given that this appears to be the most prevalent behavioural function, it is probable that some examples of challenging behaviours may also function as *avoidance* behaviours, i.e. they may serve to prevent, postpone or delay the presentation of (aversive) negative reinforcers. For example, carers may have learned to avoid presenting negative reinforcers (e.g. social demands) under conditions in which the person with intellectual disabilities appears distressed (e.g. by exhibiting low-level repetitive self-injurious behaviour). In such a situation, self-injurious behaviour would serve to avoid (postpone or prevent) the occurrence of demands.

If this were the case, then we would expect (assuming that the avoidance behaviour was under some form of discriminative control) the behaviour to occur under conditions in which the negative reinforcer (demands) was more likely to occur. If it operated as a *successful* avoidance behaviour, however, we would not see *any* environmental consequences of the behaviour as the maintaining contingency involves the nonoccurrence of a potential event (the negative reinforcer). To an observer, therefore, the person's challenging behaviour would appear to have no consequence and, unless very precise discriminative control had been established, to have no clear antecedents. Nevertheless, it would still be an example of operant behaviour maintained by its environmental consequences.

Processes of negative reinforcement can also be used to account for the process of 'benevolent enslavement' (Carr, Taylor & Robinson, 1991; Hastings & Remington, 1994b; Hastings, 1995; Oliver, 1993; Taylor & Carr, 1993, 1994). In both of the hypothetical examples with which we started this section, the cessation of an individual's challenging behaviour may be thought of as negatively reinforcing the action of care staff. In these examples, the person's challenging behaviour may act as a negative reinforcer which is withdrawn contingent on the 'helping' behaviours of care staff (providing food, withdrawing demands). The staff behaviour which reinforces the person's challenging behaviour is itself reinforced by the termination of the challenging behaviour. Thus, carer and user get locked in a vicious circle (or negative reinforcement trap) which perpetuates the person's challenging behaviour.

If this is the case, then we may expect two further things to happen. Firstly, carers and care staff are likely to habituate (get used) to particular intensities or forms of challenging behaviour over time. Thus, they may begin to only respond (and hence provide contingent reinforcement) when the person shows *more intense* or *more complex* forms of challenging behaviour. This is, of course, the basis of all shaping procedures in which new behaviours are taught by differentially reinforcing particular aspects of the behaviour that the person already shows. In this case, however, the possibility of carers and care staff habituating to 'ordinary' levels of challenging behaviour may lead to the systematic (but unplanned) shaping of more and more intense or complex forms of the behaviour. Such a process may partially account for the development of challenging behaviour (cf. Guess & Carr, 1991; Oliver, 1993).

Secondly, if the termination of challenging behaviour acts as a negative reinforcer, we may also expect carers and care staff to develop strategies for *avoiding* the occurrence of such behaviours. So, people may come to avoid interacting with users whose challenging behaviours are maintained by processes of negative social reinforcement (e.g. escape from demands, escape from social attention), while increasing their rates of interaction with users whose challenging behaviour is maintained by processes of positive social reinforcement (e.g. access to social attention). Taylor and her colleagues have demonstrated that such a pattern is quite rapidly established and is sufficiently robust to be used to predict the functions served by challenging behaviours (Carr et al., 1991; Taylor & Carr, 1993, 1994; Taylor & Romanczyk, 1994).

## Automatic reinforcement

It is clear that not all behaviour is shaped by its environmental consequences. Some behaviours are innate (e.g. salivating at the sight of food when hungry). Others are learned reflexive behaviours which are elicited by environmental stimuli (e.g. salivating at the sound of a dinner bell when hungry). Others appear to be maintained by private events or consequences internal to the person (e.g. clenching your teeth may attenuate the pain from a sprained ankle, scratching an insect bite may temporarily relieve the sensation of itching).

It has been suggested that this latter class of behaviours may be thought of as examples of operant behaviour maintained by a process of automatic or perceptual reinforcement, in which the reinforcing stimuli are private or internal to the person (Berkson, 1983; Carr, 1977; Kennedy, 1994a; Lovaas et al., 1987; Vollmer, 1994). Potential internal or automatic reinforcers include perceptual feedback from the response itself (e.g. visual effects of eye poking, kinaesthetic feedback from rocking, auditory feedback from spinning toys), modulation of levels of arousal, relief from itching and the attenuation of pain.

This approach is not without its problems for behaviour analysts (Kennedy, 1994a). Mace, Lalli and Shea (1992) point out that if the (internal) reinforcer is integral to the response (as would be the case if the reinforcer was perceptual feedback from the behaviour), discriminative control of the behaviour cannot develop as the reinforcer is always contingent on the occurrence of the behaviour.[1] In addition, if the maintaining stimuli are internal and private they will not be amenable to manipulation. Given the lack of discriminative control and inability to manipulate the hypothesized contingencies, how are we to provide a 'believable demonstration' that these unobservable events really are responsible for maintaining behaviour?

Circumstantial support for the notion of automatic or perceptual reinforcement is provided by a number of studies. Firstly, studies have indicated that the

---

[1] It is important to keep in mind that discriminative control develops through the association of (discriminative) stimuli with *variations* in the probability of a response being reinforced. Thus, if the response is always reinforced, discriminative control simply cannot develop. The behaviour would, however, be expected to vary across contexts due to (motivational) variations in the extent to which the perceptual feedback was reinforcing.

probability of occurrence of some forms of challenging behaviour (primarily stereotypy and self-injury) varies with the level of general environmental stimulation. As has been discussed above, a significant proportion of challenging behaviours occur at their highest rates under conditions of social and material deprivation. In Iwata's large-scale study, 21% of people showed their highest rates of self-injury in the 'alone' condition (Iwata et al., 1994a); 15% of the 79 people in the Derby study also showed their highest rates of challenging behaviour in this condition (Derby et al., 1992). Similarly, a number of studies have shown that increasing the level of environmental stimulation may lead to reductions in stereotypic and other forms of challenging behaviour (e.g. Favell, McGimsey & Schell, 1982; Horner, 1980; Ringdahl et al., 1997; Steege et al., 1989). These results are consistent with predictions made from the study of behavioural choice if we assume that the challenging behaviours in question are maintained by (positive) automatic reinforcement (Mace et al., 1992; Vollmer, 1994).

Interestingly, however, exactly the opposite results have been obtained in other studies. Duker and Rasing (1989), for example, found that *decreasing* the level of stimulation in the classroom by removing furniture, pictures and extraneous materials led to a reduction in stereotyped behaviour (and increase in on-task behaviour) of three young adults with severe intellectual disabilities and autism. These results are consistent with an alternative explanation – that some forms of challenging behaviour may be maintained by a process of negative automatic reinforcement in that they serve actively to dampen (aversive) levels of overarousal (cf. Isaacson & Gispin, 1990; Murphy, 1982).

This notion is akin to viewing challenging behaviour as a *coping response* which reduces the aversiveness of extraneous sources of stimulation. If this is the case, then we would expect such behaviours to occur at their highest rates under conditions of stressful external stimulation (e.g. the 'academic demand' condition typically employed in experimental functional analyses). Thus, evidence of contextual control can only ever provide circumstantial evidence in support of operant hypotheses. The key difference between coping and escape responses is that a coping response would reduce the aversiveness of an external event. An escape response would remove the event itself.

Further circumstantial evidence for the operation of automatic reinforcement is provided by the impact of *sensory extinction* in reducing some forms of challenging behaviour (e.g. Iwata et al., 1994b; Rincover & Devany, 1982; Rincover et al., 1979; Rincover, Newsom & Carr, 1979). This procedure involves masking the sensory consequences arising from the behaviour. Rincover and Devany (1982), for example, used foam padding to mask the sensory consequences arising from head banging. Unfortunately, as well as masking the sensory consequences, such procedures may also exert discriminative control over behaviours maintained by external consequences, lead to changes in environmental contingencies or reduce challenging behaviour through punishment (e.g. Mazaleski et al., 1994). Let us, for the sake of argument, make the alternative assumption that the person's head banging had been maintained by a process of positive social reinforcement. If this were the case, it is plausible to suggest that their previous experience with self-injuring in different environments may have taught them that head banging against foam padding was unlikely to be reinforced (i.e. foam padding exerts discriminative control over self-injury). Alternatively, the foam padding may directly alter the behaviour of others by reducing the aversiveness of the person's self-injury and hence reducing the probability of them intervening. In this case, the foam padding initiates the unplanned extinction of a socially reinforced behaviour.

Of course, none of this evidence is particularly convincing, due to the inability or failure to measure independently the hypothesized internal consequences of the challenging behaviour. While, in some situations, this is clearly either impossible or pointless, in that the internal consequence is guaranteed to occur (e.g. independent measurement of the perceptual feedback from the behaviour), in other cases it is both viable and necessary to provide independent measures of potential processes of automatic reinforcement. While the physiological monitoring of levels of arousal is itself a highly complex area, Romanczyk and his colleagues discussed some of the relatively simple approaches to monitoring levels of arousal which are commonly used in the analysis of issues related to anxiety in non-disabled people (Freeman, Horner & Reichle, 1999; Romanczyk & Matthews, 1998; Romanczyk, Lockshin & O'Connor,1992).

## Respondent behaviour

Respondent behaviours are those reflexive or conditioned behaviours which are primarily 'involuntary' in nature (e.g. blinking, salivating, changes in heart rate, skin conductance). A considerable amount of behavioural theorizing about issues of arousal and anxiety in nondisabled people has viewed them as examples of acquired or conditioned respondent behaviours. Phobic fear, for example, has been viewed as a form of conditioned response acquired through previous association between the feared object (the conditioned stimulus) and another aversive event.

As Romanczyk et al. (1992) point out, however, there has been remarkably little attention paid to issues of anxiety and arousal among people with severe intellectual disabilities (see also Benson, 1990; Romanczyk & Matthews, 1998). Romanczyk and his colleagues have suggested that anxiety and arousal may play some role in the maintenance of self-injurious behaviour (Freeman et al., 1999; Romanczyk, 1986; Romanczyk & Matthews, 1998; Romanczyk et al., 1992). They suggest that self-injury may be elicited as a reflexive response to high levels of arousal generated by environmental stressors. They also point out that self-injury can itself generate high levels of arousal. Similarly, evidence from basic research has indicated that aggression may be elicited as a reflexive response by punishment (e.g. Hutchinson, 1977).

These are not presented as models of challenging behaviour which stand on their own, but as additional processes within complex models (Romanczyk, 1986; Romanczyk & Matthews, 1998; Romanczyk et al., 1992). We will return to them in the concluding section of this chapter.

## Schedule-induced behaviour

Under conditions involving the repetitive delivery of food on a fixed-time schedule, or under some examples of fixed-interval schedules of reinforcement, schedule-induced behaviours may appear. These are behaviours which occur in the period immediately following reinforcement, are excessive, stereotyped in appearance, unrelated to the demands of the situation and often highly persistent over time (Staddon, 1977). The majority of studies of schedule-induced behaviour have taken place in the animal laboratory, focussing on polydipsia (over-drinking) in rats and aggression in pigeons. Studies undertaken with people, however, have led to reports of schedule-induced eating, drinking, aggression, cigarette smoking, grooming, pacing and fidgeting (Emerson & Howard, 1992; although see also Overskeid, 1992).

The potential importance of this phenomenon to the understanding of challenging behaviour shown by people with severe intellectual disabilities has not gone unnoticed (e.g. Epling & Pierce, 1983; Lewis & Baumeister, 1982). It has, however, generated remarkably few studies. Emerson and Howard (1992) investigated the possibility of schedule induction in an experimental study involving five children and three adults with severe intellectual disabilities. The results indicated that seven of the eight participants demonstrated evidence of schedule induction for at least one stereotypic behaviour. In addition, for five of the eight individuals, these behaviours occurred at a significantly greater rate in the period immediately following reinforcer presentation. Subsequent analysis of observational data collected at a special school attended by the five children indicated that: (1) none of the behaviours which appeared to be socially mediated in the classroom was evident as induced behaviours under experimental conditions; (2) none of the behaviours which were experimentally induced appeared to be socially mediated in the classroom; and (3) for the one participant for whom sufficient examples of teacher-mediated reinforcement were observed in the classroom, stereotypic arm-flapping behaviour, which had been experimentally induced, also occurred at significantly higher rates following reinforcement in the classroom

(Emerson, 1993). Similar results have been reported by Lerman et al. (1994b). While some data are available to suggest that self-injurious and disruptive behaviours may be induced under appropriate conditions (Emerson et al., 1996d), it would appear at present that this model is primarily applicable to the analysis of stereotyped behaviour.

## Neurobiological models

Over the last decade, significant gains have been made in identifying some of the potential neurobiological mechanisms which might underlie challenging behaviour. As was indicated in Chapter 1, the primary concern of this book is to present and evaluate approaches to the understanding, assessment and treatment of challenging behaviour which arise from behavioural psychology. However, to attempt to do this in isolation from a consideration of the biological bases of our behaviour would be counter-productive.

Most recent neurobiological theories have focussed on the role of various classes of endogenous neurotransmitters in modulating behaviour. These are the chemical messengers of our central nervous system which produce an effect by binding to the receptor sites on the cell surfaces of neurones. Different types of neurones are activated by different types of neurotransmitters. Recent research has focussed on three different classes of neurotransmitters: dopamine, serotonin (5-hydroxytryptamine) and the opioid peptides (in particular, β-endorphin). A number of detailed reviews are available of this area and its relation to drug treatments of challenging behaviour (e.g. Aman, Arnold & Armstrong, 1999; Aman & Madrid, 1999; Baumeister & Sevin, 1990; Lewis & Bodfish, 1998; Harris, 1992; Hellings, 1999; Racusin, Kovner-Kline & King, 1999; Reiss & Aman, 1998; Ruedrich & Erhardt, 1999; Sandman & Hetrick, 1995; Sandman, Spence & Smith, 1999; Schroeder et al., 1986; Schroeder & Tessel, 1994; Tessel et al., 1995; Thompson et al., 1994a; Thompson et al., 1995; Verhoeven & Tuinier, 1999; Werry, 1999). Below is a summary of some of the main points arising from this complex field of study.

### Dopamine

The dopaminergic system is closely involved in the regulation of motor activity. Five subtypes of dopamine receptors have been identified which are commonly grouped into two receptor 'families' (D1-like and D2-like). Some evidence suggests that abnormalities in the D1 receptor subsystem family may be implicated in the development and maintenance of some forms of self-injurious behaviour.

- People with Lesch–Nyhan syndrome, *all* of whom display injurious self-biting, show a significant deficiency in dopamine pathways in certain areas of the brain, and decreased levels of dopamine and its metabolites (Breese et al., 1995; Nyhan, 1994).

- Animal studies have shown that, if dopamine pathways are destroyed in unborn rat pups, the administration of dopamine *agonists* (substances which bind to the receptor site and reproduce the effect of dopamine) produces severe self-biting. This can be blocked by the administration of dopamine *antagonists,* substances which displace agonist compounds from the receptor sites and hence stop them producing their biological effect (Breese et al., 1995).
- Rearing rhesus monkeys in isolation almost inevitably produces self-injurious behaviour. This behaviour emerges at 3–4 months, persists into adulthood, involves multiple topographies, some of which lead to severe injury, and is most likely to occur in response to environmental stressors (Kraemer & Clarke, 1990). It is associated with long-term alterations in dopamine receptor sensitivity and destruction of dopaminergic pathways (Lewis, 1992).
- Preliminary reports suggest that fluphenazine and clozapine (D1 and D2 antagonists) may produce significant reductions in self-injury for some people (Aman & Madrid, 1999; Gualtieri & Schroeder, 1989; Hammock, Schroeder & Levine, 1995; Schroeder et al., 1995).

The accumulated evidence implicates the destruction of some D1 pathways and supersensitivity (or reduced thresholds for activation) in the remaining D1 receptors in the genesis of self-biting and, perhaps, other forms of self-injury. This effect appears to be tied to crucial developmental stages since later damage to the dopaminergic system (as occurs in Parkinson's disease and Huntington's chorea) does not lead to self-injury. It is also possible that the effect results not from dysregulation of the dopaminergic system as such, but from an imbalance between dopamine and serotonin activity (Schroeder & Tessel, 1994). Similar evidence has accumulated to suggest that abnormalities in the D2 receptor system may underlie the development of stereotyped behaviour (Cooper & Dourish, 1990).

The observation that rearing nonhuman primates in isolation can produce permanent destruction of dopaminergic pathways, long-lasting supersensitivity to dopamine agonists and very high rates of self-injury may have implications for preventative interventions. If severe social and sensory deprivation were to have similar irreversible effects in humans, there would exist a clear case for the provision of intensive social and sensory stimulation to 'at risk' infants. This may be particularly relevant to people with more severe and complex disabilities, who, because of the severity of their impairments, may have some difficulty in bonding with their parents and may have restricted repertoires for exploring the world around them.

## Serotonin (5-hydroxytryptamine)

The serotoninergic system is closely linked with a number of processes including arousal, appetite control, anxiety and depression. Disturbances in the system have been linked with insomnia, depression, disorders of appetite control and obsessive–compulsive disorders (Bodfish & Madison, 1993; Gedye, 1993; Verhoeven & Tuinier, 1999). There are at least 11 different types of serotonin receptors, some of which are inhibitory (Class 1), while others are excitatory (Class 2 and 3) (Gedye, 1993). Accumulating evidence points to a relationship between serotonin and aggression, although links have also been made between serotonin and self-injurious behaviour (Baumeister & Sevin, 1990).

- In nonhumans, lesions in areas which contain serotoninergic neurones or lesions which inhibit serotonin synthesis can lead to an increase in aggression. Similarly, interventions which increase serotonin synthesis or administration of serotonin agonists lead to a reduction in aggression (Baumeister & Sevin, 1990).
- In nondisabled humans, there is some evidence of a negative correlation between levels of serotonin or its metabolites in the cerebral spinal fluid or blood plasma and aggression (Baumeister & Sevin, 1990; Thompson et al., 1994a).
- Evidence also suggests that serotoninergic agonists or reuptake inhibitors (e.g. fluoxetine) can reduce obsessive–compulsive disorders, self-injurious behaviour and aggression in people with intellectual disabilities (Aman et al., 1999; Racusin et al., 1999; Sovner et al., 1998; Verhoeven & Tuinier, 1999).
- Dietary increases in serotonin have been implicated in the reduction of self-injurious behaviour (Ellis, Singh & Ruane, 1999; Gedye, 1990, 1991).

## Opioid peptides (β-endorphin)

Opioid peptides are structurally and functionally related to the opioid alkaloids morphine and heroin and play an important role in pain control systems. There are three general groups of opioid peptides (encephalins, dynorphins and endorphins) and four types of receptor (mu, kappa, sigma and delta). β-endorphin, which binds to mu receptors, has the greatest analgesic and antinocicoptive (blocking of pain receptors) properties, and may produce a euphoric mood state. Sandman and his colleagues (e.g. Sandman & Hetrick, 1995; Sandman, Spence & Smith, 1999) have proposed two models in which β-endorphin activity may be related to self-injurious behaviour. In the *congenital opioid excess* model, it is proposed that excess opioid activity leads to permanently raised pain thresholds. In the *addiction* hypothesis, is proposed that self-injurious behaviour leads to the release of β-endorphin which, through its analgesic, antinocicoptive and euphoria-inducing properties, acts as an automatic reinforcer for the self-injury (see also Thompson et al., 1995). Over time, it is suggested that physical dependence (with associated withdrawal symptoms) may develop.

Evidence in support of a link between β-endorphin and self-injurious behaviour includes:

- levels of β-endorphin are raised in the cerebral spinal fluid of people with severe intellectual disabilities who self-injure when compared with appropriate controls (Sandman et al., 1990a);
- levels of β-endorphin are raised in the cerebral spinal fluid of people with severe intellectual disabilities following an episode of self-injury (Sandman et al., 1997);
- suggestive associations exist between self-injurious behaviour and paradoxical responses to sedatives (Sandman & Barron, 1992), diet (Neri & Sandman, 1992), the menstrual cycle (Taylor et al., 1993a) and body site preference (Symons & Thompson, 1997);
- the β-endorphin antagonist naltrexone hydrochloride has brought about significant reductions in self-injury for some people (Sandman et al., 1998; Sandman, Spence & Smith, 1999);
- the effect of naltrexone hydrochloride is associated with the location of injury (Thompson et al., 1994b) and the extent to which levels of β-endorphin metabolites are raised in the blood plasma of people with severe intellectual disabilities following an episode of self-injury (Sandman et al., 1997; Sandman, Spence & Smith, 1999).

As noted above, neurobiological models also need to take account of the interaction between neurotransmitter systems. So, for example, Corbett and Campbell (1980) point out a possible link between serotonin and opioid peptides, in that tryptophan (a precursor of serotonin) enhances the tolerance for, and the development of dependence on, morphine. Oliver (1993) draws links between chronic β-endorphin release and increased sensitivity in dopamine receptors. In this context, and given the probable importance of the timing of damage to dopaminergic systems, it is interesting to note that there is a reported association between fetal distress and increased β-endorphin levels in amniotic fluid (Cataldo & Harris, 1982).

## Psychiatric disorders and challenging behaviour

Emerson, Moss and Kiernan (1999b) have identified three possible ways in which psychiatric disorders may be associated with challenging behaviour; (1) challenging behaviours may represent the atypical presentation of the core symptoms of a psychiatric disorder in people with severe intellectual disabilities; (2) challenging behaviours may occur as secondary features of psychiatric disorders among people with severe intellectual disabilities; and (3) psychiatric disorders may act as establishing operations for operant-maintained challenging behaviour.

### Challenging behaviour as the atypical presentation of a psychiatric disorder

It is possible that psychiatric disorders may be manifested in atypical ways among people with highly restricted linguistic and adaptive behaviours. For example, two sources of circumstantial evidence suggest that some forms of self-injurious behaviour may constitute the atypical presentation of obsessive–compulsive disorder among people with severe intellectual disabilities (King, 1993). Firstly, there are clear topographical similarities between obsessive–compulsive disorder and self-injurious behaviour in that both categories of 'challenging' behaviour are repetitive, stereotyped, ritualistic, apparently unrelated to the immediate demands of the person's situation and are extremely resistant to change (Emerson et al., in press c; Kiernan et al., 1997). Secondly, there is growing evidence to suggest that serotoninergic agonists or reuptake inhibitors (e.g. fluoxetine, clomipramine) can reduce obsessional compulsive disorders in people without intellectual disabilities (Lader & Herrington, 1996) and self-injurious behaviour in people with severe intellectual disabilities (Aman et al., 1999; Bodfish & Madison, 1993; Lewis et al., 1996; Markowitz, 1992; Sovner et al., 1993; Sovner et al., 1998).

Bodfish and Madison (1993), for example, reported that fluoxetine (at a dosage of 40 mg/day) significantly reduced self-injurious and aggressive behaviours which had a 'compulsive' nature in seven out of ten participants. None of the six participants who showed 'noncompulsive' aggression or self-injury responded positively. These results are particularly interesting in that they appear to point to possible behavioural 'markers' which may discriminate between responders and nonresponders. These markers include the person also showing self-restraint and other compulsive behaviours (e.g. ordering, touching, hoarding) which interfere with ongoing activities and the person showing distress on the interruption of their 'ritualistic' self-injurious behaviour (see also Bodfish et al., 1995; Lewis et al., 1996).

### Challenging behaviour as a secondary feature of psychiatric disorders

It has previously been suggested that a range of challenging behaviours (including aggression and self-injurious behaviour) may occur as secondary features of affective disorders among people with severe intellectual disabilities (Reid, 1982; Sovner & Hurley, 1983). Reid (1982), for example, suggests a variety of clinical features which may be indicative of depression among people whose level of disability makes it difficult to verbalize their feelings. These features include somatic symptoms (e.g. headache and abdominal ache), hysterical fits, agitation, and disturbances of physiological functions such as sleep, appetite and bowel movements.

A number of recent studies have attempted to quantify the diagnostic significance of challenging behaviours and loss of self-care skills in depression. Meins (1995), for example, identified major depression in adults with mental retardation using a two-phase method of screening followed by detailed assessment of potential cases. Additional potential symptoms, including a range of problem behaviours and loss of self-care skills, were also observed. Meins showed that, in people with more severe intellectual disabilities, the severity of existing behaviour problems was higher in the presence of depression as defined by the Diagnostic and Statistical Manual of Mental Disorders II(R) criteria. He points specifically to the diagnostic significance of aggressive and self-injurious behaviour, stereotypies, screaming and spontaneous crying. Similarly, Reiss and Rojahn (1993), using the Reiss Screen, found criterion levels of depression to be evident in four times as many aggressive as nonaggressive subjects.

### Psychiatric disorders may establish a motivational basis for the expression of challenging behaviours maintained by operant processes

Emerson et al. (1999b) suggest that some psychiatric disorders may function as establishing operations and thereby provide a motivational basis for the expression of challenging behaviour maintained by operant processes. Depression, for example, may be associated with an unwillingness to participate in educational or social activities, thus establishing such activities as negative reinforcers (i.e. events whose termination is reinforcing). If the person has previously learned that challenging behaviours can terminate such aversive events, we would expect an episode of depression to be associated with an increase in challenging behaviour. It is worth noting that, unlike in the previous section, depression is not seen as 'causing' challenging behaviour (i.e. is not a sufficient condition for the expression of challenging behaviour). Rather, the occurrence of challenging behaviour is determined by the combination of: (1) the motivational influence of depression in establishing negative reinforcers; and (2) the pre-existence in the individual's repertoire of challenging behaviours which have previously served an escape function. Such a conceptualization suggests two complementary approaches to intervention: (1) change the motivating condition (e.g. treat the person's depression); and (2) change the 'functionality' of the person's challenging behaviour.

Lowry and Sovner (1992) describe two case studies in which this type of process appeared to be operating. In both cases, rapid cycling bipolar mood disorder (assessed through detailed behavioural recording of affect and activity) appeared to be closely associated with variations in self-injury (Case 1) or aggression (Case 2). For both cases, however, anecdotal information was presented to suggest that: (1) specific environmental events (demands from care staff) precipitated episodes of challenging behaviour, but only during particular mood states (depression for

Case 1, mania for Case 2); and (2) the person's challenging behaviour may have functioned within such states to terminate or delay such precipitating stimuli.

## Summary

The studies which have been reviewed in this chapter provide strong evidence that many examples of challenging behaviours shown by people with severe intellectual disabilities are maintained by behavioural processes. In particular, evidence suggests that challenging behaviours may be members of discriminated operant-response classes. The operant model also provides a coherent account of the types of reciprocal influences between user and carer behaviour which may lead to the development of challenging behaviour (Guess & Carr, 1991; Oliver, 1993) and its maintenance through the process of 'benevolent enslavement' (Taylor & Carr, 1993, 1994).

Romanczyk and his colleagues, however, warn us that to label challenging behaviour as functional and purposeful

provides a perspective superior to viewing it simply as a psychotic behavior but also lends itself to a simplistic and naive understanding as well. That is, self-injurious behavior represents a classification of behavior, and therefore, one cannot assume that the causal and maintaining factors are (1) similar across individuals, (2) consistent for the same individual at different points in time, and (3) similar for different topographies of self-injurious behavior both within and across individuals (Romanczyk et al., 1992, p. 93).

To this, it could be added that we cannot assume that causal and maintaining factors are: (4) consistent for the same individual across different contexts; and (5) not complex and diverse within specific topographies. Indeed, the variety of possible behavioural functions and aetiological processes, the frequent co-occurrence of different forms of challenging behaviours and the importance of the contextual control of behavioural relationships should all serve to guard us against such naivety.

In the sections below, the studies which highlight the need for such cautions will be reviewed. In addition, evidence relating to the possible interface between behavioural and neurobiological models will be discussed.

### Causal and maintaining factors may be dissimilar across individuals

The evidence which was reviewed earlier in this chapter suggests that challenging behaviours may be maintained by:

- positive reinforcement involving the presentation of attention from carers (e.g. Derby et al., 1992; Iwata et al., 1982, 1994a; Lovaas & Simmons, 1969; Mace et al., 1986; Paisey et al., 1991) or material reinforcers such as food or access to materials (e.g. Durand & Crimmins, 1988; Marcus & Vollmer, 1996; Wacker et al., 1996a);

- negative reinforcement involving escape from the attention or presence of carers (Emerson, 1990), the demands of carers (Carr et al., 1976, 1980; Derby et al., 1992; Iwata et al., 1982, 1994a; Mace et al., 1986; Paisey et al., 1991), ambient noise (Iwata et al., 1994a; O'Reilly, 1997) and medical examinations (Iwata et al., 1990a);
- automatic positive reinforcement resulting from perceptual feedback from the behaviour itself (Lovaas et al., 1987; Vollmer, 1994) or from the mood-altering effects of β-endorphin release (Sandman & Hetrick, 1995); and
- automatic negative reinforcement involving the attenuation of states of over-arousal (Duker & Rasing, 1989) or pain reduction (Carr & McDowell, 1980; Romanczyk et al., 1992).

In addition, the challenging behaviour shown by some individuals may result primarily from disturbances in neurotransmitter systems (Baumeister & Sevin, 1990; Lewis & Bodfish, 1998; Harris, 1992; Sandman & Hetrick, 1995; Schroeder & Tessel, 1994; Thompson et al., 1994a, 1995; Verhoeven & Tuinier, 1999) or the presence of underlying psychiatric disorders (King, 1993; Meins, 1995; Reid, 1982; Reiss & Rojahn, 1993; Sovner & Hurley, 1983).

### Maintaining factors may vary over time

It is important when considering the development of challenging behaviour to distinguish between causal and maintaining factors; those factors which lead to the initial emergence of challenging behaviour may be very different from those which, at later points in time, are responsible for their maintenance. While the behavioural model may provide a convincing account of the processes shaping and maintaining challenging behaviour, it is less convincing when attempting to account for its initial emergence.

Indeed, very little is known about the early development of challenging behaviour in people with severe intellectual disabilities (Murphy et al., 1999). The following accounts are, therefore, primarily speculative. To understand the emergence of challenging behaviour, it is probably important to address the natural occurrence during development of repetitive, potentially injurious or minor aggressive/tantrum behaviours in the specific developmental context provided by intellectual disabilities (Guess & Carr, 1991; MacLean, Stone & Brown, 1994; Tröster, 1994).

In both nondisabled children and children with intellectual disabilities, repetitive movements commonly occur at transition points in motor development. Thus, for example, rocking on hands and knees occurs prior to the onset of crawling. A number of studies have also indicated that head banging occurs in up to 20% of nondisabled children between the age of 5 and 17 months (e.g. de Lissovoy, 1962; Werry, Carlielle & Fitzpatrick, 1983), possibly in response to ear infections or teething (de Lissovoy, 1963).

As most parents will know, tantrums, aggression and property destruction are extremely common in nondisabled children, reaching a peak at 2 to 3 years of age. They then gradually diminish in both severity and frequency, probably as a combined result of the punishment of these behaviours, the development of verbal self-regulation and, perhaps most importantly, because the child learns alternative ways of solving life's problems.

The specific developmental context provided by having an intellectual disability may be important in a number of ways.

- Children with severe intellectual disabilities may, as a result of their slower pace of development, exhibit behaviours which are developmentally appropriate, but inappropriate to their chronological age. They may also exhibit such behaviours for a longer period of time (MacLean et al., 1994).
- Specific impairments associated with the child's severe intellectual disability (e.g. specific sensory impairments, language delay, physical disabilities) may result in the child having an additionally restricted behavioural repertoire. As such, they may have greater difficulty in developing alternative ways of responding to challenging situations – particularly relevant may be the occurrence of restricted receptive and expressive communication skills among children with severe intellectual disabilities (e.g. Sigafoos, in press).
- Syndromes associated with intellectual disabilities (e.g. destruction of dopamine pathways in Lesch–Nyhan syndrome) may increase an individual's vulnerability to developing particular behaviours (e.g. self-biting). Indeed, the recent explosion of interest in the 'new genetics' is likely to lead to a substantial growth in knowledge about the behavioural manifestations or 'phenotypes' of a range of syndromes (Clarke et al., 1996; Clarke & Boer, 1998; Dykens, 1995; Dykens et al., 1999; Dykens & Hodapp, 1999; Dykens & Kasari, 1997; Dykens & Smith, 1998; Einfeld et al., 1999; Hodapp, 1997; Holland, 1999; Howlin, Davies & Udwin, 1998; Symons et al., 1999b; Turk, 1998).
- Similarly, specific disorders which are more common among people with intellectual disabilities (e.g. feeding difficulties, autism) may be associated with difficulties in establishing bonding with carers and an increased risk of experiencing common events (e.g. eating, interactions with carers) as stressful and/or aversive.
- The social consequences of having an intellectual disability may result in reduced opportunity for learning appropriate adaptive behaviours and may put the child at greater risk of experiencing adverse life events. These may, again, help establish common events as stressful or aversive.

The above points illustrate the potential for minor challenging behaviours, whose expression is part of the normal process of development, to occur more commonly, with a greater severity and for a longer period of time among children with intellectual disabilities. This, in itself, provides greater opportunity for alternative maintaining mechanisms to come into play. Thus, for example, the 'comforting' reaction of carers to stress-induced tantrums may, over time, come to play an important role in maintaining the behaviour, i.e. behaviours which emerge as part of a normal developmental process may, at a later stage, come to be maintained by operant processes (Guess & Carr, 1991). The reciprocal nature of these processes may then, through a process of shaping, act to select more extreme, abnormal and severe variants of the initial behaviour (Hastings & Remington, 1994b; Oliver, 1993; Taylor & Carr, 1993, 1994).

It is also possible that the nature of the maintaining operant processes may vary over time. Carr and McDowell (1980), for example, describe the treatment of self-injurious scratching shown by a nondisabled 10-year-old boy. While first arising in response to contact dermatitis, the scratching was apparently maintained by positive social attention at the time of referral. More recently, Lerman and her colleagues examined the possibility that transfer of behavioural function may have been responsible for treatment relapse in four people with self-injurious behaviour (Lerman et al., 1994a). Re-analysis of behavioural function following relapse was rather inconclusive, but suggested that, for two people, self-injury had acquired an additional function (positive reinforcement in addition to negative reinforcement; automatic reinforcement in addition to negative reinforcement), while for another it had acquired an alternative function (automatic reinforcement rather than positive social reinforcement).

For self-injurious behaviour, the importance of operant processes may, at a later point in time, be replaced in whole or in part by automatic reinforcement through the contingent release of β-endorphin; as the self-injury becomes more severe, it is more likely to lead to the release of β-endorphin which, over time, may result in physical dependency. Thus, during the course of a person's self-injury that 'same' behaviour may be maintained by a variety of different processes, all of which may be functionally unrelated to the original cause(s) of the behaviour.

### Causal and maintaining factors may vary across different forms of challenging behaviour shown by the same individual

As has been discussed, the behavioural approach is primarily interested in the relationship between response classes and environmental events, rather than in the topographical form of the behaviour itself. It does not assume that similar topographies serve similar functions. This is an important point given the common co-occurrence of different forms of challenging behaviour (see Chapter

3). Unfortunately, much applied research has implicitly made the assumption that similar forms of behaviour are likely to serve similar functions. Thus, for example, many studies have investigated the relationship between environmental events and broad classes of self-injurious, aggressive or disruptive behaviour.

A few studies, however, have examined the relationships between different forms of challenging behaviour shown by individuals. Emerson et al. (1995, 1996b) provided descriptive and experimental analysis of multiple forms of challenging behaviour shown by five children and one young adult with severe intellectual disabilities. The results indicated the existence of distinct response classes *within* the various forms of challenging behaviour shown by some of the participants. Thus, for example, one participant showed three forms of self-injurious behaviour (hair pulling, back poking and ear poking), which appeared to be maintained by a process of negative reinforcement involving escape from teacher demands, and two forms of self-injury (fist-to-cheek hitting and body digging) which appeared to be maintained by a process of automatic reinforcement.

Derby et al. (1994) used extended and brief experimental analyses to identify aspects of the contextual control of multiple forms of challenging behaviour shown by four people with intellectual disabilities. They presented results which indicated that apparently random responding across experimental conditions was attributable to adding together the results relating to different behaviours shown by the person which served different behavioural functions (see also Day, Horner & O'Neill, 1994; Kern, Carberry & Haidara, 1997; Mace et al., 1986; Richman et al., 1998; Sigafoos & Tucker, in press; Slifer et al., 1986; Sprague & Horner, 1992).

### Maintaining factors may vary across contexts

If maintaining factors can vary over time, it is also likely that they can vary across contexts. Firstly, as we have seen, the presence or absence of a functional relationship is contextually controlled by establishing operations (McGill, 1999; Smith & Iwata, 1997). Above, we reviewed a number of recent studies that have identified a wide range of variables which appear to operate in this way for particular individuals. In addition, a range of studies have investigated personal and environmental correlates of challenging behaviour. Such studies may indicate further classes of variables which are capable of acting as establishing operations. Taken together, the results from these two types of studies suggest that establishing operations may involve such factors as:

- *bio-behavioural states* such as alertness, fatigue and sleep/wake patterns (Brylewski & Wiggs, 1999; Espie, 1992; Green et al., 1994; Guess et al., 1990, 1993; Horner et al., 1997; Kennedy & Meyer, 1996; O'Reilly, 1995), hormonal changes (Taylor et al., 1993a), drug effects (Kalachnik et al., 1995; Taylor et al.,

1993a), caffeine intake (Podboy & Mallery, 1977), seizure activity (Gedye, 1989a,b), psychiatric disorders (Emerson et al., 1999b; Lowry & Sovner, 1992), food deprivation (Talkington & Riley, 1971; Wacker et al., 1996a), mood (Carr et al., 1996), illness or pain (Bosch et al., 1997; Carr et al., 1996; Carr & Smith, 1995; Gardner & Whalen, 1996; Kennedy & Meyer, 1996; O'Reilly, 1997; Peine et al., 1995);

- *preceding interactions* including such factors as preceding compliance (Harchik & Putzier, 1990; Horner et al., 1991; Mace et al., 1988), task repetition (Winterling, Dunlap & O'Neill, 1987), critical comments from others (Gardner et al., 1986), the cancelling or delay of previous activities (Horner et al., 1997), immediately preceding interactions (O'Reilly, 1999; O'Reilly & Carey, 1996; O'Reilly, Lancioni & Emerson, in press), temporally distant social interactions (Gardner et al., 1986; O'Reilly, 1996), physical exercise (Lancioni & O'Reilly, 1998), the route taken to a setting (Kennedy & Itkonen, 1993) and time of awakening (Gardner, Karan & Cole, 1984; Kennedy & Itkonen, 1993).

- The *current context* for behaviour including such factors as noise, temperature, levels of demand and positive comments from staff (Kennedy, 1994b; O'Reilly, 1997), location (Adelinis et al., 1997), music (Durand & Mapstone, 1998), crowding (McAfee, 1987), preference and choice regarding concurrent activities (Cooper et al., 1992; Dunlap et al., 1994; Dunlap et al., 1995; Dyer, Dunlap & Winterling, 1990; Ferro, Foster-Johnson & Dunlap, 1996; Foster-Johnson, Ferro & Dunlap, 1994; Lindauer, DeLeon & Fisher, 1999; Ringdahl et al., 1997; Vaughn & Horner, 1997), the amount of noncontingent reinforcement available in the setting (Derby et al., 1998; Hagopian, Fisher & Legacy, 1994; Hanley, Piazza & Fisher, 1997; Roscoe, Iwata & Goh, 1998; Vollmer et al., 1993; Vollmer, Marcus & Ringdahl, 1995a), concurrent social interactions and the nature of surrounding activities (Carr et al., 1976), and the presence of idiosyncratic variables such as small balls, puzzles and magazines (Carr et al., 1997).

Secondly, the form of the functional relationship may be sensitive to establishing operations. Romanczyk et al. (1992), for example, described a case in which severe self-injury appeared to either increase or decrease levels of arousal dependent on the context in which the behaviour occurred. Haring and Kennedy (1990) reported that the effectiveness of two approaches to intervention (differential reinforcement of other behaviours and time-out) varied across contexts. They demonstrated that the differential reinforcement procedure was effective in reducing stereotypy for two students in the context of academic instruction, but ineffective in a leisure context. Conversely, they demonstrated that while a time-out procedure was ineffective during academic instruction, it was effective in a leisure context. While clearly demonstrating the contextual control of intervention efficacy, these results also suggest that the differential efficacy may be related to challenging behaviour serving different functions across settings (see also Carr & Durand, 1985a; Emerson et al., 1996b).

### Causal and maintaining factors may be complex

Finally, it is possible that operant behaviours may be under multiple control (Skinner, 1953), i.e. they may be controlled by more than one reinforcement contingency. Day et al. (1994), for example, demonstrated that the challenging behaviours (aggression or self-injury) of three people with severe intellectual disabilities were maintained by contingencies of negative reinforcement (escape from difficult tasks) *and* positive reinforcement (access to preferred materials, e.g. food, coffee, a necklace). Similarly, Smith et al. (1993a) identified the multiple control of self-injurious behaviour shown by two people with severe intellectual disabilities. Automatic reinforcement and positive social reinforcement were shown to be maintaining the self-injurious behaviour shown by a 19-year-old nonambulatory man, while automatic reinforcement and negative reinforcement (involving escape from social demands) were shown to underlie the self-injury shown by a 37-year-old woman with Down's syndrome. Further examples of multiply controlled challenging behaviour are provided by Lalli & Casey (1996), Piazza et al. (1997c) and Thompson et al. (1998).

As we have suggested above, it is also possible that self-injurious behaviour may be multiply controlled by external (operant) processes and automatic reinforcement involving the release of β-endorphin (Oliver, 1993). This, in itself, may involve components of both positive (automatic) reinforcement arising from the euphoric mood state induced by opioid release and negative (automatic) reinforcement arising from the analgesic and antinociceptive properties of β-endorphin. Indeed, the face validity of such a suggestion is quite strong in that it would possibly lower the response cost or effort associated with self-injury to the extent that it could be more easily selected as an operant behaviour (cf. Friman & Poling, 1995). The possibility of multiple control by operant and neurobiological processes is also indicated by evidence of the effectiveness of behavioural approaches in partially reducing the self-injurious biting in people with Lesch–Nyhan syndrome (Grace, Cowart & Matson, 1988; Hile & Vatterott, 1991).

### Summary

In this chapter, some of the behavioural and neurobiological evidence which is currently available regarding the aetiology and maintenance of challenging behaviours shown by people with severe intellectual disabilities has been reviewed. There can be no doubt that behavioural (operant) processes are important in the maintenance of many examples of such behaviours. It is also clear, however, that this is not the sole explanation. Challenging behaviour is a complex phenomenon. Neurobiological and psychiatric factors are clearly implicated in some examples of challenging behaviour and it seems plausible to suggest that a fuller understanding of challenging behaviour will be provided by more comprehensive bio-behavioural models which address the interface between developmental, operant, neurobiological, psychiatric and ecological processes (e.g. Emerson et al., 1999b; Guess & Carr, 1991; Lewis, Silva & Silva, 1995; Mace & Mauk, 1995; Murphy, 1994; Oliver, 1993).

The complexity of the issues is also apparent within behavioural and neurobiological models. Behavioural accounts need to attend to issues arising from the multiple and contextual control of different forms of challenging behaviour and the interaction of these behaviours with other components of the person's behavioural repertoire. They also need to consider the role played by respondent and induced behaviours (Emerson & Howard, 1992; Freeman et al., 1999; Romanczyk et al., 1992). Similarly, neurobiological models may also need to take into account complex interactions *between* neurotransmitter systems.

# 5

# The bases of intervention

In this chapter, some of the general characteristics of current 'best practice' in approaches to intervention will be discussed. It will be argued that, wherever possible, interventions, whether behavioural, psychopharmacological or based on alternative approaches, should be constructional, functionally based, socially valid and, of course, ethical.

## The constructional approach

Israel Goldiamond, in one of the classic contributions to the development of applied behaviour analysis, identified two broad orientations which characterize most approaches to intervention (Goldiamond, 1974). Firstly, he identified a *pathological* approach which focusses on the elimination of behaviours (e.g. self-injury) or states (e.g. anxiety, distress). As he pointed out:

such approaches often consider the problem in terms of a pathology which, regardless of how it was established, or developed, or is maintained, is to be eliminated (Goldiamond, 1974, p. 14).

He contrasted this with what he termed a *constructional* approach, an orientation:

whose solution to problems is the construction of repertoires (or their reinstatement or transfer to new situations) rather than the elimination of repertoires (Goldiamond, 1974, p. 14).

Take, for example, the case of John, a young man with severe intellectual disabilities who displays aggression when attempts are made to teach him new skills. A pathological approach would pose the question: how can we stop John being aggressive? A constructional approach would formulate the problem in terms of: how can we support John in responding more appropriately to the types of situations which evoke his aggression? As can be seen, while the pathological approach is simply concerned with the *elimination* of aggression, the constructional approach is concerned with the *establishment* of new ways of acting which would be more appropriate in the situations which currently evoke his aggression.

There may, of course, be situations in which it is easier and simpler to adopt a pathological rather than a constructional approach. Consider, for example, the case in which challenging behaviour only occurs in response to a particular situation which is not itself particularly important for the person's health, development or quality of life (e.g. travelling to school by a particular route; Kennedy & Itkonen, 1993). An unintrusive and potentially effective pathological approach to such a situation would be simply to avoid the eliciting stimuli. It is likely, however, that such situations are relatively rare and that pathological approaches should be considered the exception rather than the rule.

Cullen, Hattersley and Tennant (1981) identify three reasons for adopting a constructional approach. Firstly, and as Goldiamond (1974) argued, constructional interventions may be more consistent with notions of human rights. This is perhaps best illustrated by the tendency for critics of behavioural approaches to focus on the questionable ethical value of eliminative procedures (e.g. Repp & Singh, 1990; Winnet & Winkler, 1972). A constructional approach would certainly appear to offer some safeguards against the more blatant examples of the abuse of therapeutic power which can occur when therapeutic procedures are applied to vulnerable populations.

Secondly, most basic and applied behavioural research concerns the establishment of new behaviours or repertoires (cf. Bailey et al., 1987; Iversen & Lattal, 1991a,b; Lattal & Neef, 1996; Stromer, Mackay & Remington, 1996). Indeed, the particular strength of the behavioural approach – and its greatest contribution to the field of intellectual disabilities – is its store of knowledge concerning the establishment, maintenance and generalization of behaviour. This, in effect, provides a very strong empirical foundation for constructionally based interventions.

Finally, a successful pathological intervention *must* involve a constructional component. If a particular behaviour is eliminated, new behaviour(s) will take their place. Behaviour is a dynamic process and (like nature) abhors a vacuum. On the face of it, a pathological orientation leaves this aspect of the intervention process to chance; a constructional intervention addresses it directly and some of the potential benefits of doing so are demonstrated by Sprague and Horner (1992). They examined the effects of a pathological intervention and a constructional intervention on the aggression and tantrums shown by Alan, a 15-year-old boy with intellectual disabilities. Assessment had indicated that his aggression and tantrums were maintained by a process of negative reinforcement, in that they elicited teacher help when presented with a difficult task. Each intervention was applied in sequence to only one of Alan's challenging behaviours: his hitting out. While the pathological intervention (verbal reprimands and response blocking) markedly reduced his hitting out, other problem behaviours (head and body shaking, screaming, hitting objects and putting his hands to his face) all increased so that, overall, there was no change in the total rate of challenging behaviours. The constructional intervention (prompting Alan to ask for help in response to difficult tasks) eliminated all problem behaviours, a result which was maintained after 2 months. Given the very real risks of response covariation or 'symptom substitution' in response to intervention (Schroeder & MacLean, 1987), an approach which centres on the introduction of alternative behaviours would appear to have much to offer.

## The functional perspective

Perhaps the single most significant development in behavioural practice in relation to intellectual disabilities during the 1980s was the re-emergence of a *functional approach* to analysis and intervention (Axelrod, 1987; Carr, Robinson & Palumbo, 1990a; Mace & Roberts, 1993; Mace, Lalli & Lalli, 1991; Mace, Lalli & Shea, 1992). This approach is based on a belief that *the selection or design of approaches to intervention should reflect knowledge of the causal and maintaining factors underlying the person's challenging behaviour.*

Such a belief is, of course, axiomatic to much medical practice. If we are interested in moving beyond symptomatic relief, diagnosis must precede treatment. Indeed, a similar concern with analysis providing the foundation for intervention was evident in the earlier days of applied behaviour analysis. In the intervening period, however, 'behaviour modification' took precedence. As Mace and Roberts point out this approach:

relied largely on [the use of] potent reinforcers or punishers to override the reinforcement contingencies or biologic processes that maintained problem behavior. The treatments were effective, but they were often artificial, conspicuous, difficult to implement for long periods of time, and deemed unacceptable by some caregivers. (Mace & Roberts, 1993, p. 113).

They were also primarily pathological in orientation. The significance of adopting a functional approach can be simply illustrated by considering the use of time-out procedures. The logic of such procedures is that, by arranging the person's environment to ensure that occurrence of challenging behaviour reliably results in reduced *opportunity* for reinforcement, challenging behaviour should become less frequent over time. Indeed, this is the most likely outcome if time-out were applied to a challenging behaviour maintained by positive reinforcement (e.g. contingent adult attention). In such a case, the time-out procedure would effectively combine extinction (preventing access to adult attention) with a temporary reduction in the background rate of reinforcement. However, what would happen if the person's challenging behaviour was maintained by negative re-inforcement (e.g. escape from aversive tasks or unwanted attention)? In this case, application of a traditional 'time-out' procedure would *guarantee* that each episode of the challenging behaviour was (negatively) reinforced by the contingent removal of aversive materials and/or attention (e.g. teacher demands). At best, such an intervention would be ineffective; at worst, it could lead to a significant strengthening of the behaviour (cf. Durand et al., 1989; Solnick, Rincover & Peterson, 1977).

Certain approaches to intervention, including much of the emerging technol-ogy of positive behavioural support (Carr et al., 1999a; Koegel, Koegel & Dunlap, 1996a), are dependent for their success on accurate knowledge about the factors which maintain an individual's challenging behaviour. Those approaches, which can be applied in the absence of knowledge of underlying processes, tend to be either relatively ineffective (e.g. simple differential reinforcement procedures: Lancioni & Hoogeveen, 1990; O'Brien & Repp, 1990) or procedurally unaccept-able in many contexts (e.g. punishment). Indeed, one of the potential benefits of adopting a functional approach is that it may lead to a reduced reliance on such intrusive methods (Axelrod, 1987; Carr et al., 1990a; Pelios et al., 1999). There is also some evidence to suggest that functionally based procedures may be preferred by people with severe intellectual disability and challenging behaviour (Hanley et al., 1997).

The discussion in the preceding chapter regarding the potential complexity of underlying mechanisms indicates that the adoption of a functional approach may be demanding in that:

- there is no clear link between the topography and function of challenging behaviour – indeed, very similar topographies shown by the same person may serve different behavioural functions;
- the maintaining factors underlying a person's challenging behaviour may vary over time and across contexts;
- challenging behaviours may be multiply controlled by different contingencies of reinforcement and may reflect a combination of biological and behavioural processes.

The viability of this approach, therefore, lies in the availability of reliable, valid and user-friendly approaches to assessment. This issue will form the basis for the next chapter.

## Social validity

In Chapter 2, the notion of social validity was introduced. An intervention which is socially valid should: (a) address a socially significant problem, (b) do so in a manner which is acceptable to the main constituencies involved and (c) result in socially important outcomes or effects. In that chapter, some time was spent discussing the social significance of challenging behaviours and approaches to measuring the 'meaningful outcomes' of intervention (Evans & Meyer, 1985; Fox & Emerson, in press; Meyer & Evans, 1993a,b; Meyer & Janney, 1989). We will return to the latter topic in Chapter 6. The remaining component of social validity – the acceptability of intervention procedures – generated much controversy in the 1980s and early 1990s.

## The 'aversives' debate

Many thousands of words were written on the acceptability (or not) of using 'aversive' or 'intrusive' procedures to reduce challenging behaviour (e.g. G. Allan Roeher Institute, 1988; Guess et al., 1987; LaVigna & Donnellan, 1986; McGee et al., 1987; Mulick, 1990; O'Brien, 1991; Repp & Singh, 1990; Van Houten et al., 1988). Opinions ranged from suggestions that the use of such procedures may be the most ethically appropriate course of action in certain situations (Van Houten et al., 1988), to calls for a blanket condemnation of the use of intrusive interventions (G. Allan Roeher Institute, 1988). An indication of the intensity of the debate was provided by a number of organizations sponsoring a 'call to action' to Amnesty International to investigate the use of such procedures as a form of torture (Weiss, 1992).

One unfortunate outcome of this controversy was the implicit (and at times explicit) assumption that the use of intrusive procedures was inherent to behavioural theory and/or practice. Evans and Meyer (1990), for example, suggested that the 'narrow' and 'rigid' approach of applied behaviour analysis was characterized by 'the use, refinement, and fascination with procedures for delivering aversives to people with disabilities' (p. 135). On the face of it, such a statement clearly failed to reflect the diverse activities of applied behaviour analysts (e.g. Bailey et al., 1987; Remington, 1991).

In other ways, however, it is easy to see how such an apparent association may have come about. A number of accounts had been published in the behavioural literature of what can only be considered degrading practices (e.g. Altmeyer, Williams & Sams, 1985; Conway & Butcher, 1974; Freagon, 1990). In addition, the behavioural community had taken a lead in supporting the individual's right to effective treatment in contentious situations (Etzel et al., 1987) and some leading behaviour analysts played a very visible role indeed in contributing to the continued development of punitive procedures or 'default technologies' (e.g. Iwata, 1988; Linscheid et al., 1990). Further, reviews of the behavioural research literature undertaken at that time did indicate a major reliance, at least in research studies, on punitive procedures focussing on the reduction of challenging behaviour (cf. LaGrow & Repp, 1984; Lennox et al., 1988; Lundervold & Bourland, 1988; Scotti et al., 1991b).

The association between behavioural techniques and intrusive procedures was in some ways rather ironic since behavioural theorists have, in general, been forceful advocates of the use of procedures based on positive reinforcement rather than punishment in many areas of human affairs (e.g. Sidman, 1989; Skinner, 1971). As Skinner himself pointed out:

> to remain satisfied with punishment without exploring nonpunitive alternatives is the real mistake . . . I have been proud of the success we have had in finding many alternatives to punishment and I regret that this controversy is likely to renew the view that behaviorism means punishment. It is, I believe, the only hope for the eventual elimination of punitive control in all fields (Griffin et al., 1988, p. 105).

## The emergence of positive behavioural support

The last decade has seen major changes in behavioural practice, changes which in many respects were driven by changing conceptions among practitioners, families and advocates about the social acceptability of behavioural procedures. Most notably, the latter half of the 1990s saw the emergence of the discipline of 'positive behavioural support' (Koegel, Koegel & Dunlap, 1996a), a development marked by the launch of the new *Journal of Positive Behavior Interventions*.

In the context of a recent meta-analysis, Carr et al. (1999a) identified the defining characteristics of positive behavioural support in terms of independent and dependent variables:

> From the standpoint of the independent variable, the PBS [positive behavioral support] approach refers to those interventions that involve altering deficient environmental conditions (e.g. activity patterns, choice options, prompting procedures) and / or deficient behavior repertoires (e.g. communication, self-management, social skills) . . . increases in positive behavior, lifestyle change and decreases in problem behavior define the core of PBS with respect to the dependent variables (Carr et al., 1999a, pp. 7–8).

Much of the content of the following two chapters will address the methods and procedures associated with this emerging discipline.

## The ethics of intervention

As noted above, stances taken by contributors to the 'aversives' debate ranged from blanket condemnation of the use of such procedures (e.g. Endicott, 1988; Ewen, 1988; Freagon, 1990; O'Brien, 1991) to arguments that, under certain circumstances, the costs to the person and others in terms of distress experienced may be justified given the likely benefits of intervention when compared with either no intervention or currently available alternatives (e.g. Van Houten et al., 1988).

It is important to note that, in all cases, the conclusions reached reflect a set of beliefs regarding the actual or likely effects of intrusive and alternative procedures. Thus, for example, Endicott (1988) stated that the use of any form of aversive procedure 'is unacceptable because it undercuts the factor that is most likely to lead to permanent freedom from serious destructive behaviour, namely bonding based on affection and trust between one human being and another' (p. 100). The central issue of the debate, therefore, was one of defining the conditions under which a set of procedures, of a given level of intrusiveness and with certain predictable outcomes, could be justified.

This is, of course, central to consideration of the ethics of intervention. Meinhold and Mulick (1990) made a useful contribution to the debate by drawing on the literature of 'comparative risk assessment'. This approach involves careful consideration of the risks, costs and benefits of the alternative courses of action which are open to us when confronted by a difficult social problem. The stages involved in this process are: identifying the problem; conducting a feasibility assessment of potential solutions; assessing the risks, costs and benefits of potential solutions and of inaction; and making a decision. Some of the issues involved in these four stages will be briefly discussed below.

### Identifying the problem

As was indicated in Chapter 2, the problem, or social significance, of challenging behaviour needs to be conceptualized broadly. It involves significant social and financial costs to the person themselves, to carers and to other family members, co-residents and co-workers, and to care staff and agencies responsible for the purchase and provision of health and welfare services. We will discuss ways of identifying and assessing the challenge presented by challenging behaviours in the following chapter.

### Feasibility assessment of potential solutions

Potential solutions to the problem must satisfy two criteria. Firstly, they must be technically feasible, i.e. it must be possible to design a solution using a particular approach based on knowledge concerning the causes of the problem. Thus, for example, it is not technically feasible to replace self-injurious behaviour maintained by β-endorphin release with an alternative communicative response (communicative responses do not lead to β-endorphin release). Secondly, potential solutions must be practically feasible, i.e. the human and other resources necessary for the successful implementation of the approach need to be identified and

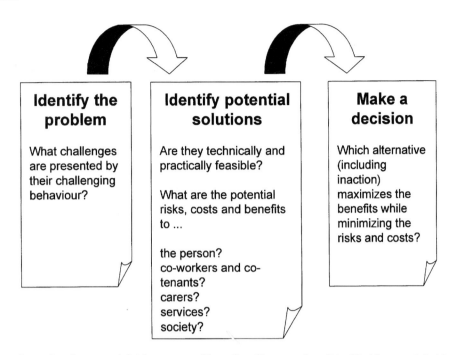

Figure 5.1.   Assessing the potential risks, costs and benefits of intervention. (Modified from Meinhold & Mulick, 1990.)

compared with what is actually or potentially available. Advocating solutions which are not feasible in a given context is equivalent to advocating inaction.

**Assessing risks, costs and benefits**

Identifying the nature of the problem indicates the areas in which the risks, costs and benefits of potential solutions need to be evaluated. Figure 5.1 illustrates the application of this approach to the selection of interventions to reduce challenging behaviour. Unfortunately, much of the information which is required in such an analysis is not currently available. Thus, while much is known about the short-term effects of intervention on the targeted behaviour, relatively little is known regarding such issues as: the generalization and long-term maintenance of reductions in challenging behaviour; positive or negative changes in collateral behaviours in response to interventions; the impact of interventions on the social ecology of service settings; and the impact of intervention procedures on the social status of participants.

It is also important that the 'costs' of interventions are considered in context. From a behavioural perspective, of course, stimuli are neither intrinsically reinforcing nor aversive. Stimuli act as punishers or reinforcers dependent on factors such as prior experience, current levels of deprivation or satiation, or the nature of the individual's access to an activity in relation to free operant baselines (Konarski et al., 1981). Thus, stimuli which common consensus may regard as aversive, for example being mechanically restrained, do, for some individuals, act as powerful reinforcers (e.g. Favell et al., 1981). Similarly, some nominally 'nonaversive' procedures may involve components which some individuals may find distressing, e.g. procedures involving sustained social interaction, such as Gentle Teaching (e.g. McGee et al., 1987), may be aversive to people with autism. Paisey, Whitney and Moore (1989), for example, reported higher levels of both self-injury and collateral 'distress' behaviours for one of their two clients during Gentle Teaching when compared with other intervention approaches. These observations suggest that the 'aversiveness' of procedures, including more humanistic procedures such as psychotherapy or the creative therapies, can only be considered in the context of their actual implementation. The aversiveness of a procedure is a product of the interaction between the individual, the context of intervention and the intervention process – it is not inherent in the procedure itself.

## Decision making

The final stage in the process of comparative risk assessment involves the weighing up of the risks, costs and benefits of the potential courses of action and the 'default' option of inaction. Obviously, this will be a complex process with different stakeholders in the intervention process placing different weights on the importance of the range of possible outcomes. Normally, of course, the person themselves would take the main role in this process by giving consent to a treatment selected out of a range of proffered options. Situations in which an adult with severe intellectual disabilities is defined as legally incompetent raise some complex issues regarding the giving of consent or approval (Kiernan, 1991; Murphy, 1993).

# 6

# Assessment and analysis

Approaches to assessment which take account of the issues discussed in the previous chapter will need to address a number of factors. Firstly, adopting a functional perspective implies that a key task of assessment will be to identify the behavioural (and other) processes responsible for maintaining the person's challenging behaviours. This process will be referred to as functional assessment. Secondly, taking a constructional approach to intervention suggests that it will be necessary to evaluate aspects of the individual's existing repertoire and to identify potential reinforcers which may be employed in establishing new behaviours. Finally, the requirement that interventions be ethical and socially valid indicates the need to evaluate the feasibility and potential risks, costs and benefits of the intervention process.

## Functional assessment

In recent years, a number of reviews and practical guides have focussed on the procedures and techniques which may be involved in functional assessment (e.g. Carr et al., 1994; Demchak & Bossert, 1996; Durand, 1990; Feldman & Griffiths, 1997; Halle & Spradlin 1993; Lalli & Goh, 1993; McBrien & Felce, 1994; Meyer & Evans, 1989; Miltenberger, 1998; O'Neill et al., 1997; Pyles & Bailey, 1990; Romanczyk & Matthews, 1998; Vollmer & Van Camp, 1998; Wacker et al., 1998; Zarkowska & Clements, 1994). In the following sections, some of the key issues and important trends in this burgeoning area will be discussed. The process of conducting a comprehensive functional assessment may be conceptualized as comprising four interlinked processes:

- the selection and definition of challenging behaviours as potential targets for intervention;
- the description of relationships between the occurrence of challenging behaviour, environmental events and bio-behavioural states;
- the generation of hypotheses concerning the nature of the contingencies

maintaining the person's challenging behaviours, the establishing operations and discriminative stimuli which set the occasion for challenging behaviour to occur, and aspects of the organization of behaviour; and

• the further evaluation of these hypotheses prior to intervention.

In general, the second stage involves the descriptive (or structural) analysis of challenging behaviour; the fourth stage involves the functional analysis of challenging behaviour (Axelrod, 1987). Descriptive or structural analyses focus on the description of relationships between the rate and form of a behaviour and aspects of the context within which it occurs. A functional analysis extends this descriptive process by providing an experimental analysis (i.e. a 'believable demonstration') of the contextual control of behaviour.

It is important to see these aims as interlinked processes, rather than as distinct stages. The relationship between hypothesis formulation and data collection is not linear. Descriptive analyses are themselves based on hypotheses regarding the kinds of processes which may underlie challenging behaviours; one cannot just 'observe'. The results of descriptive and experimental analyses are likely to feed back into refining the definition of response classes. Nevertheless, for the sake of simplicity, these four areas will be addressed separately in the sections below.

## The identification and definition of behaviours

Four issues need to be considered in relation to the identification and definition of behaviours:

• the selection of targets for intervention on the basis of their personal and social impact;
• the importance of assessing the function of separate forms of challenging behaviour;
• the inclusion within the assessment process of functionally equivalent behaviours; and
• choice of the unit of assessment.

### Selecting socially valid targets for intervention

If interventions are to be socially valid, then the selection of target behaviours should reflect their personal and social significance, i.e. they should include those behaviours which, if reduced, would result in the most socially significant (or 'meaningful') outcomes. This will require an assessment of the extent to which the challenging behaviour(s) shown by the person have, or are likely to have, a direct impact on such factors as:

• the short- and medium-term physical risk to the person and others;
• the restriction of access to functional age-appropriate community-based activities;

- exclusion from their family or community-based services;
- stress and strain experienced by carers and care staff;
- the quality of relationships between the service user and others; and
- the need for more restrictive management practices (e.g. restraint, sedation, seclusion).

Unfortunately, this area has received scant attention. While attention has been drawn to the importance of these issues and some *general* measurement strategies outlined (e.g. Evans & Meyer, 1985; Meyer & Evans, 1989, 1993a,b; Meyer & Janney, 1989), no structured approaches are currently available which seek to identify the broader impact of the person's challenging behaviour in their particular context. Approaches to assessing change in these broader outcomes were introduced in Chapters 2 and 5 and will be discussed in more detail in the final section of this chapter.

### The form and function of behaviour

The selection and definition of intervention targets should also be guided by knowledge about the potential types of relationship which may exist between behaviour and maintaining processes. As discussed in Chapter 4, the relationship between the form and function of challenging behaviours is far from straightforward; maintaining factors may be complex, are likely to vary significantly across individuals and may vary within individuals over contexts and time.

It is also possible that different forms or topographies of the person's challenging behaviour may be maintained by different processes (e.g. Day et al., 1988; Derby et al., 1994; Emerson et al., 1995; Kern et al., 1997; Richman et al., 1998; Sigafoos & Tucker, in press; Slifer et al., 1986; Sprague & Horner, 1992). This has considerable implications for the selection and definition of target behaviours, strongly suggesting that the assessment process should aim to identify the function of each topographically distinct form of challenging behaviour shown by the individual, rather than aggregate challenging behaviours together under such general terms as 'self-injury' or 'disruption'. The latter option runs the risk that the results of the assessment process may be contaminated by summing together behaviours which are maintained by different processes. This may result in apparently undiscriminated patterns of responding in the results of assessment (e.g. Derby et al., 1994). Alternatively, it may overlook the functions of behaviours which occur at a relatively lower rate within the person's repertoire. This latter risk is illustrated in Figures 6.1 and 6.2.

Figure 6.1 displays the rate of self-injurious behaviours shown by Susan, a 13-year-old girl with multiple severe self-injury, during a brief experimental functional analysis (see Chapter 4 for a description of the conditions). The data suggest that her self-injury is maintained by a process of automatic reinforcement,

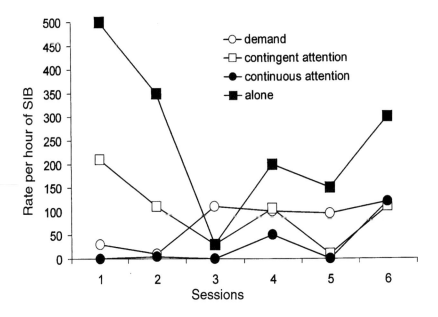

Figure 6.1.   Rate of occurrence of Susan's self-injurious behaviours across experimental conditions.

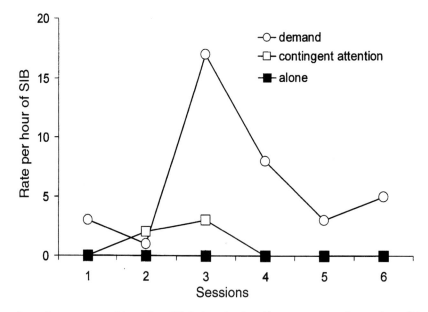

Figure 6.2.   Rate of occurrence of Susan's self-injurious back poking across experimental conditions.

in that it occurs consistently at higher rates in the 'alone' condition. Figure 6.2, however, shows the rate of one of her less frequent forms of self-injury (back poking) when disaggregated from the overall results. As can be seen, this particular behaviour appears to be maintained by a process of negative (social) reinforcement, in that it occurs consistently at a higher rate under conditions of instructional demand. In this case, relying on aggregated data would have resulted in overlooking the behavioural process maintaining at least one form of her self-injury. This could have been proven problematic, since a logical approach to intervention for behaviours maintained by (positive) automatic reinforcement would be to provide alternative external stimulation (Vollmer, 1994). While this may have reduced the rate of those forms of self-injury maintained by automatic reinforcement (Favell et al., 1982), it may well have *increased* the rate of those behaviours maintained by negative reinforcement.

One of the tasks of assessment is to identify relationships *between* behaviours (e.g. identifying which behaviours belong to which response classes). This can only be achieved, of course, if assessment begins by defining the separate and topographically distinct forms of challenging behaviour shown by the person. The decision of whether to aggregate behaviours together into larger units is an empirical issue which will be determined by the results of the assessment process.

### Including functionally equivalent behaviours in the assessment process

A focus on the function, rather than the form, of behaviour also draws attention to the potential value of including behaviours in the assessment process which may be functionally equivalent to the targeted challenging behaviour. This has two possible advantages. Firstly, if it is possible to identify existing socially appropriate functionally equivalent behaviours, these may be used during intervention to substitute for and displace the target behaviour (Carr, 1988; Carr et al., 1994).

Secondly, it may increase the opportunity for examining aspects of the contextual control of low frequency challenging behaviours. Functional assessment (and, in particular, experimental functional analysis) is often problematic when applied to behaviours which occur at a very low rate. In such instances, it may be possible to identify members of the same response class which occur at a higher rate than the challenging behaviour. This would then allow us to examine the contextual control of the more frequent behaviours as indicators for the main intervention target. For example, a preliminary descriptive analysis may suggest that screaming (which occurs relatively frequently) and aggression (which occurs much more rarely) are members of the same response class – that is, they both appear to be controlled by the same contingencies. Assessment could then proceed by gathering more detailed information on the contextual control of the person's screaming as a 'proxy' indicator for aggression. At the end of the day, of course, it would be necessary to demonstrate, rather than simply assume, the applicability of hypotheses generated from descriptive and functional analyses of such proxy indicators to the target behaviour of interest.

Richman et al. (1999) provide an illustration of such an approach in the functional analysis of aggression shown by three children with intellectual disabilities. During initial experimental functional analyses, aggression either did not occur or occurred sporadically at extremely low rates. However, less severe challenging behaviours (disruption, screaming) were reliably associated with particular assessment conditions (escape from tasks for two participants, access to toys for the third). A subsequent extinction analysis indicated that aggression was, in fact, a member of the same response class as the less severe forms of challenging behaviour (see also Lalli et al., 1995).

## The unit of assessment

The functional classification of behaviours also has implications for the size of the behavioural 'unit' selected for analysis. As Scotti et al. (1991a) point out, there is probably no greater truism in psychology than 'behaviour consists of a complex stream within which elements are defined and abstracted by the human observer' (p. 140). Obviously, the way in which we abstract units or chunks of behaviour for the purpose of assessment may have significant implications.

A functional approach will attempt to abstract units on the basis of their functional integrity, i.e., it will aim to identify chunks of behaviour which are controlled by their end-point maintaining consequences. So, for example, the sequence of behaviours involved in making a cup of coffee, including all behaviours from getting up to go to the kitchen to sitting down with a freshly brewed cup of coffee, is probably, for most of us, a single functional unit controlled by the reinforcing consequences of coffee drinking. This is only the case, however, when the chain of behaviours is under the control of a specific end-point contingency. In a teaching programme to make coffee, of course, this may not be the case. In such instances, this larger sequence may be comprised of any number of separate functional units each controlled by, for example, instructor praise or, alternatively, escape from instructor prompts.

Applying this approach to the identification of challenging behaviours does mean that we need to be constantly aware of the possibility that the composition of functional units containing challenging behaviours may vary across individuals and settings. While, for one person, a blow to the face may consist of a functional unit maintained by social attention, for another person the functional unit may consist of a complete 'tantrum' of which self-injury is but one part. Hall and Oliver (1992) illustrated this point with regards to the self-injurious behaviour shown by a 28-year-old man with severe intellectual disabilities. They presented descriptive data which indicated that high-rate bursts of self-injury were maintained by positive social reinforcement. No such relationship was apparent, however, when they examined the relationship between low-rate bursts or single occurrences of self-injury and carer attention. There are, of course, plausible reasons to suggest that issues such as behavioural rate, intensity and the presence of concurrent behaviours may be important in defining functional units or operants.

## Summary

In summary, then, it has been suggested that:

- the targets for intervention (of which assessment is the first stage) should be primarily guided by the current personal and social impact of the behaviours and the possibility of bringing about more widespread change as a result of successful intervention;
- a key aim of assessment is to identify which of the challenging behaviours shown by the person belong to which response classes – as such, it is important that assessment begins by identifying the behavioural function associated with individual behaviours;
- there may be practical value in including in the assessment process behaviours which may be functionally equivalent to the primary targets of intervention; and
- the definition of the target behaviours should aim to capture a functionally integrated unit of behaviour, the nature of which is likely to vary between people and, possibly, across contexts.

## Descriptive analyses

The primary objective of descriptive analyses is to identify the processes responsible for maintaining the person's challenging behaviour; that is, they are approaches to 'behavioural diagnosis' (Pyles & Bailey, 1990). They differ from techniques of functional analysis in that they do not involve the systematic manipulation of environmental variables in order to demonstrate experimental control over the person's challenging behaviour. The value of informant-based approaches will be considered first, followed by an examination of the use of more complex observational methods. It will be shown that, while informant-based approaches are simple to administer and provide comprehensive preliminary information, concerns regarding the accuracy of informant reports suggest that they will need to be combined with more detailed observational or experimental methods in order to arrive at reliable and valid conclusions.

## Informant-based approaches

Structured and semi-structured interviews with key informants form the most widely used approach to the descriptive analysis of challenging behaviour (Desrochers, Hile & Williams-Moseley, 1997). They are easy to conduct and can provide a wealth of information on a broad range of topics of direct relevance to both the primary and secondary objectives of a functional assessment. Indeed, their use should be considered a logical prerequisite to more complex observational and experimental approaches. A number of structured approaches to collecting information from third parties are now available (e.g. Demchak & Bossert, 1996; Donnellan et al., 1988; Durand & Crimmins, 1988; Matson et al., 1999; McBrien & Felce, 1994; Meyer & Evans, 1989; O'Neill et al., 1997; Pyles & Bailey, 1990; Wieseler et al., 1985; Zarkowska & Clements, 1994).

O'Neill et al. (1997), for example, describe the use of a structured interview for collecting information from key informants in relation to:

- the topography, frequency, duration, intensity, impact and covariation of the person's challenging behaviours;
- potential setting events (e.g. medications, medical complaints, sleep cycles, eating routines and diet, daily schedule of activities, predictability, control and variety of activities, crowding, staffing patterns) which may be correlated with general variations in the probability of occurrence of the challenging behaviours;
- specific events or situations (e.g. time of day, setting, activity, identity of carer) which are predictive of either high or low rates of occurrence of the challenging behaviours;
- the environmental consequences of the challenging behaviours;
- the efficiency of the challenging behaviours in relation to physical effort, rate and delay of reinforcement;
- alternative communicative strategies used by the person in the context of everyday activities;
- potential reinforcers;
- existing functionally equivalent behaviours; and
- the history of previous approaches to intervention.

In addition to these topics, it may be desirable for the clinical interview to cover such issues as:

- the resources (human and material) available in the settings in which challenging behaviours occur;
- staff beliefs about the causes and/or functions of the person's challenging behaviour (Hastings, 1996, 1997; Oliver et al., 1996);
- the pattern (including its consistency) of the physical and emotional responses of staff to episodes of challenging behaviour (e.g. Mitchell & Hastings, 1998); and

- informal strategies adopted by staff to prevent the occurrence of challenging behaviour.

Structured interview formats are of considerable value in providing a series of prompts to guide the process of behavioural interviewing and, as noted above, they are undemanding of resources and capable of addressing a broad range of issues. Unfortunately, however, the reliability or validity of information collected with such schedules are unknown. Research evidence, however, suggests that such information should be treated with extreme caution.

Green et al. (1988, 1991), for example, report a series of studies examining the correspondence between: (1) staff rating of the preference of students with profound multiple handicaps for specific stimuli; (2) actual student approach to, and use of, these stimuli; and (3) the extent to which they functioned as positive reinforcers in a teaching task. They reported that, while student approach predicted the reinforcing potential of stimuli, the considerable majority of care staff was unable to predict either student approach or the reinforcing potential of stimuli at greater than chance levels (although see also Newton, Ard & Horner, 1993; Reid, Everson & Green, 1999). Similarly, Durand and Crimmins (1988) found a nonsignificant correlation between teachers' opinions regarding the motivational basis of self-injury shown by their pupils and the results of the Motivation Assessment Scale (MAS), which, in their study, predicted the results of more detailed experimental analyses of the children's self-injury.

These few studies, limited in scope as they are, do suggest that the global opinions of informants on such varied topics as student preference for specific stimuli and the function of challenging behaviour may be of highly questionable validity. Durand (1990) suggests that consistency of responding across informants may increase the confidence with which the resulting data are viewed; that is, increased levels of inter-informant agreement may be taken as an indicator of validity. While such a suggestion has a certain intuitive appeal, it does presuppose that the development of an *inaccurate* consensus of opinion among informants is a rare event. At present, we simply do not know whether or not this is likely to be the case.

Durand and Crimmins (1988) described the development of the MAS (see also, Durand, 1990; Durand & Crimmins, 1992). This is a 16-item questionnaire, each item of which is designed to ascertain the extent to which challenging behaviour occurs under stimulus conditions associated with behaviours maintained by: sensory consequences; positive social reinforcement; positive tangible reinforcement; or negative social reinforcement. They reported acceptable levels of inter-informant agreement for individual items and acceptable test–retest reliability over a 30-day period. They also reported 100% correspondence between the results of the MAS and more detailed functional analyses of the self-injury shown by eight randomly selected pupils (see also Durand & Carr, 1992).

More recently, however, conflicting evidence has accumulated concerning the utility of the MAS as a clinical tool. Firstly, studies investigating the factorial structure of the MAS have provided conflicting results (Bihm et al., 1991; Duker & Sigafoos, 1998; Singh et al., 1993a). Secondly, numerous studies have questioned the reliability of the data generated by the MAS (Duker & Sigafoos, 1998; Kearney, 1994; Newton & Sturmey, 1991; Sigafoos, Kerr & Roberts, 1994; Spreat & Connelly, 1996; Thompson & Emerson, 1995; Zarcone et al., 1991; although see Akande, 1998). Finally, Emerson et al. (1995) have reported unacceptably low levels of correspondence between the results of the MAS and the results of more detailed descriptive and experimental analyses (see also Toogood & Timlin, 1996).

These concerns regarding the reliability and validity of data derived from informant-based approaches do suggest that the behavioural interview should *only* be considered an initial stage in functional assessment and should *always* be followed by the use of more detailed observational and/or experimental analyses.

However, while information collected from carers and staff may not provide accurate data concerning the processes underlying a person's challenging behaviour, it will provide useful information regarding staff or carer beliefs about the behaviour's cause or function. Marked discrepancies between the demonstrated function of a behaviour and staff or carer beliefs about its function will need to be taken into account when planning interventions (Hastings & Remington, 1994a,b).

## Observational methods

The use of nonparticipant observation in functional assessments raises a number of methodological issues. These include: the selection and definition of target behaviours; the selection and definition of concurrent behaviours and environmental events; the selection of recording methods and sampling strategies; the reliability and validity of observational methods; observer training; the assessment of inter-observer agreement; subject reactivity; observer drift; and the use of graphical and statistical methods of data analysis (e.g. Kratochwill & Levin, 1992; Suen & Ary, 1989; Thompson, Felce & Symons, 2000). To review these issues is beyond the scope of the present book. Instead, discussion will be restricted to an examination of some of the observational methods which have been used in descriptive analyses of challenging behaviours in applied settings.

### ABC charts

The most frequently used observational approach to descriptive analysis in clinical practice involves the recording by care staff of descriptions of a sample of occurrences of antecedent (A) events, the target challenging behaviour (B) and

NAME: Sophie          OBSERVER: Eric          DATE: 9 January 2000

GENERAL CONTEXT: Home                          TIME: 4:30 pm

INTERPERSONAL CONTEXT: Sophie was watching TV. Chris walked in and asked her to tidy her room.

CHALLENGING BEHAVIOUR: Sophie begins to moan, shout and stamp her feet.

SOCIAL IMPACT: Chris looked exasperated and walked out muttering to herself. Sophie went back to watching TV.

NAME: Nick          OBSERVER: Eric          DATE: 10 January 2000

GENERAL CONTEXT: Pub                          TIME: 4:30 pm

INTERPERSONAL CONTEXT: Nick, Vicky and Sophie are having a coffee. Vicky and Sophie are deep in conversation with each other.

CHALLENGING BEHAVIOUR: Nick begins to moan, shout and stamp his feet.

SOCIAL IMPACT: Vicky looks concerned, pats Nick on the shoulder and included him in the conversation.

Figure 6.3.   Examples of index cards used for recording episodes of challenging behaviour during functional assessment. (Modified from Carr et al., 1994.)

consequent (C) events (Desrochers et al., 1997). Carr et al. (1994), for example, suggest using index cards to record occurrences of challenging behaviour (see Figure 6.3).

The data generated by ABC recording may be summarized to provide, depending on the sampling strategy employed, three types of information. Firstly, they may provide estimates of the rate or probability of occurrence of episodes of challenging behaviour within specified periods of time (e.g. days) or possibly contexts (e.g. sessions of group instruction). Secondly, they may highlight aspects of environmental context which appear to be common across episodes of challenging behaviour (e.g. being asked to participate in a nonpreferred activity). Finally, they may identify general classes of impact that episodes of challenging behaviour may have on ongoing social or other types of activities (e.g. withdrawal of requests, comforting attention from care staff). As such, these descriptions of antecedent and consequent events may generate some tentative hypotheses for further investigation (e.g. Lalli et al., 1993). However, due to the questionable accuracy of informant reports (see above), they are far from providing a 'believable demonstration' of underlying behavioural processes.

In a more structured approach to ABC analysis, Gardner et al. (1984, 1986) described the use of conditional probabilities over a 1-month period to identify antecedent conditions which set the occasion for aggression to occur in a young man with intellectual disabilities. These events included staff reminders, corrections, repeated prompts, demands, praise and teasing by peers. The conditional probability of aggression following such events ranged from 0.01 (aggression following praise) to 0.32 (aggression following teasing). In addition, information was collected regarding a range of potential establishing operations including weekend visits from his family, difficulty in getting up in the morning, the presence of a particular member of staff and arguments with peers prior to arriving at his day programme. Their results indicated that: (1) 81% of all aggressive outbursts occurred on the 43% of days which included one of these setting events; (2) the mean rate of occurrence of the recorded antecedent conditions was 21.7 per day for days including setting events, compared with 8.3 per day on the remaining days; and (3) the overall conditional probability of antecedent events eliciting aggression was 0.17 for days including setting events, compared with 0.07 on the remaining days (Gardner et al., 1984, 1986).

*Sequential analysis*

Some of the interpretative problems associated with ABC charts (cf. Emerson, 1995) can be resolved by the use of more complex approaches to recording and analysis (e.g. Bijou, Peterson & Ault, 1968; Emerson, Reeves & Felce, 2000; Emerson et al., 1996b; Hall & Oliver, 1992, 2000; Lalli et al., 1993; Lerman & Iwata, 1993; Sasso et al., 1992; Symons & MacLean, 2000).

As described in Chapter 4, Edelson et al. (1983) used a 10-second partial interval observational procedure to record the occurrence of self-injurious behaviours and staff demands, denials or punishment for approximately 5 hours for each of 20 institutionalized young people with intellectual disabilities. They reported sharp increases in the rates of staff contact prior to episodes of self-injury for 19 of the 20 participants. Similar procedures have been employed more recently by Lalli et al. (1993), Lerman and Iwata (1993), and Mace and Lalli (1991). Lalli et al. (1993), for example, used a continuous 10-second partial-interval recording procedure to monitor environmental events occurring antecedent and subsequent to challenging behaviours shown by three students with severe intellectual disabilities. Five hours of observational data were collected for each child. The resulting data suggested that the challenging behaviour of two participants was maintained by positive (social) reinforcement. The challenging behaviour of the third participant appeared to be multiply controlled by both positive and negative (social) reinforcement.

A limited number of studies have examined agreement between these types of descriptive approaches and the results of experimental functional analyses. Overall, they suggest that descriptive approaches tend to identify a greater number of potential functions for a given behaviour than experimental approaches (Lerman

& Iwata, 1993; Mace & Lalli, 1991; although see also Crawford et al., 1992) and may fail to discriminate between processes of positive and negative social reinforcement (Lerman & Iwata, 1993; Mace & Lalli, 1991). A number of factors may account for this apparent insensitivity of descriptive analyses including: the application of descriptive analyses in relatively barren settings in which carer responses to challenging behaviour may be inconsistent (Lerman & Iwata, 1993); the inherent difficulties of using descriptive analyses to identify relatively 'thin' schedules of reinforcement (Iwata, Vollmer & Zarcone, 1990b; Mace et al., 1991); failure to identify the appropriate functional unit in descriptive analyses (Hall & Oliver, 1992); failure to identify distinct response classes among topographically similar behaviours (Emerson et al., 1995); and the use of relatively unsophisticated approaches to the identification of behavioural sequences.

This last issue may be addressed by the use of portable computers to undertake more sophisticated observational and statistical analyses (Thompson et al., 2000). Emerson et al. (1995, 1996b, 1999c, 2000), for example, have illustrated the use of time-based lag sequential analysis (Sackett, 1979, 1987) to identify relationships between challenging behaviours and environmental events. This approach involves the calculation of the conditional probability of the onset, occurrence or termination of one event (e.g. self-injury) at specific points in time in relation to the onset or termination of a second event (e.g. instructional demands). Emerson et al. (1996b) used this method in the analysis of multiple forms of challenging behaviour shown by two girls and one boy with severe intellectual disabilities. Eight hours of videotape per child was transformed into a real-time event record using hand-held computers. They reported that 11 of the 12 topographies of challenging behaviours shown by the three children demonstrated statistically significant variation under particular environmental conditions. For ten of these behaviours, the variations were consistent with possible behavioural functions including: socially mediated positive and negative reinforcement; automatic reinforcement; and schedule induction.

Emerson et al. (1995) compared the results obtained by this approach with the results of experimental functional analysis for 21 topographies of challenging behaviour shown by five people with severe intellectual disabilities. They reported that: (1) descriptive analyses were more likely to identify a function for behaviours than experimental analyses (86% compared with 67%); and (2) there was a high degree of agreement (85%) between the results of sequential and experimental analyses in the 13 examples in which both procedures positively identified a function of the behaviour. This level of agreement compares well with previous comparisons between the results of descriptive and experimental analyses (although see also Toogood & Timlin, 1996).

*Scatter plots and related techniques*

A key aim of descriptive analysis is to identify patterns of variation in the occurrence of challenging behaviour in order to identify possible establishing operations. Touchette, MacDonald and Langer (1985) described the use of a *scatter plot* to identify temporal and contextual variations in the occurrence of challenging behaviour. Due to the simplicity of this technique, which involves the graphical display of partial-interval observational data over successive days to identify those times of day or settings associated with high rates of challenging behaviour, the use of scatter plots has become relatively common (Desrochers et al., 1997). However, (Kahng et al., 1998) in a recent study reported that visual analysis by experienced behaviour analysts of scatter plot data for 15 adults with challenging behaviour failed to identify any temporal relationships, even though temporal patterning was revealed by statistical control procedures for 12 of the participants.

## Generating hypotheses

The primary objectives of descriptive analyses are to generate hypotheses regarding the processes maintaining the person's challenging behaviour, including the identification of establishing operations which set the occasion for the behaviour to occur (Lalli & Goh, 1993). As indicated in the introduction to this chapter, the relationship between hypothesis formulation and data collection is interactive. Descriptive analyses are based on hypotheses regarding the kinds of processes which may underlie challenging behaviours. Nevertheless, a mid-point stage in a functional assessment requires the specification of more precise hypotheses regarding:

- the process(es) responsible for maintaining the person's challenging behaviour(s);
- the contextual control of these processes; and
- the interrelationships between different forms of challenging behaviour shown by the person.

As noted in Chapter 4, these relationships may be complex; maintaining factors may vary across behaviours, time and settings. In addition, challenging behaviours may be multiply controlled. It is appropriate, therefore, to attempt to identify the processes underlying each form of the person's challenging behaviours and to examine the extent to which this underlying process is constant across contexts. Table 6.1 illustrates the types of context–behaviour–consequence relationships which may be indicative of various underlying processes.

As indicated above, a host of variables may influence the extent to which these underlying processes are operational in particular contexts. These include aspects of the individual's bio-behavioural state, preceding interactions and aspects of the current context for behaviour.

**Table 6.1.** Relationships between antecedent events, challenging behaviours and consequent events which may suggest particular underlying processes

---

*Socially mediated positive reinforcement*

Does the person's challenging behaviour sometimes result in them receiving more or different forms of contact with others (e.g. while the episode is being managed or while they are being 'calmed down') or having access to new activities?

Is the behaviour more likely when contact or activities are potentially available but not being provided (e.g. situations in which carers are around but are attending to others)?

Is the behaviour less likely in situations involving high levels of contact or during preferred activities?

Is the behaviour more likely when contact or preferred activities are terminated?

*Socially mediated negative reinforcement (escape or avoidance)*

Do people respond to the behaviour by terminating interaction or activities?

Is the behaviour more likely in situations in which demands are placed on the person or they are engaged in interactions or activities they appear to dislike?

Is the behaviour less likely when disliked interactions or nonpreferred activities are terminated?

Is the behaviour less likely in situations involving participation in preferred activities?

Is the behaviour more likely in those situations in which they may be asked to participate in interactions or activities they appear to dislike?

*Positive automatic reinforcement (sensory stimulation, perceptual reinforcement or opioid release)*

Is the behaviour more likely when there is little external stimulation?

Is the behaviour less likely when the person is participating in a preferred activity?

Does the behaviour appear to have no effect upon subsequent events?

*Negative automatic reinforcement (de-arousal)*

Is the behaviour more likely when there is excessive external stimulation or when the individual is visibly excited or aroused?

Is the behaviour less likely when the individual is calm or in a quiet, peaceful environment?

Does the behaviour appear to have no effect on subsequent events?

---

- *Bio-behavioural state* includes such factors as alertness, fatigue and sleep/wake patterns (Brylewski & Wiggs, 1999; Espie, 1992; Green et al., 1994; Guess et al., 1990, 1993; Horner et al., 1997; Kennedy & Meyer, 1996; O'Reilly, 1995), hormonal changes (Taylor et al., 1993a), drug effects (Kalachnik et al., 1995; Taylor et al., 1993b), caffeine intake (Podboy & Mallery, 1977), seizure activity (Gedye, 1989a,b), psychiatric disorders (Emerson et al., 1999b; Lowry &

Sovner, 1992), food deprivation (Talkington & Riley, 1971; Wacker et al., 1996a), mood (Carr et al., 1996), illness or pain (Bosch et al., 1997; Carr et al., 1996; Carr & Smith, 1995; Gardner & Whalen, 1996; Kennedy & Meyer, 1996; O'Reilly, 1997; Peine et al., 1995).

- *Preceding interactions* include such factors as preceding compliance (Harchik & Putzier, 1990; Horner et al., 1991; Mace et al., 1988), task repetition (Winterling et al., 1987), critical comments from others (Gardner et al., 1986), immediately preceding interactions (Horner et al., 1997; O'Reilly, 1999; O'Reilly & Carey, 1996; O'Reilly et al., in press), temporally distant social interactions (Gardner et al., 1986; O'Reilly, 1996), physical exercise (Lancioni & O'Reilly, 1998), the route taken to a setting (Kennedy & Itkonen, 1993), and time of awakening (Gardner et al., 1984; Kennedy & Itkonen, 1993).

- The *current context* for behaviour includes such factors as noise, temperature, levels of demand and positive comments from staff (Kennedy, 1994b; O'Reilly, 1997), location (Adelinis et al., 1997), music (Durand & Mapstone, 1998), crowding (McAfee, 1987), preference and choice regarding concurrent activities (Cooper et al., 1992; Dunlap et al., 1994, 1995; Dyer et al., 1990; Ferro et al., 1996; Foster-Johnson et al., 1994; Lindauer, DeLeon & Fisher, 1999; Ringdahl et al., 1997; Vaughn & Horner, 1997), the amount of noncontingent reinforcement available in the setting (Derby et al., 1998; Hagopian et al., 1994; Hanley et al., 1997; Roscoe et al., 1998; Vollmer et al., 1993, 1995a), concurrent social interactions and the nature of surrounding activities (Carr et al., 1976), and the presence of such idiosyncratic variables as small balls, puzzles and magazines (Carr et al., 1997).

### Hypothesis testing: experimental functional analysis

Experimental functional analyses involve the demonstration, through the experimental manipulation of environmental conditions, of the stimulus control of challenging behaviour. Experimental control is demonstrated if important aspects of the challenging behaviour (e.g. its rate, duration, intensity) systematically vary as a result of planned environmental changes. The methods employed in functional analyses form a subset of single subject experimental designs (Barlow & Hersen, 1984). Most frequently, functional analyses employ either withdrawal designs (e.g. Carr et al., 1976; Carr & Durand, 1985a) or alternating treatment (multielement) designs (e.g. Iwata et al., 1982, 1994a).

The general model of functional analysis is illustrated in the work of Iwata and colleagues. As described in Chapter 4, Iwata et al. (1982) used an alternating treatment design to examine the effect of social context on self-injurious behaviour. They recorded the rates of self-injury under four different conditions, which were selected as representing three *general* cases of the types of contexts under which self-injury maintained by operant processes may occur ('social disapproval', 'academic demand' and 'alone') and one control condition. In the *social disapproval* condition, an adult was present throughout, but did not interact with the child except to express concern or mild disapproval (e.g. 'don't do that') on the occurrence of self-injury. It is assumed that self-injury maintained by positive social reinforcement is more likely to occur under this condition. In the *academic demand* condition, an adult was present throughout and encouraged the child to complete an educational task using a graduated (ask–show–guide) prompting procedure. However, the adult withdrew their attention for 30 seconds contingent on the child's self-injury. This condition was assumed to be discriminative for self-injury maintained by negative social reinforcement. In the *alone* condition, no adults or materials were present. This condition was assumed to be discriminative for behaviours maintained by automatic or perceptual reinforcement. The *control* condition consisted of a stimulating environment in which social attention was delivered contingent on the nonoccurrence of self-injury.

Each condition lasted for 15 minutes and was presented on at least four occasions, the order of presentation being randomized. Visual inspection of the consistency of responding across conditions was used as evidence of behavioural function. Figures 6.1 and 6.2 above illustrate the use of this procedure.

Over the past decade, this approach has been used increasingly in the functional assessment of self-injurious behaviours (e.g. Day et al., 1988; Derby et al., 1992, 1994; Durand & Crimmins, 1988; Emerson et al., 1995; Hagopian et al., 1994; Iwata et al., 1994a; Lerman et al., 1994a; Steege et al., 1989, 1990; Toogood & Timlin, 1996; Vollmer, Marcus & LeBlanc, 1994; Wacker et al, 1990a; Zarcone et al., 1994) and has been extended to different forms of challenging behaviour, including aggression and destructive behaviours (e.g. Bowman et al., 1997; Derby et al., 1992; Emerson, 1990; Emerson et al., 1995; Fisher et al., 1998a; Hagopian et al., 1994; Hall et al., 1997; Mace et al., 1986; Paisey et al., 1991; Toogood & Timlin, 1996; Wacker et al., 1990a), pica (Goh et al., 1999; Mace & Knight, 1986; Piazza et al., 1996, 1998a), running away (Piazza et al., 1997a), inappropriate social behaviour (Frea & Hughes, 1997), bizarre speech and screaming (Mace & Lalli, 1991; Toogood & Timlin, 1996), breath holding (Kern et al., 1995) and stereotypy (e.g. Derby et al., 1994; Emerson et al., 1995; Goh et al., 1995; Mazaleski et al., 1994; Sturmey et al., 1988; Toogood & Timlin, 1996).

In addition to the types of conditions listed above, studies have also examined covariation between the target behaviour and a range of other environmental conditions, including continuous social attention (Emerson et al., 1995; Oliver, 1991; Toogood & Timlin, 1996), delayed access to food (Durand & Crimmins,

1988), contingent access to individually defined reinforcers (Day et al., 1988), medical examination (Iwata et al., 1990a), self-restraint (Vollmer & Vorndran, 1998), response cost (Steege et al., 1989) and differing forms of instructional demands (Fisher et al, 1998a).

More recently, research has begun to address such issues as optimal session length (Wallace & Iwata, 1999), the association between brief and extended experimental analyses (Kahng & Iwata, 1999; Tincani, Castrogiavanni & Axelrod, 1999; Vollmer et al., 1995b), the effects of equal and unequal reinforcer duration (Fisher, Piazza & Chiang, 1996), the effect of reinforcer preference and idiosyncratic preferences on assessment outcomes (Carr et al., 1997; Lalli & Kates, 1998; Richman & Hagopian, 1999), the effects of pre-session activity on assessment outcomes (O'Reilly et al., in press; O'Reilly & Carey, 1996), the use of within-session analyses to clarify results (Roane et al., 1999), procedures for clarifying ambiguous results (Kuhn et al., 1999), the stability of assessment outcomes over time (Martin, Gaffan & Williams, 1999) and the development of standard criteria for evaluating results (Hagopian et al., 1997; Martin et al., 1999).

The value of experimental functional analyses is that: (1) they provide a direct method for identifying functional relationships; (2) they require only brief changes to the person's environment, which is of particular value when sustaining systematic environmental changes may be impractical and/or unethical; (3) they are particularly suitable for examining the effects of stimulus conditions which may be conceptually important, but which only occur rarely in the person's normal setting (e.g. demands in institutional settings); (4) they involve a high degree of quantitative precision; and (5) they provide a practical method of testing hypotheses regarding the role of establishing operations in the contextual control of challenging behaviour (Smith et al., 1995a; Vollmer & Van Camp, 1998; Wacker et al., 1998).

The use of these procedures does, however, have a number of limitations (Halle & Spradlin, 1993; Iwata et al, 1990b; Mace, 1994b; Oliver, 1991; Sturmey, 1995; Vollmer & Van Camp, 1998; Wacker et al., 1998). In general, they are demanding of resources and expertise, both of which may be in short supply in many settings (Durand & Crimmins, 1988: although see Derby et al., 1992; Northup et al., 1991). In such instances, the opportunity costs involved in conducting a detailed experimental analysis need to be balanced against the likely benefits accruing from such an activity. For individuals with seriously challenging behaviours, investment in rigorous analysis may well be justified given the personal and social consequences of introducing inefficient or ineffective treatments. In addition, the resources and commitment required are likely to be less than that required during intervention (Iwata et al., 1990b). As such, functional analyses may provide a valuable behavioural test of staff compliance.

More serious is the possibility that experimental analyses may overlook important variables which might be operating in the person's natural environment,
including, for example, the operation of situationally specific or idiosyncratic
reinforcers (Carr et al., 1997; Lalli & Kates, 1998; Richman & Hagopian, 1999),
discriminative stimuli or setting events, and all examples of elicited behaviour
(Emerson & Howard, 1992; Romanczyk et al., 1992). This could lead to the
assessment process either failing to identify maintaining contingencies (lack of
internal validity) or to it providing results which may not generalize beyond the
analogue conditions (lack of external validity: cf. Conroy et al., 1996; Emerson et
al., 1995; Lerman & Iwata, 1993; Shirley, Iwata & Kahng, 1999; Toogood & Timlin,
1996). These potential limitations argue for the use of hypothesis-driven approaches to functional analysis in which experimental analysis is preceded by a
detailed descriptive or structural analysis (Carr, 1994).

## Summary

In the sections above, some of the more common descriptive and experimental
approaches to the functional assessment of challenging behaviour have been
reviewed. Table 6.2 summarizes some of the key advantages and disadvantages of
these approaches.

As can be seen, there is a clear (and unsurprising) relationship between the ease
of use of different approaches and the detail, reliability and validity of the
information generated. While structured interviews are easy to use and comprehensive, the information generated must be treated with considerable caution.
While demanding of resources, the combination of descriptive analyses (e.g.
scatter plots, structured observation) with hypothesis-driven experimental
analyses may provide the best chances of generating clear, reliable and valid
information.

Of course, functional assessments are often conducted in situations with limited
resources and under conditions in which there may be an obvious need to
intervene as quickly as possible. In deciding whether to invest more resources and
time in further assessment, it is important to keep in mind the aim of the
assessment process: to identify the processes maintaining or underlying the
person's challenging behaviour. The role of specific techniques is to generate and
test hypotheses about potential processes. Thus, the value of any particular
approach is determined by its effect in terms of reducing uncertainty about the
processes underlying the person's challenging behaviour. At times, these may
become painfully obvious through the use of simple descriptive techniques. In
such a situation, investing additional resources in order to achieve a minimal
reduction in uncertainty could not be justified.

In other situations, however, the use of simple descriptive techniques will reveal

**Table 6.2.** Descriptive and experimental approaches to functional assessment

|  | Advantages | Disadvantages |
| --- | --- | --- |
| Structured interviews (e.g. O'Neill et al., 1997) | Ease of use<br>Comprehensive<br>Applicable to low frequency behaviours | Unknown (but probably poor) reliability and validity |
| Rating scales (e.g. Durand & Crimmins, 1992) | Ease of use<br>Focus on specific maintaining factors<br>Applicable to low frequency behaviours | Poor reliability and validity |
| ABC charts (e.g. Carr et al., 1994) | Ease of use<br>Provide some information about event–behaviour–event sequences<br>Applicable to low frequency behaviours | Unknown (but probably poor) reliability and validity |
| Scatter plots (e.g. Touchette et al., 1985) | Ease of use<br>Provide information about broad aspects of contextual control<br>Can be reliable<br>Applicable to low frequency behaviours | Do not provide detailed information of maintaining contingencies<br>Possibly difficult to interpret |
| Setting event questionnaires (e.g. O'Neill et al., 1997) | Ease of use<br>Provide easily interpretable information about broad aspects of contextual control<br>Can be reliable<br>Applicable to low frequency behaviours | Do not provide information about maintaining contingencies |
| Structured partial-interval records (e.g. Lalli et al., 1993) | Can be highly reliable<br>Provide detailed information about immediate event–behaviour–event sequences<br>Precise measurement | More demanding of resources<br>Difficult to apply to low frequency behaviours<br>May have difficulty in distinguishing between positive and negative reinforcement, hence questionable validity |

**Table 6.2.** (*cont.*)

|  | Advantages | Disadvantages |
| --- | --- | --- |
| Structured real-time record with sequential analyses (e.g. Emerson et al., 1996b) | Can be highly reliable<br>Provide extremely detailed information about immediate event–behaviour–event sequences<br>Sound statistical basis for decision making<br>Precise measurement | Highly demanding of resources<br>Difficult to apply to low frequency behaviours |
| Standardized experimental analyses (e.g. Iwata et al., 1982) | Provide experimental demonstration of contextual control<br>Precise measurement | More demanding of resources<br>Difficult to apply to low frequency behaviours<br>May overlook important variables operating in natural environment |
| Brief standardized experimental analyses (e.g. Derby et al., 1992) | Provide experimental demonstration of contextual control<br>Precise measurement | Difficult to apply to low frequency behaviours<br>Limited internal validity<br>May overlook important variables operating in natural environment |
| Hypothesis-driven experimental analyses (e.g. Carr et al., 1976) | Link to descriptive analyses<br>Provide experimental demonstration of contextual control<br>Precise measurement | More demanding of resources<br>Difficult to apply to low frequency behaviours |

complex and confusing patterns of contextual control over the person's challenging behaviour. In such instances, to intervene prior to more detailed analysis would be ethically unjustifiable. As was discussed in Chapter 5, failure to match intervention to analysis may be either ineffective or potentially harmful.

## Assessing existing skills, competencies and potential reinforcers

The constructional approach looks for solutions to problems in the 'construction of repertoires (or their reinstatement or transfer to new situations) rather than the elimination of repertoires' (Goldiamond, 1974, p. 14). As a result, three additional aims of an initial assessment will be:

- to evaluate the broad range of skills and competencies the person possesses and to identify any additional impairments which may limit the establishment of new behaviours;
- to identify discrepancies between the person's current behaviour in key situations and what are more desirable alternative responses; and
- to identify the person's preferences with regard to potential alternative activities.

### General competencies

A large number of questionnaires and checklists have been developed to help assess the general competencies or adaptive behaviours of people with severe intellectual disabilities (Schalock, 1999). In addition to specific instruments, a number of more comprehensive overviews are available to provide guidance to practitioners regarding the assessment of adaptive behaviours (e.g. Browder, 1991), including texts which focus on the application of such methods to people with challenging behaviour (e.g. Carr et al., 1994; Meyer & Evans, 1989; Zarkowska & Clements, 1994).

Over the past decade, a number of authors have suggested that challenging behaviours may be conceptualized as examples of socially inappropriate communication strategies or interactional styles (Carr & Durand, 1985a,b; Carr et al., 1994; Day, Johnson & Schussler, 1986; Donnellan et al., 1984, 1988; Durand, 1986, 1990; Evans & Meyer, 1985; Meyer & Evans, 1989). Furthermore, as indicated above, evidence has begun to accrue to suggest that some challenging behaviours may be rapidly eliminated by providing the individual with an alternative communicative response which serves the same function as the challenging behaviour (see Chapter 7).

As such, the evaluation of the person's communicative competencies and style is of particular significance. Donnellan et al. (1984) described an observational procedure for recording 'ongoing impressions regarding the possible communicative function(s) of the behavior(s) of interest' (p. 205). More recently, Duker (1999) has described the development of the Verbal Behavior Assessment Scale (VerBAS), a 15-item scale containing three subscales for evaluating the verbal ability of people with severe intellectual disability in relation to requesting, labelling and echoing. Other instruments of potential value include the Receptive–Expressive Emergent Language Scale (Bzoch & League, 1991), which has been shown to correlate with some indicators of challenging behaviour (Sigafoos, in press).

### Discrepancy analysis

One of the specific aims of a functionally based constructional approach to remediating challenging behaviour is to identify behavioural deficits specific to conditions known to evoke challenging behaviour. Evans and Meyer (1985) suggested that 'discrepancy analysis' be employed to identify skill deficiencies (and hence targets for intervention) associated with the person's challenging behaviour. A discrepancy analysis involves the comparison of the individual's performance in a problematic situation with that of a more competent peer. On the basis of such a qualitative comparison, specific skill deficiencies may be identified as targets for intervention (Browder, 1991; Meyer & Evans, 1989). Such an approach has many similarities with some procedures for assessing the social validity of intervention outcomes and targets (Schwartz & Baer, 1991).

## Identifying preferences

The establishment or generalization of alternative responses to challenging behaviours may require the identification of activities or materials which are highly preferred by the person. For example, one possible strategy to reduce challenging behaviours maintained by perceptual reinforcement is to teach the use of and provide access to preferred materials or activities (Mace & Roberts, 1993; Vollmer, 1994). Of course, a functional assessment may well identify some extremely powerful reinforcers and contingencies – those maintaining the challenging behaviour itself. Approaches to intervention based on the notion of functional displacement (Carr, 1988) seek to use these contingencies to support alternative behaviours (see Chapter 7).

In other situations, however, the reinforcers maintaining the challenging behaviour may be unclear or not readily accessible by other means (e.g. β-endorphin release). In these cases, the identification of alternative highly preferred activities assumes a greater significance. There are three possible approaches for identifying the preferences of people with severe intellectual disabilities: indirect approaches involving informant interviews; theory-driven approaches; and empirical approaches.

*Indirect approaches* involve soliciting judgements from key informants regarding the person's preference for particular activities. As noted above, however, the validity of such judgements may be questionable (Green et al., 1988, 1991). Nevertheless, indirect approaches have an obvious role to play in selecting potential stimuli or activities for more detailed evaluation (Newton et al., 1993; Reid et al., 1999).

*Theory-driven approaches* can be used to identify potential reinforcing contingencies on the basis of predictions from either the Premack Principle (Premack, 1959) or molar equilibrium theory (Timberlake, 1980). The Premack Principle suggests that the opportunity to engage in high probability behaviours can be used to reinforce the performance of low probability behaviours. Molar equilibrium theory extends this notion to suggest that, in effect, the opportunity to engage in any behaviour shown by the organism under a free-operant baseline can be used to reinforce or punish the performance of any other behaviour, depending on the constraining conditions imposed (see Chapters 4 and 7). An interesting application of these approaches was reported by Charlop, Kurtz and Casey (1990) who demonstrated that the opportunity to engage in high probability stereotypy following completion of an academic task acted as a more powerful reinforcer than food for autistic children. Furthermore, they reported no negative side-effects of this procedure (Charlop et al., 1990).

Finally, *empirical approaches* may be used to identify preferences by examining the actual impact that materials or activities have on behaviour (Fisher & Mazur, 1997; Lancioni, O'Reilly & Emerson, 1996; Lohrmann-O'Rourke & Browder, 1998). A number of strategies have been employed to do this including measuring: approach responses to individual stimuli presented in an array (e.g. Green et al., 1988, 1991; Pace et al., 1985; Sigafoos & Dempsey, 1992; Steege et al., 1989); approach responses in a forced-choice situation (e.g. Fisher et al., 1992; Piazza et al., 1996); approach responses to materials presented in an array with (Windsor, Piche & Locke, 1994) or without (DeLeon & Iwata, 1996) the replacement of chosen stimuli; time allocation under free-operant baselines (Roane et al., 1998); and the extent to which stimuli presented contingently would increase the rate of motor behaviours for people with profound multiple handicaps (e.g. Wacker et al., 1985; Wacker et al., 1988). The available evidence suggests that the measurement of approach responses to materials presented in an array without the replacement of chosen stimuli may constitute the most efficient procedure for selecting preferred activities (DeLeon & Iwata, 1996).

## Evaluating the risks, costs and benefits of intervention

At a number of points throughout this book, attention has been drawn to the need to address the social validity of intervention. It has been argued that:

- challenging behaviour needs to be understood in its social context, including the impact it may have on broader aspects of the quality of life of the person, their family and friends, co-residents and co-workers, care staff and the public;
- socially valid interventions should involve procedures acceptable to the main stakeholders in the intervention process; and
- socially valid interventions should result in socially significant outcomes, which need to be framed in a broader social context than is usually the case and may involve a trade-off between procedural acceptability and the speed and magnitude of outcome.

These observations indicate the need for the assessment process to collect baseline information on a range of potential outcomes in order for the risks, costs and benefits of intervention to be thoroughly evaluated. As has been indicated, however, it is important that the process is individualized and that it focusses on the *legitimate outcomes of intervention*. This requires, among other things, that the goals of intervention are separated from more general life-planning processes.

Let us take, for example, the situation of a young woman who shows self-injurious behaviour and lives in a small house with two other women with severe intellectual disabilities. None of the women attend any sort of day programme. Indeed, most of the people served by that particular agency have very restricted lives. In terms of lifestyle, the young woman does not stand out from her peers.

In this instance, it would appear that her challenging behaviour is not functionally related to her poor lifestyle. Rather, her social and physical isolation stem from the failing of the service agency. It would seem inappropriate, then, to judge the success of an intervention programme to reduce self-injury on the basis of such general lifestyle variables as earned income, and social and physical integration.

Fox and Emerson (in press) have attempted to identify the outcomes of intervention which were considered particularly salient by a number of stakeholder groups including people with intellectual disability, parents of people with intellectual disability, clinical psychologists, psychiatrists, nurses, managers and direct support workers. The outcomes which were considered most salient across stakeholder groups are listed in Table 6.3, along with possible approaches to evaluating such 'meaningful outcomes' (see also Emerson, 1995; Meyer & Janney, 1989).

Lucyshyn, Olson and Horner (1995) provide an example of the use of a broad range of measurement approaches to evaluate the social validity of community-based supports for a young woman with life-threatening self-injury. They employed a variety of quantitative and qualitative approaches to measure outcomes in such areas as: frequency of self-injury and aggression; participation in community-based activities; activity preferences; social integration; relationships with her family; expressed satisfaction; medication use; and staff turnover.

## Summary

In the sections above, some of the key techniques and issues involved in the assessment of challenging behaviour have been examined. It has been argued that

**Table 6.3.** Assessing the socially significant outcomes of intervention

| Outcomes | Potential approaches |
| --- | --- |
| Reductions in severity of challenging behaviour | Observational methods (see *Journal of Applied Behavior Analysis*, 1967 onwards) |
| | Inspection of injuries (e.g. Iwata et al., 1990c) |
| | Structured interview with person and/or informants |
| | Analysis of incident reports |
| | Inspection of injuries received |
| Family and/or care staff have a better understanding of why the behaviour occurs | Structured interview |
| | Visual analogue or Likert rating scale |
| | Modified versions of checklists designed for staff (cf. Hastings, 1997; Oliver et al., 1996) |
| Increased participation in community-based activities | Diaries |
| | Structured interview with person/informants |
| | Visual analogue or Likert rating scale |
| | Checklists or questionnaires (e.g. Raynes et al., 1994) |
| Increased engagement within the home | Direct observation (e.g. Felce & Emerson, 2000) |
| | Diaries |
| | Visual analogue or Likert rating scale |
| | Structured interview with person/informants |
| | Checklists or questionnaires (e.g. Raynes et al., 1994) |
| Improved interpersonal environment in the home | Visual analogue or Likert rating scale |
| | Structured interview with person/informants |
| | Checklists or questionnaires (e.g. Albin et al., 1996) |
| Person learns alternative way of getting needs met | Observational methods |
| | Structured interview with person and/or informants |
| Increased friendships and relationships | Diaries |
| | Visual analogue or Likert rating scale |
| | Structured interview with person/informants |
| | Checklists or questionnaires (e.g. Tracey & Whittaker, 1990) |
| Family members and/or care staff learn effective coping strategies | Visual analogue or Likert rating scale |
| | Structured interview with person/informants |
| | Checklists or questionnaires (e.g. Albin et al., 1996) |
| Improved relationships between family members and/or care staff | Visual analogue or Likert rating scale |
| | Structured interview with person/informants |
| | Checklists or questionnaires (e.g. Albin et al., 1996) |
| Person is able to stay living with their family or in local community | Visual analogue or Likert rating scale |
| | Structured interview with person/informants |
| | Checklists or questionnaires |

**Table 6.3.** (*cont.*)

| Outcomes | Potential approaches |
| --- | --- |
| Person has greater control, more empowered | Visual analogue or Likert rating scale |
| | Structured interview with person/informants |
| | Checklists or questionnaires (e.g. Robertson et al., in press c) |
| Person has more frequent social contact | Direct observation (e.g. Felce & Emerson, 2000) |
| | Diaries |
| | Visual analogue or Likert rating scale |
| | Structured interview with person/informants |
| | Checklists or questionnaires (e.g. Tracey & Whittaker, 1990) |
| Effective supports are put in place | Diaries of service contacts |
| | Visual analogue or Likert rating scale |
| | Structured interview with person/informants |
| | Checklists or questionnaires (e.g. Beecham & Knapp, 1992) |
| Person is more contented, more self-esteem | Direct observation (e.g. Green, Gardner & Reid, 1997) |
| | Visual analogue or Likert rating scale |
| | Structured interview with person/informants |
| | Checklists or questionnaires (e.g. Schalock, 1996) |
| Others change their perception of the person | Visual analogue or Likert rating scale |
| | Structured interview with person/informants |
| Reduction in use of aversive methods and restrictive procedures | Analysis of medication records |
| | Recording of time spent in restraint/seclusion |
| | Analysis of records detailing restriction of liberty |
| | Analysis of risk-taking policies for person |

the assessment process will need to:
- identify and prioritize socially significant targets for intervention;
- determine the processes underlying the challenging behaviour(s) shown by the person;
- assess general and specific aspects of the person's existing skills and competencies;
- identify preferences; and
- collect information which will allow the attainment of the legitimate targets of intervention to be evaluated.

  In the next chapter, behavioural approaches to intervention will be considered.

# 7

# Behavioural approaches

In this chapter, a range of behavioural approaches to reducing challenging behaviour will be examined. It is not the intention, however, to provide a comprehensive meta-analysis of this vast area. Instead, attention will be directed to those approaches which form important components of the emerging technology of positive behavioural support (Carr et al., 1999a; Koegel et al., 1996a).

Those who are looking for more comprehensive or detailed reviews of specific areas are referred to the plethora of publications relating to this topic which has appeared over the last decade (e.g. Ball & Bush, 2000; Bouras, 1999; Carr et al., 1990b; Carr et al., 1999a; Cataldo, 1991; Cipani & Spooner, 1997; Didden, Duker & Korzilius, 1997; Emerson, 1998; Kiernan, 1993; Koegel et al., 1996a; Konarski et al., 1992; Lehr & Brown, 1996; Luiselli & Cameron, 1998; Luiselli, Matson & Singh, 1992; Matson et al., 1996; McGill, Clare & Murphy, 1996; Murphy, 1996; Oliver, 1995; Reichle & Wacker, 1993; Repp & Singh, 1990; Schlosser & Goetze, 1992; Schroeder, 1991; Schroeder, Rojahn & Oldenquist, 1991; Scotti et al., 1991b; Singh, 1997).

The contents of the chapter have been organized in terms of the general rationale behind particular approaches to intervention. Thus, approaches will be discussed which are based on: manipulating antecedent stimuli or changing the context to prevent the occurrence of challenging behaviour; behavioural competition or response covariation; disruption of maintaining contingencies; and punishment or other default technologies. In practice, of course, intervention programmes are likely to consist of a number of distinct approaches. The chapter will, therefore, be concluded by an examination of multicomponent strategies.

## Preventing the occurrence of challenging behaviours through the modification of establishing operations

The results of a comprehensive functional assessment should indicate: (1) contexts or settings in which challenging behaviour is significantly more likely to occur;

(2) establishing operations which may either activate or abolish the contingencies maintaining the person's challenging behaviour; and (3) the nature of the contingencies themselves. This knowledge opens up possibilities for either preventing or reducing the occurrence of challenging behaviours by the 'indirect' manipulation of antecedent variables.

As we noted previously, it is rare that challenging behaviours consistently occur in response to particular situations. More commonly, while the behaviour of interest may be more likely to occur in certain situations (e.g. during a specific type of instructional task), its actual occurrence can show considerable variability over time – people have good days and bad days. The identification of establishing operations which account for such variability and their modification, allows for the development of highly effective nonintrusive approaches to intervention which, in effect, undercut the motivational basis underlying challenging behaviours (Carr et al., 1990b, 1994, 1996, 1998, 1999a; Carr & Smith, 1995; Horner et al., 1996; Kennedy & Meyer, 1998a; McGill, 1999; Smith & Iwata, 1997).

For example, a functional assessment may indicate that a person's aggression is maintained by escape from social demands. Further analysis may help to identify those establishing operations *which establish demands as aversive stimuli* (and, consequently, as negative reinforcers). These could include such diverse factors as fatigue, illness, sedation, hangover, caffeine ingestion, the nature of preceding activities, the presence of preferred competing activities, and the pacing or style of demands. The modification of any establishing operations which might be identified could, therefore, prevent social demands acquiring aversive properties and, hence, reduce aggression by undercutting its motivational base (if demands are no longer aversive why would someone wish to escape from them?). This possibility is illustrated by Carr et al. (1976). In the study described in Chapter 4, rates of self-injury were immediately and significantly reduced by embedding demands in the context of a story. In all probability, these startling results reflect the operation of establishing operations.

As indicated above, a host of variables may influence the extent to which these underlying processes are operational in particular contexts, including aspects of the individual's bio-behavioural state, preceding interactions and aspects of the current context for behaviour.

- *Bio-behavioural state* includes such factors as alertness, fatigue and sleep/wake patterns (Brylewski & Wiggs, 1999; Espie, 1992; Green et al., 1994; Guess et al., 1990, 1993; Horner et al., 1997; Kennedy & Meyer, 1996; O'Reilly, 1995), hormonal changes (Taylor et al., 1993a), drug effects (Kalachnik et al., 1995; Taylor et al., 1993b), caffeine intake (Podboy & Mallery, 1977), seizure activity (Gedye, 1989a,b), psychiatric disorders (Emerson et al., 1999b; Lowry & Sovner, 1992), food deprivation (Talkington & Riley, 1971; Wacker et al.,

1996a), mood (Carr et al., 1996), illness or pain (Bosch et al., 1997; Carr et al., 1996; Carr & Smith, 1995; Gardner & Whalen, 1996; Kennedy & Meyer, 1996; O'Reilly, 1997; Peine et al., 1995).

- *Preceding interactions* include such factors as preceding compliance (Harchik & Putzier, 1990; Horner et al., 1991; Mace et al., 1988), task repetition (Winterling et al., 1987), the delay or cancelling of previous activities (Horner et al., 1997), critical comments from others (Gardner et al., 1986), immediately preceding interactions (O'Reilly, 1999; O'Reilly & Carey, 1996; O'Reilly et al., in press), temporally distant social interactions (Gardner et al., 1986; O'Reilly, 1996), physical exercise (Lancioni & O'Reilly, 1998), the route taken to a setting (Kennedy & Itkonen, 1993), and time of awakening (Gardner et al., 1984; Kennedy & Itkonen, 1993).

- The *current context* for behaviour includes such factors as noise, temperature, levels of demand and positive comments from staff (Kennedy, 1994b; O'Reilly, 1997), location (Adelinis et al., 1997), music (Durand & Mapstone, 1998), crowding (McAfee, 1987), preference and choice regarding concurrent activities (Cooper et al., 1992; Dunlap et al., 1994, 1995; Dyer et al., 1990; Ferro et al., 1996; Foster-Johnson et al., 1994; Lindauer et al., 1999; Ringdahl et al., 1997; Vaughn & Horner, 1997), the amount of noncontingent reinforcement available in the setting (Derby et al., 1998; Hagopian et al., 1994; Hanley et al., 1997; Roscoe et al., 1998; Vollmer et al., 1993, 1995a), concurrent social interactions and the nature of surrounding activities (Carr et al., 1976), and the presence of such idiosyncratic variables as small balls, puzzles and magazines (Carr et al., 1997).

A wide range of antecedent manipulations have been shown to decrease the rate of various types of challenging behaviour. It is probable that many of these have their effect by reducing the potency of the reinforcers responsible for maintaining challenging behaviour; that is, they involve the modification of establishing operations or stimuli which set the occasion for the behaviour to occur. A number of specific techniques and general approaches are outlined below.

## Modification of bio-behavioural state

As noted above, a range of bio-behavioural states have been shown to be correlated with the occurrence of challenging behaviour. These include such factors as alertness, fatigue, sleep/wake patterns, hormonal changes, drug effects, seizure activity, psychiatric disorders, mood, and illness or pain. Carr et al. (1996) and Carr and Smith (1995), for example, report preliminary data to suggest that the pain associated with menses established the negatively reinforcing capacity of staff demands (i.e. make staff demands 'aversive' and thus evoke escape-motivated aggression). Similarly, O'Reilly (1997) reported data suggesting that otitis media established ambient noise as a negative reinforcer for a young girl with self-injury. The results of these and other studies suggest that, in some instances, effective reductions in challenging behaviours may be achieved by modification of bio-behavioural states *when such states have been linked through functional assessment to increased rates of challenging behaviour.* Such 'indirect' approaches to intervention could include the treatment of sleep disorders (e.g. Durand, Gernert-Dott & Mapstone, 1996; Kennedy & Meyer, 1996; Lancioni, O'Reilly & Basili, 1999; O'Reilly, 1995; Piazza et al., 1998b), appropriate treatment of medical conditions (Bosch et al., 1997; Kennedy & Meyer, 1996; Peine et al., 1995) and changes to medication regimens (Kalachnik et al., 1995).

## Changing the nature of preceding activities

The nature of preceding activities may have a significant impact on people's responses to ongoing events. Krantz and Risley (1977), for example, identified some effects of the scheduling of activities on disruptive behaviour in a preschool setting. They reported that levels of disruption during a storytelling period were markedly reduced if the activity was preceded by a rest period rather than by a period of vigorous activity. In a similar vein, Wahler (1980) presented data to suggest that aversive interactions between low-income parents and their relatives or workers from service agencies set the occasion for subsequent aversive interactions between parents and children.

Studies have examined the relationship between a variety of types of preceding activities and subsequent rates of challenging behaviour. These include studies of the effects of: behavioural momentum in increasing compliance and reducing challenging behaviours associated with noncompliance; choice making; task variety and stimulus fading; exercise; and a variety of idiosyncratic establishing operations.

Mace et al. (1988) described the application of the phenomenon of *behavioural momentum* to the reduction of challenging behaviour. Behavioural momentum refers to the temporary, but marked, increase in response probability for a general response class following a period of reinforcement; that is, following repeated reinforcement, behaviour appears to gain a 'momentum' which makes it temporarily resistant to change. Mace et al. (1988) applied the notion of behavioural momentum to increase the compliance of four men with intellectual disabilities. They first identified requests which either elicited high (high probability requests) or low (low probability requests) rates of compliance. They reported that compliance with low probability requests was significantly increased by preceding them with a series of high probability requests. Subsequent studies have also demonstrated that this procedure is effective in reducing challenging behaviours associated with noncompliance. For example, preceding a request to take medication (which often led to challenging behaviour) with a series of requests to 'give me five' resulted in increased compliance and reduced challenging behaviour (Harchik & Putzier, 1990). It would appear that the generalized response class of complying with requests had gained a momentum from prior reinforcement which 'carried over' to the more problematic request. A number of studies since then have illustrated the viability of this procedure across a range of settings (e.g. Davis et al., 1992; Horner et al., 1991; Mace & Belfiore, 1990; Singer, Singer & Horner, 1987).

Winterling et al. (1987) reported that increasing task variety (and decreasing repetition) was associated with immediate and significant reductions in aggression and tantrums for three young people with intellectual disabilities and autism. These results are consistent with the suggestion that *repeated exposure* to the task within a short period of time acts as an establishing operation, leading to subsequent presentations acting as negative reinforcers. However, Lancioni et al. (1998) reported that, while three of four participants with severe intellectual disabilities expressed strong preferences for task variety (over task repetition), the other participant expressed strong preferences for task repetition. As with the results of studies on environmental enrichment, these data highlight the need for interventions to be based on individualized functional assessments.

A small number of studies have examined the potentially therapeutic effects of *stimulus fading* (e.g. Heidorn & Jensen, 1984; Kennedy, 1994b). Stimulus fading refers to the temporary withdrawal and gradual reintroduction of stimuli which set the occasion for challenging behaviour. This technique has been combined with the use of negative extinction in the treatment of escape-motivated self-injurious behaviour. The results of these studies suggest that, while stimulus fading may help avoid the occurrence of an extinction burst (Zarcone et al., 1993), it does not necessarily appear to increase the effectiveness of the extinction procedure itself (Zarcone et al., 1993; although see also Pace et al., 1993).

The technique of stimulus fading is procedurally similar to the techniques of systematic desensitization and reinforced graded practice in the treatment of fears and phobias (cf. Marks, 1987). This, when combined with the suggestion that conditioned arousal may be implicated in the maintenance of self-injury and aggression (Freeman et al., 1999; Romanczyk, 1986; Romanczyk et al., 1992), suggests that the effectiveness of stimulus fading may be increased if combined with procedures incompatible with arousal (e.g. relaxation, massage, eating). While there have been no tests of this specific hypothesis, a few case studies have reported the beneficial effects of including relaxation training or massage as a component of more complex treatment packages (Bull & Vecchio, 1978; Dossetor, Couryer & Nicol, 1991; Steen & Zuriff, 1977). Steen and Zuriff (1977), for example, describe the use of relaxation training and reinforced practice during the phased removal of restraints from a 21-year-old woman with severe intellectual disabilities. Prior to intervention, she had been kept in full restraint (involving tying her ankles and wrists to her bed) for the previous 3 years in an attempt to control her self-injurious finger biting and the scratching of her legs, face and scalp. Within 115 sessions over a total time of 17 hours, her self-injury was virtually eliminated.

Kennedy (1994b) combined the stimulus fading of instructor demands with high rates of noncontingent praise to reduce the escape-motivated challenging behaviour of two 20-year-old men and one 20-year-old woman with severe intellectual disabilities. He also reported that, for two of the participants, a repetition of the preliminary functional assessment after intervention indicated that teacher demands no longer served as antecedents to challenging behaviour.

Numerous studies have reported that physical exercise may result in reductions in stereotypic (Bachman & Fuqua, 1983; Bachman & Sluyter, 1988; Baumeister & MacLean, 1984; Kern, Koegel & Dunlap, 1984; Kern et al., 1982), self-injurious (Baumeister & MacLean, 1984; Lancioni et al., 1984) and aggressive or disruptive behaviours (Jansma & Combs, 1987; McGimsey & Favell, 1988; Tomporowski & Ellis, 1984, 1985) during immediately subsequent activities. Greater reductions in challenging behaviour have been reported for more strenuous activities (e.g. jogging compared with ball games, Kern et al., 1984). These results cannot be accounted for by overall reductions in activity since some studies also report increases in the amount of time spent on task and work performance (e.g. Kern et al., 1982). Schroeder and Tessel (1994) suggest that the results may reflect the impact of exercise on dopamine turnover. Whatever the mechanism, the accumulated evidence points to a consistent, although not inevitable (e.g. Larson & Miltenberger, 1992), short-term effect of aerobic exercise on subsequent activity (Lancioni & O'Reilly, 1998).

As we saw in Chapter 6, a number of studies have presented data to link idiosyncratic, temporally distant events (e.g. difficulty getting up, the choice of route to school) with an increased probability of challenging behaviour (Gardner et al., 1984, 1986; Kennedy & Itkonen, 1993; O'Reilly, 1996). Figure 7.1 shows the effect of travelling to college via the 'city route' (dark squares) versus the 'highway route' (light squares) on the frequency of subsequent aggressive and disruptive behaviours shown by Kelly, a 20-year-old woman with severe intellectual disabilities, cerebral palsy and visual impairments. The 'travel programme' solely consisted of travelling by the 'highway route'. As can be seen, marked and systematic changes were associated with choice of route. The 'intervention' resulted in rapid and significant reduction in challenging behaviour, these gains being maintained $2\frac{1}{2}$ months later. Similarly, O'Reilly (1996) reported the long-term elimination of the episodic self-injury shown by a 25-year-old man with intellectual disabilities

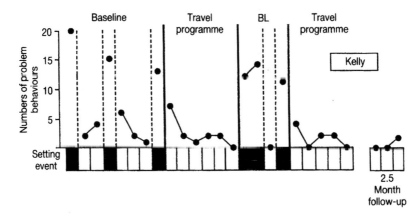

Figure 7.1.   Results for Kelly in Study 2. The data are presented as the frequency of problem behaviour per school day. Closed rectangles arrayed along the horizontal axis indicate the occurrence of a setting event. (From Kennedy & Itkonen, 1993.)

by changing the form of respite care he received. Clearly, descriptive and experimental analyses are essential for identifying the operation of such idiosyncratic establishing operations.

Finally, Horner et al. (1997) describe the use of *neutralizing routines* to eliminate the effects of establishing operations. They demonstrated that, for each of three children with severe intellectual disability, their aggression and self-injury reliably occurred only following the occurrence of an establishing operation (a poor night's sleep for one participant, the cancelling of or delay in previous activities for the other two) *and* a discriminative stimulus (error correction or interruption by staff). They demonstrated that following the establishing operation with an individually designed 'neutralizing routine' (a 1-hour sleep for one participant, participation in highly preferred activities for the other two) immediately led to the virtual elimination of challenging behaviour.

### Changing the nature of concurrent activities

A number of studies have indicated that challenging behaviour may be substantially reduced by changing the nature or context of concurrent activities.

### Curricular design and supported routines

Touchette et al. (1985) described the use of a scatter plot (see Chapter 6) to identify the settings associated with high rates of aggression shown by a 14-year-old girl with autism and severe intellectual disabilities. The results of this descriptive analysis indicated that the majority of episodes of aggression were associated with certain activities, in particular her attendance at pre-vocational and community living classes. Following the rescheduling of her weekly timetable, in which activities associated with low rates of aggression were substituted for these class activities, the girl's aggression rapidly reduced to near-zero levels. Similarly, Touchette et al. (1985) demonstrated the rapid elimination of the serious self-injurious behaviour shown by a 23-year-old man with autism following the reallocation of care staff. In both examples, it proved possible over time to gradually reintroduce (or fade in) the activity or person which had been associated with high rates of challenging behaviour while maintaining the treatment gains.

In an illustration of a 'molar' approach to identifying antecedent influences on challenging behaviour (Carr et al., 1998), Ferro et al. (1996) used nonparticipant behavioural observations to examine the association between curricular activities and challenging behaviour among 288 students with intellectual disabilities in 64 classrooms in the south-eastern United States. Their results indicated significantly greater occurrence of challenging behaviours during activities which were either nonfunctional, age-inappropriate or nonpreferred.

Using a similar approach, several studies have reported reductions in challenging behaviour as a result of using assessments of participant preferences to design educational or vocational curricula (e.g. Cooper et al., 1992; Dunlap et al., 1991, 1993, 1994, 1995; Dyer, 1987; Dyer et al., 1990; Foster-Johnson et al., 1994; Kern & Dunlap, 1998; Vaughn & Horner, 1997; Wolery & Winterling, 1997). For example, Foster-Johnson et al. (1994) used an observational procedure to assess preference for curricular activities with three children with intellectual disabilities (cf. Dyer, 1987). Subsequent experimental analysis using a withdrawal design revealed higher rates of challenging behaviour during nonpreferred activities and, for two of the three participants, higher rates of desirable behaviours during the preferred activities.

A small number of studies have also suggested that the actual act of choosing may be important in increasing participation (Bambara, Ager & Koger, 1994; Mithaug & Mar, 1980; Parsons et al., 1990; Sigafoos, 1998) and reducing challenging behaviour (Dyer et al., 1990). Dunlap et al. (1994), for example, attempted to untangle the effects of the act of choosing and the results of choosing (gaining access to preferred activities) in a study involving three young boys with severe emotional and behavioural difficulties. They found that when the children chose tasks they showed greater engagement and less challenging behaviour than when simply presented with identical tasks at other times (although see also, Kahng et al., 1997; Smith, Iwata & Shore, 1995b). While this obviously does not account for momentary fluctuations in preferences, it does suggest that the act of choosing itself may be important (Bannerman et al., 1990; Sigafoos, 1998).

Such an approach has obvious attractions for the treatment of challenging behaviour in that: (1) it can result in rapid and marked reductions in the challenging behaviour; and (2) it may be relatively easy to sustain (if not intro-duce) since it requires general organizational change rather than changes in the way that carers or support staff respond to episodes of challenging behaviour. Its primary disadvantages, however, are that: (1) the settings which evoke behaviour may be either important for the person's health and safety, development or quality of life (e.g. interaction with other people, requests to participate in an activity); or (2) it may be difficult to avoid the eliciting circumstances.

### Environmental enrichment and noncontingent reinforcement

A number of studies have indicated that generally enriching the environment by, for example, increasing interaction with materials or introducing materials into barren environments may lead to a reduction in the rate of challenging behaviours. Thus, for example, increasing social contact (Baumeister et al., 1980; Mace & Knight, 1986) and providing toys (Favell et al., 1982; Finney, Russo & Cataldo, 1982; Horner, 1980), individually preferred activities (Lindauer et al., 1999; Ringdahl et al., 1997), visual stimulation (Forehand & Baumeister, 1970), leisure activities (Sigafoos & Kerr, 1994) and music (Mace, Yankanich & West, 1989) have been associated with increased compliance (Nordquist, Twardosz & McEvoy, 1991), reduced rates of stereotypy (Baumeister et al., 1980; Forehand & Baumeis-ter, 1970; Horner, 1980; Mace & Knight, 1986; Mace et al., 1989) and self-injury (Favell et al., 1982; Finney et al., 1982; Lindauer et al., 1999; Ringdahl et al., 1997). Similarly, moving from materially and socially deprived institutional settings into enriched community-based residential provision is commonly associated with a reduced rate of stereotypic (although not more seriously challenging) behaviour (Emerson & Hatton, 1994; Larson & Lakin, 1989; Young et al., 1998).

These results are consistent with predictions made from behavioural theory. As McDowell (1982) has pointed out, a hyperbolic relationship exists between the rate of response-contingent reinforcement and behaviour (cf. Martens & Houk, 1989; Martens, Lochner & Kelly, 1992). The relationship is moderated, however, by the rate of background or response-independent reinforcement. One implica-tion of this observation is that a particular rate of reinforcement will sustain a greater response rate in an impoverished environment than in an enriched environment. Put another way, increasing the rate of 'free' or response-indepen-dent reinforcement should decrease response rate for a given rate of contingent reinforcement. Thus, the rate of behaviours maintained by positive reinforcement (external or automatic) should reduce as the background level of reinforcement increases.

As was noted in Chapter 4, however, other studies have indicated that increas-ing the level of stimulation in the environment through visual displays (Duker & Rasing, 1989), television (Gary, Tallon & Stangl, 1980) and crowding (McAfee,

1987) can lead to *increased* rates of stereotypy (Duker & Rasing, 1989; Gary et al., 1980) and aggression (McAfee, 1987) and to decreased task performance (Duker & Rasing, 1989). The results suggest that, for some individuals, environmental enrichment may be associated with increased rates of negative reinforcement (e.g. overarousal, increased rates of negative peer contact). The contradictory nature of the results highlights the importance of basing interventions on prior functional assessment (e.g. Lindauer et al., 1999; Ringdahl et al., 1997), since the same environmental changes may have very different effects on topographically similar behaviours (cf. Duker & Rasing, 1989; Nordquist et al., 1991).

A more specific illustration of reducing the rate of challenging behaviour by increasing the rate of background reinforcement is provided by studies of the effects of noncontingent (or response-independent) reinforcement (e.g. Derby et al., 1998; Fischer, Iwata & Mazaleski, 1997; Gaylord-Ross, Weeks & Lipner, 1980; Hagopian et al., 1994; Hanley et al., 1997; Lalli et al., 1997; Mace & Lalli, 1991; Marcus & Vollmer, 1996; Piazza et al., 1997a,c; Roscoe et al., 1998; Vollmer et al., 1993, 1995a, 1997, 1998). In these studies, the background rate of the *specific reinforcer maintaining the challenging behaviour* is increased, often on a fixed-time schedule. Of course, if the background rate of reinforcement is sufficiently high, it will abolish the deprivational condition which establishes the stimulus as reinforcing and consequently eliminate challenging behaviour; that is, it should prevent maintaining stimuli acting as reinforcers in that particular context.

Mace and Lalli (1991), for example, demonstrated that the bizarre 'delusional and hallucinatory' speech of a 46-year-old man with moderate intellectual disabilities was maintained by attention. Subsequently, the provision of noncontingent attention on a conjunctive fixed-time, DRO schedule (reinforcer presented after a set period of time has elapsed as long as the target behaviour did not occur) resulted in the immediate reduction of bizarre speech to near zero levels. Hagopian et al. (1994) examined the effects of dense and lean schedules of noncontingent reinforcement on the attention-maintained aggressive, disruptive and self-injurious behaviour shown by four 5-year-old identical quadruplets with intellectual disabilities and pervasive developmental disorder. They reported that: (1) the dense (fixed-time–10 second) schedule resulted in greater reductions in disruptive behaviour (virtual elimination) than the lean (FT–5 minute) schedule; (2) it was possible to fade gradually from the dense to lean schedule over a period of 55–85, 20-minute sessions while maintaining treatment gains; and (3) once established on the FT–5 minute schedule, it was possible to generalize treatment gains to the home setting using the children's mother as the therapist. These gains were maintained at 1 and 2 month follow-up.

Vollmer et al. (1995) demonstrated the use of noncontingent negative reinforcement to reduce the rate of escape-maintained self-injury shown by two young men with intellectual disabilities by scheduling frequent breaks in tasks which had previously elicited challenging behaviour. The length of time between breaks was gradually increased from 10 seconds to 10 minutes for one participant ($2\frac{1}{2}$ minutes for the other) while maintaining near zero rates of self-injury.

Satiation involves allowing free access to the reinforcer maintaining challenging behaviour for a specified period of time. This technique has been used successfully to reduce rumination (the regurgitation and chewing of food). Rast et al. (1981) and Rast, Johnston and Drum (1984) demonstrated that rumination in people with profound intellectual disabilities could be prevented if they were allowed to eat until they were full. Given that the participants in these studies were underweight, increased calorific intake was in itself beneficial.

The value of approaches based on the use of noncontingent reinforcement is that: (1) they are relatively simple to implement; (2) they appear to have few side-effects (Vollmer et al., 1997, 1998); and (3) they may prevent the development of deprivational conditions which set the occasion for challenging behaviour to occur. One general concern, however, is that while functionally based, such procedures are not constructional; that is, no new behaviours are established or generalized to the settings in which the person had learned a strategy for accessing particular stimuli. Indeed, the procedure results in an overall loss of opportunities for the person with severe disabilities to exert control over their environment. Given the generalized importance of our ability to exercise control (Bannerman et al., 1990), and the very limited opportunities for control available to people with severe disabilities, the use of noncontingent reinforcement *on its own* should be advocated with some caution.

## Embedding

As was demonstrated in Chapter 4, sometimes changing relatively superficial aspects of the context in which challenging behaviour occurs can have a significant impact (Carr et al., 1976). Similarly, a number of studies have shown that increasing the availability of positive reinforcers or preferred materials in 'high risk' situations may significantly reduce escape-motivated challenging behaviour (Carr & Newsom, 1985; Carr et al., 1980, 1997; Kennedy, 1994b). Durand and Mapstone (1998) reported substantial reductions in challenging behaviour and reduced negative affect (measured through ratings of facial expression) when 'fast-paced' music was incorporated into situations which were associated with high rates of challenging behaviour.

## Summary

Approaches which rely on the modification of antecedent or contextual factors have a number of potential advantages. Firstly, they can bring about rapid and significant reductions in challenging behaviour (e.g. Carr et al., 1976, 1980; Kennedy, 1994b; Kennedy & Itkonen, 1993; Touchette et al., 1985). Both the speed and magnitude of the reported changes compare well with more traditional approaches to intervention (Carr et al., 1990b, 1999a). Indeed, if the intervention is successful in removing those establishing operations which create the motivational basis for challenging behaviour, we would expect the intervention to *eliminate immediately* the challenging behaviour. To date, however, such dramatic effects have only been reported for escape-motivated challenging behaviour where preliminary descriptive or experimental analyses have been able to identify clear environmental establishing operations.

Secondly, approaches based on the modification of antecedent events may be relatively easy to implement and sustain over time. Such approaches place less reliance on altering the nature of carers' responses to episodes of challenging behaviour, responses which may be powerfully determined by the dynamics of the challenging behaviour itself (Taylor & Carr, 1993, 1994). Failure to sustain 'successful' intervention programmes and the re-emergence of challenging behaviour has been one of the enduring problems faced by applied behavioural approaches.

Finally, studies to date have not reported any negative 'side-effects' of interventions based on the alteration of antecedent conditions. Again, this is consistent with the underlying rationale of the approach. If the motivational bases for challenging behaviour can be removed, there is no particular reason why new challenging behaviours should emerge to replace those eliminated.

## Behavioural competition and response covariation

The second set of approaches to intervention which will be examined are all based on the notion that decreases in challenging behaviour may be brought about indirectly through increasing the rate of other behaviours. Two sets of procedures which share this common aim will be discussed: the use of *functional displacement* to replace challenging behaviour with a more appropriate member of the same response class (Carr, 1988); and other procedures involving the *differential reinforcement* of other, alternative or incompatible behaviours.

Before discussing these techniques, however, some of the concepts and evidence underlying this set of approaches will be briefly reviewed. As discussed in Chapter 4, a behavioural perspective is primarily concerned with the discovery of functional relationships between behaviours and between behaviour and environmental variables. It also views the behaviours shown by a person as the product of a dynamic system of elements which may interact in complex and unforeseen ways. The discovery of functional relationships between behaviours led to the notion of *response classes*; these are comprised of topographically distinct behaviours which have the same functional relationship to environmental events. So, for example, pressing a light switch with your thumb or index finger has the same environmental effect. As such, these two behaviours are members of the same response class. It was also suggested that different forms of challenging behaviour may be members of the same or different response classes, and that a behaviour's membership of a response class may vary over time and across settings. Intervention through functional displacement (Carr, 1988) seeks to establish and/or differentially reinforce socially appropriate members of response classes containing challenging behaviour.

Other concepts have also been developed to describe the interrelationships between behaviours (Evans et al., 1988; Koegel & Koegel, 1988; Parrish & Roberts, 1993; Rosales-Ruiz & Baer, 1997; Schroeder & MacLean, 1987; Scotti et al., 1991a; Voeltz & Evans, 1982; Wahler & Graves, 1983). These include such concepts as behavioural clusters, keystone behaviours, behavioural cusps and pivotal behaviours.

The *behavioural cluster* is a theoretically neutral term which refers to behaviours that tend to occur together in the same context. So, for example, writing an essay, drinking coffee and gazing out of the window may form a cluster of behaviours centred around the *keystone behaviour* of writing; that is, knowledge of the keystone behaviour allows us to predict the occurrence of other behaviours in the cluster. Wahler (1975), for example, examined the correlation of 19 categories of child behaviour and six categories of social–environmental events across two settings for two boys. He identified a number of naturally covarying behavioural clusters which were all specific to a particular setting. Clusters were, however, stable over time and across experimental phases. So, for example, the self-stimulatory behaviour of one participant was positively correlated with social contact at home and with sustained attention to classroom work at school. Wahler (1975) suggested that such analyses may indicate ways in which covert or low frequency behaviours may be treated indirectly and may help identify keystone behaviours whose modification may be associated with more widespread positive change.

*Pivotal behaviours* (Koegel & Koegel, 1988) or, more broadly, *behavioural cusps* (Rosales-Ruiz & Baer, 1997) are behaviour changes which have widespread effects by bringing the person's subsequent behaviour into contact with new contingencies and opportunities which may have far-reaching consequences. Examples of pivotal behaviours include enhancing motivation and increasing responsivity to multiple cues among children with autism (Schreibman, Stahmer & Pierce, 1996).

*Response chains* are sequences of behaviour where each step in the chain is dependent on the occurrence of the previous 'link'. Taking a bath, for example, includes a chain of behaviours (putting the plug in, running the water . . .) in which the completion of each step sets the occasion for the next step in the sequence. Performance of the complete chain is maintained by end-point reinforcing contingencies. It is possible that some examples of challenging behaviours which occur together may form response chains (Parrish & Roberts, 1993; Scotti et al., 1991a). If this were the case, then intervention focussed on initial components in the chain should have generalized benefits in also preventing the occurrence of later links.

### Functional displacement

As noted above, intervention through functional displacement seeks to establish and/or differentially reinforce socially appropriate members of response classes containing challenging behaviour. In other words, it does not aim to alter either the antecedents which set the occasion for the behaviour to occur or the contingencies maintaining the challenging behaviour. Rather, it seeks to introduce a new behaviour (or increase the rate of a pre-existing behaviour) which will tap in to the existing contingencies and displace the challenging behaviour (Carr, 1988; Carr et al., 1994; Dyer & Larsson, 1997).

The seminal study in this area was conducted by Carr and Durand (1985a). Firstly, they used experimental functional analyses to identify the processes underlying the disruptive behaviours (aggression, tantrums, self-injury, noncompliance) shown by four children with intellectual disabilities (Jim, Eve, Tom and Sue). Jim and Eve's disruptive behaviours appeared to be maintained by negative reinforcement involving escape from difficult tasks. Tom's disruptive behaviours appeared to be maintained by positive reinforcement involving teacher attention. Sue's disruptive behaviours appeared to be maintained by both negative reinforcement involving escape from difficult tasks *and* positive reinforcement involving teacher attention.

They then taught the children 'relevant' and 'irrelevant' communicative responses to the situations which elicited their challenging behaviour. The relevant response was functionally equivalent to their challenging behaviour. This involved either asking the teacher for help during difficult tasks by saying 'I don't understand' (Jim, Eve and Sue) or asking the teacher for feedback during easy tasks by asking 'Am I doing good work' (Tom and Sue). The irrelevant response was functionally unrelated to the child's challenging behaviour, which involved either asking the teacher for feedback during difficult tasks (Jim, Eve and Sue) or asking the teacher for help during easy tasks (Tom and Sue). The results of this study demonstrated immediate and dramatic reductions in each of the children's challenging behaviours when the child was taught the relevant (functionally equivalent) communicative response. Training on the irrelevant communicative response had no impact on their challenging behaviour.

Two studies serve to illustrate the use of functional displacement to reduce challenging behaviours shown by people with more severe disabilities. Steege et al. (1990) taught two young children with severe multiple disabilities to press a microswitch which activated a tape recording to request a break from self-care activities. Use of this assistive device was associated with significant reductions in their escape-motivated self-injurious behaviour. Bird et al. (1989) described the use of functional communication training to eliminate the severe escape-maintained challenging behaviours of two men with severe intellectual disabilities (Gregg and Jim). Gregg was taught to exchange a token for a short break from vocational tasks; Jim was taught to use the manual sign 'break'. In addition to rapid and marked reductions in challenging behaviour, spontaneous communication increased in a range of settings and, interestingly, both men spent more time on-task than they had previously and actually requested to work on tasks they had previously avoided. This suggests that one effect of the intervention was to decrease the 'aversiveness' of the negatively reinforcing tasks. This is, of course, consistent with the literature which suggests that *perceived control* over potentially aversive events is an important moderator of the level of stress experienced (cf. Bannerman et al., 1990).

A number of other studies have demonstrated the viability of the procedure across a number of settings, participants and challenging behaviours (e.g. Campbell & Lutzker, 1993; Day et al., 1994; Derby et al., 1997; Duker, Jol & Palmen, 1991; Durand, 1993, 1999; Durand & Carr, 1987, 1991, 1992; Durand & Kishi, 1987; Fisher et al., 1993; Fisher, Kuhn & Thompson, 1998b; Hagopian et al., 1998; Horner & Budd, 1985; Horner & Day, 1991; Horner et al., 1990; Kahng et al., 1997; Lalli, Casey & Kates, 1995; Northup et al., 1991; Peck et al., 1996; Shirley et al., 1997; Shukla & Albin, 1996; Smith, 1985; Smith & Coleman, 1986; Sprague & Horner, 1992; Vaughn & Horner, 1995; Wacker et al., 1990b). In addition, studies have indicated that the treatment gains achieved may generalize across settings and therapists (e.g. Durand, 1999; Durand & Carr, 1991) and may be maintained over time (e.g. Derby et al., 1997; Durand & Carr, 1992).

Studies have also begun to identify the conditions under which functional displacement is more or less likely to occur. Carr (1988) suggested that functional displacement is likely to occur if the replacement response is equivalent to the challenging behaviour and is also a relatively more 'efficient' response. He defined response efficiency as a complex construct reflecting the combined effects of response effort and the rate, delay and quality of reinforcement contingent on the response. Indeed, much basic research on behavioural choice has identified these variables as predicting allocation between two concurrently available responses (Fisher & Mazur, 1997; Friman & Poling, 1995). These experimental results have also been extended to applied studies, which have indicated that such variables as the rate of reinforcement (Martens & Houk, 1989; Martens et al., 1992; Neef et al., 1992), reinforcer quality (Neef et al., 1992), response effort (Hanley et al., 1998; Horner et al., 1990; Irvin et al., 1998) and the immediacy of reinforcement (Neef, Mace & Shade, 1993) predict behaviour in real life settings.

Horner et al. (1990) examined the effect of response effort on the displacement of escape-motivated aggression in a 14-year-old boy with intellectual disabilities and cerebral palsy. They demonstrated that, while teaching an alternative response which required substantial effort (spelling out 'help please' on a personal communicator) had no impact on aggression, training in a low effort response (pressing one key to elicit the message 'help please') resulted in marked reductions in aggression and an increased use of appropriate communication. Similarly, Horner and Day (1991) in three separate studies demonstrated the importance of response effort (signing a whole sentence compared with signing one word), the schedule of reinforcement (FR3 compared with FR1) and the immediacy of reinforcement (20-second delay compared with 1-second delay) in predicting whether a functionally equivalent communicative response would replace the challenging behaviours shown by three people with severe intellectual disabilities. In each study, only the latter alternative was associated with significant reductions in challenging behaviour. More recently, Peck et al. (1996) demonstrated that variation in both duration and quality of reinforcement similarly influenced allocation of responses to trained functionally equivalent signs and challenging behaviour.

Further support for the importance of relative response efficiency in predicting the outcomes of intervention is provided by studies which have undertaken component analyses of intervention programmes based on functional communication training. Wacker et al. (1990b), for example, demonstrated that the combination of functional communication training with DRO and time-out contingencies for the occurrence of challenging behaviour resulted in significantly greater reductions in challenging behaviour than functional communication training alone. Fisher et al. (1993) reported that functional communication training alone only reduced the severely challenging behaviours shown by one of three people with severe intellectual disabilities. However, the combination of functional communication training and punishment of the challenging behaviour (verbal reprimand plus prompting and guiding to complete five requests or 30-second physical restraint) resulted in rapid and clinically significant reductions in all challenging behaviours. More recently, Shirley et al. (1997) reported that, for each of three participants, signing could not be established and challenging behaviour was not reduced until an extinction component was introduced into the functional communication training package (see also Hagopian et al., 1998).

The accumulated evidence, therefore, suggests that a range of challenging behaviours may be rapidly and substantially reduced by establishing and/or differentially reinforcing a more socially appropriate member of the response class which includes the person's challenging behaviour. In addition, it would appear that the effects of intervention may persist over time and generalize to new settings (Durand & Carr, 1991, 1992). This approach is attractive in that it is functionally based, constructional and seeks to tap into contingencies of reinforcement which are known to be highly effective in maintaining behaviour over time and across settings (i.e. the contingencies maintaining challenging behaviour). The success of this approach, however, is dependent on the alternative response being *functionally equivalent* to the challenging behaviour and relatively more efficient than the challenging behaviour.

The first requirement highlights the importance of conducting a thorough functional assessment prior to intervention. Indeed, it is only through such an assessment that the behavioural function of the person's challenging behaviour may be established. As was noted in Chapter 4, however, this may not be a simple matter, in that the processes underlying challenging behaviour may be complex and may vary over time, behaviours and across settings.

Day et al. (1994) illustrated some of these issues in a study of multiply controlled challenging behaviours shown by a 9-year-old girl, an 18-year-old boy and a 34-year-old woman with severe intellectual disabilities. For each person, challenging behaviour (self-injury or aggression) was shown to be maintained by both escape from difficult tasks *and* access to preferred items. Teaching functionally equivalent communicative responses (signing 'want' for access to preferred items, saying 'go' or exchanging a card for escape) only brought about reductions in challenging behaviour in the appropriate condition (cf. Carr and Durand, 1985a).

The second requirement, that the replacement response be more efficient than the challenging behaviour, has two main implications. Firstly, in order to maximize the impact of intervention, it may be important to increase the response efficiency of the replacement behaviour *and* decrease the response efficiency of the challenging behaviour, i.e. it is likely to be necessary to combine functional displacement or functional communication training with more traditional reactive strategies (e.g. extinction, time-out) to weaken the challenging behaviour (Fisher et al., 1993; Hagopian et al., 1998; Shirley et al., 1997; Wacker et al., 1990b). In situations in which the challenging behaviour is multiply controlled by biological and behavioural factors (e.g. self-injury maintained by extrinsic reinforcement and $\beta$-endorphin release), this may involve the combined use of behavioural and psychopharmacological treatments (e.g. Symons, Fox & Thompson, 1998).

Secondly, evidence of the powerful effects of challenging behaviour on the performance of care staff (Taylor & Carr, 1993, 1994) suggests that it may be difficult to maintain these relative differences in response efficiency. Indeed, the behavioural account of the development of challenging behaviour through a process of shaping (see Chapter 4) suggests that such behaviours may, over time, have replaced more socially appropriate, functionally equivalent behaviours. Thus, the problem is often not that the person does not have more appropriate behaviours in his or her repertoire, but that environments have, over time, preferentially selected challenging behaviours. Decay in the implementation of 'successful' intervention programmes has long been a problem faced in applied settings. If such decay results in reducing the response efficiency of the alternative behaviour (e.g. care staff not attending to socially appropriate requests for breaks or attention), it is likely that the challenging behaviour will re-emerge (e.g. Durand & Kishi, 1987). In many ways, teaching a functionally equivalent response to a service user may be considerably easier than ensuring that carers and care staff continue to listen to and act on alternative methods of communication.

The primary disadvantages of functional displacement are, firstly, that its successful implementation requires skilled and intensive support during assessment and intervention. Secondly, it may not be appropriate in situations in which the person's challenging behaviour is maintained by either access to events which are detrimental to their health, welfare or safety (e.g. challenging behaviour maintained by sexually inappropriate contact with care staff) or, perhaps more commonly, avoidance of situations which are important to their health, welfare or quality of life (e.g. social interaction). Take, for example, the situation in which, following sexual abuse, a person with severe intellectual disabilities develops challenging behaviour to escape from physical or social contact with all carers. Would it be appropriate to simply provide the person with an alternative way of avoiding contact or should the aim of intervention also be to help the person overcome their fear/distress of nonabusive contact?

## Differential reinforcement

A more general set of approaches based on the notion of differential reinforcement also seeks to intervene indirectly on challenging behaviour by increasing the rate of other behaviours (Carr et al., 1990b; Jones, 1991; Vollmer & Iwata, 1992; Whitaker, 1996). These include DRO and the *differential reinforcement of alternative* (DRA) or *incompatible* (DRI) behaviour.

The differential reinforcement of other behaviour, also known as omission training, is a nonconstructional procedure involving the delivery of a reinforcement contingent on the nonoccurrence of the targeted challenging behaviour during an interval of time or, more unusually, at a specific point in time (momentary DRO: Lindberg et al., 1999). Under a DRO schedule, the nature of the 'other' behaviours is not specified. Reinforcement is provided as long as the challenging behaviour does not occur. In effect, a DRO schedule is equivalent to time-out from a newly imposed contingency of positive reinforcement (Rolider & Van Houten, 1990).

The differential reinforcement of alternative or incompatible behaviour involves the delivery of reinforcement contingent on the occurrence of a specified alternative behaviour (DRA) or a behaviour which is physically incompatible with the challenging behaviour (DRI). Functional displacement is, in effect, a particular form of DRA in which the reinforcing contingency is identical to that maintaining the challenging behaviour.

Individual studies have reported marked variability in the outcomes associated with differential reinforcement procedures, with results ranging from complete suppression, through marginal improvements to increases in the rate of challenging behaviour over baseline (Carr et al., 1990b). In general, however, it would appear that such procedures may not be particularly effective in reducing severely challenging behaviours (Carr et al., 1990b; Didden et al., 1997; Scotti et al., 1991b). There are, however, some notable exceptions to this generalization. Luiselli et al. (1985), for example, used a 5-minute DRO schedule involving food and tactile reinforcement to reduce to near zero levels the frequent aggression shown by a 15-year-old girl with severe intellectual disabilities and dual sensory impairments. As intervention progressed, the schedule was faded from 5 to 30 minutes. Russo, Cataldo and Cushing (1981) reported the use of a DRA procedure to reinforce compliance with requests among three preschool children with intellectual disabilities. As compliance increased, challenging behaviours, which included aggression and self-injurious behaviour, rapidly decreased to near zero levels.

As has been discussed above, studies of behavioural choice suggest that a person's allocation of time between concurrently available alternatives (e.g. attending to a task, engaging in self-injurious behaviour, gazing out of the window) is a function of response effort and the rate, quality and immediacy of reinforcement (Fisher & Mazur, 1997). As such, these factors should predict the effectiveness of differential reinforcement procedures as well as functional displacement. Thus, an effective procedure should aim to ensure that:

- the alternative behaviour requires less effort than the person's challenging behaviour;
- the rate of reinforcement delivered contingent on the alternative behaviour is greater than the rate of reinforcement maintaining the challenging behaviour;
- reinforcement is delivered immediately on occurrence of the alternative behaviour; and
- the reinforcers selected are more powerful than those maintaining the challenging behaviour, preferably through the use of empirical procedures to identify reinforcer selection.

The effectiveness of differential reinforcement procedures may also be enhanced by selecting alternative behaviours which show a natural negative covariation with the targeted challenging behaviour. Parrish et al. (1986), for example, demonstrated the natural negative covariation of compliance and challenging behaviours, including aggression, property destruction, pica and disruption, among four children with intellectual disabilities. As compliance increased, due to the effects of either differential reinforcement and/or guided compliance, challenging behaviours decreased (see also Koegel & Frea, 1993; Lalli, Kates & Casey, 1999). These suggestions for improving the effectiveness of differential reinforcement procedures again highlight the importance of preceding intervention with a thorough functional assessment.

Such procedures are relatively simple to administer in that they do not require skilled performance from care staff. The main drawbacks of these procedures, however, are that reinforcer satiation may occur at brief inter-reinforcement intervals and that their implementation requires intensive monitoring of user behaviour.

## Modification of maintaining contingencies: extinction

The approaches discussed so far have not involved any *direct* alteration of the contingencies maintaining the person's challenging behaviour. Antecedent manipulations and differential reinforcement may both, of course, indirectly influence the power of the maintaining contingencies through modifying establishing operations, by increasing the rate of 'free' reinforcement or reinforcement available for competing behaviours. Extinction procedures involve the direct modification of the contingencies responsible for maintaining the challenging behaviour.

Specifically, extinction procedures involve ensuring that the contingencies responsible for maintaining the person's challenging behaviour are no longer operative. Thus, for example, if functional assessment has indicated that an individual's aggression is maintained by positive social reinforcement involving attention from care staff, an extinction procedure would ensure that such positive reinforcers were no longer delivered contingent on the person's challenging behaviour.

Lovaas and Simmons (1969), for example, used an extinction procedure to reduce the attention-maintained severe self-injurious behaviour shown by two boys with severe intellectual disabilities. The procedure involved leaving each boy alone in an observation room for 90-minute sessions. The results of this procedure are shown in Figure 7.2.

As can be seen, within eight sessions (12 hours), John's self-injury had been eliminated. Prior to this, however, he had hit himself 9000 times during the extinction sessions. Gregg's self-injury clearly took much longer to extinguish.

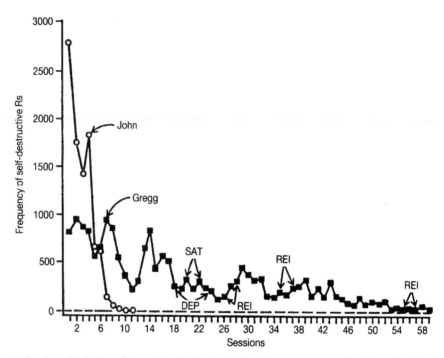

Figure 7.2.    Extinction of John's and Gregg's self-injurious behaviour, over successive days of extinction, during 90-minute sessions with total number of self-injurious acts on any one day given on the ordinate. SAT stands for satiation, DEP for deprivation and REI for reinforcement. (From Lovaas & Simmons, 1969.)

These effects were, however, situationally specific, in that treatment gains failed to generalize to other settings.

*Escape extinction* involves ensuring that negative reinforcers are not withdrawn contingent on the person's challenging behaviour (e.g. preventing escape from an aversive situation contingent on challenging behaviour). Such procedures have been used to reduce successfully escape-maintained challenging behaviour (e.g. Iwata et al., 1990b, 1994b; Repp, Felce & Barton, 1988).

*Sensory extinction* procedures involve attempting to block the sensory or perceptual feedback from challenging behaviours maintained by automatic reinforcement (Rincover & Devany, 1982). Such procedures have been employed to reduce self-injurious and stereotypic behaviours apparently maintained by automatic reinforcement (e.g. Iwata et al., 1994b; Rincover & Devany, 1982). As was noted in Chapter 4, however, the effectiveness of sensory extinction may be attributable to a number of factors including antecedent control and punishment (cf. Mazaleski et al., 1994).

While extinction may be effective, its use does have a number of significant problems. Firstly, the rate, intensity and variability of challenging behaviour is likely to increase in a significant minority of cases during the initial stages of an extinction programme (Lerman & Iwata, 1995, 1996). Such *extinction bursts* may place the physical safety of the person in jeopardy and are likely to be distressing to carers and care staff. Secondly, extinction procedures may need to be implemented with a high degree of consistency. Otherwise, the procedure would be equivalent to simply reducing the rate of reinforcement for the person's challenging behaviour. While this may have the effect of reducing response rate (see above), it may not bring about socially or clinically significant improvement. Thirdly, as noted above, the effects of extinction procedures may not generalize to new situations. Finally, as a nonconstructional approach, extinction may be associated with unwanted changes in collateral behaviours. Given the problems associated with extinction procedures, it is highly unlikely that they would be implemented on their own. They are often, however, included as an important component in complex treatment packages.

## Default technologies: punishment

There are two types of contingent relationship between behaviour and reinforcers which are sometimes important in directly *reducing or eliminating* operant behaviour. *Positive punishment* refers to a decrease in the rate of a behaviour as a result of the contingent *presentation* of a (negatively) reinforcing stimulus (positive punisher). Illustrative examples of positive punishment include the use by parents of reprimands to reduce the unruly behaviour of their children. *Negative punishment* refers to a decrease in the rate of a behaviour as a result of the contingent *withdrawal* of a (positively) reinforcing stimulus (negative punisher). Examples of negative punishment include the use of fines to prevent inappropriate parking (negative punisher: loss of money) and the withdrawal of attention to reduce the overbearing or rude behaviour of colleagues.

Over the past three decades, numerous studies have demonstrated that punishment procedures can produce socially and clinically significant reductions in severe challenging behaviours shown by people with severe intellectual disabilities (Axelrod & Apsche, 1983; Cataldo, 1991; Didden et al., 1997; Luiselli et al., 1992; Repp & Singh, 1990; Scotti et al., 1991b). Indeed, meta-analyses of the intervention literature indicate that extinction and punishment-based procedures are the most effective approaches available, both immediately and at follow-up, if the goal is to eliminate challenging behaviour (e.g. Didden et al., 1997; Scotti et al., 1991b).

In terms of the criteria which perhaps should underpin intervention, however, the use of punishment-based procedures poses considerable problems. Firstly, they are neither constructional nor functionally based. Secondly, the procedures (if not the outcomes) are increasingly being seen as socially unacceptable (e.g.

G. Allan Roeher Institute, 1988; Guess et al., 1987; O'Brien, 1991; Repp & Singh, 1990). This combination of factors has led to a situation in which punishment procedures may be best viewed as 'default technologies' (Iwata, 1988) and as approaches which should only be considered when: (a) alternative approaches have failed or are not feasible, and (b) the costs of not intervening outweigh the costs and risks associated with the use of such procedures.

In the sections below, some of the approaches to punishment which have been successfully used to reduce severely challenging behaviours will be briefly reviewed.

### Response cost: time-out and visual screening

Response cost (or negative punishment) refers to the reduction in the rate of a behaviour resulting from the *withdrawal* of positive reinforcers contingent on its occurrence. *Time-out* is a clinical procedure in which opportunity for positive reinforcement is removed or reduced for a set period following the occurrence of a target behaviour (Hobbs & Forehand, 1977). This may involve the brief seclusion of the person in a barren environment (e.g. Wolf, Risley & Mees, 1964), removal to a less stimulating part of the current setting (e.g. Mace et al., 1986) or the withdrawal of potentially positively reinforcing activities or events from the vicinity of the person (e.g. Foxx & Shapiro, 1978).

Time-out has been shown to be successful in reducing challenging behaviours shown by people with severe intellectual disabilities (Cataldo, 1991). Mace et al. (1986), for example, used a time-out procedure involving sitting in a chair facing a wall for 2 minutes to bring about rapid and significant reductions in the aggressive and disruptive behaviours shown by three children with intellectual disabilities. As we noted in Chapter 5, however, 'time-out' may also lead to an increase in the rate of escape-motivated challenging behaviour (e.g. Durand et al., 1989; Solnick et al., 1977). For such behaviours, the implementation of a typical exclusionary time-out procedure is likely to reinforce negatively the targeted behaviour. Research conducted on the parameters of time-out has suggested that short durations are as effective as long durations, the use of contingent delay for release from time out (i.e. release is delayed until challenging behaviours have stopped) may be unnecessary and the effectiveness of the procedure may be enhanced by combining time-out with differential reinforcement of more appropriate behaviour (Hobbs & Forehand, 1977; Murphy & Oliver, 1987). While potentially effective, the implementation of time-out and response-cost procedures may themselves set the occasion for the occurrence of challenging behaviour as the person seeks to avoid, or escape from, the punishing contingency.

*Visual* or *facial screening* involves the brief (5–15 seconds) blocking of vision contingent on the occurrence of challenging behaviour (Rojahn & Marshburn,

1992). This procedure has been shown to bring about rapid, significant and, at times, persistent reductions in self-injurious behaviour (e.g. Lutzker, 1978; Singh, Watson & Winton, 1986), screaming (e.g. Singh, Winton & Dawson, 1982) and stereotypy (e.g. Jordan, Singh & Repp, 1989). Similarly with the use of time-out, visual screening may set the occasion for the occurrence of challenging behaviour as the person seeks to avoid, or escape from, the punishing contingency (Rojahn & Marshburn, 1992).

## Positive punishment

Positive punishment refers to the reduction in the rate of a behaviour as a result of the contingent presentation of a punishing stimulus. A wide range of punishing stimuli have been employed to reduce challenging behaviour. Apart from verbal reprimands, all approaches have been shown to be effective in some instances in bringing about short- and medium-term reductions in severe challenging behaviour (Axelrod & Apsche, 1983; Cataldo, 1991; Luiselli et al., 1992; Repp & Singh, 1990).

Azrin et al. (1988), for example, demonstrated that the combination of DRI, response interruption and contingent manual restraint for a 2-minute period brought about rapid and significant reductions in the severe long-standing self-injurious behaviour shown by one girl, two women and six men with severe intellectual disabilities. Across all participants, self-injury was reduced to 11% of baseline levels. The combined treatment package was shown to be significantly more effective than its constituent components, each of which reduced self-injury to approximately 50% of baseline levels (see also Luiselli, 1992b; Van Houten, Rolider & Houlihan, 1992).

Controversially, Linscheid et al. (1990) described the development and evaluation of the Self-Injurious Behavior Inhibiting System (SIBIS; see also Iwata, 1988; Linscheid, 1992; Linscheid et al., 1994; Ricketts, Goza & Matese, 1992; Williams, Kirkpatrick-Sanchez & Iwata, 1993). This is an automated device which delivers electric shock contingent on self-injury which is automatically detected by a piezoelectric impact detector. The use of punishment-based procedures raises a number of issues. Several commentators have suggested that the use of punishment may be associated with unacceptably high rates of negative 'side-effects' (e.g. Guess et al., 1987; Meyer & Evans, 1989). Indeed, negative outcomes associated with the use of punishment have included increases in nontargeted challenging behaviour, increased incontinence and decreased appetite (Cataldo, 1991). However, reviews of applied research have consistently noted that: (a) reporting of side-effects is often anecdotal; and (b) the reporting of positive side-effects (e.g. increased sociability, increased responsiveness, reduced medication, reduced use of restraints) consistently outweighs the reporting of negative side-effects in the applied literature (Carr & Lovaas, 1983; Cataldo, 1991; see also Duker & Seys, 1996; Linscheid et al., 1990, 1994). Nevertheless, as with procedures based on negative punishment, the implementation of punishment-based procedures may set the occasion for the occurrence of challenging behaviour as the person seeks to avoid, or escape from, the punishing contingency (Linscheid, 1992). In addition, problems may be encountered in the maintenance of treatment gains, especially over the longer term (e.g. Murphy & Wilson, 1980; although also see McGlynn & Locke, 1997).

## Cognitive–behavioural approaches, self-management and self-control

Over the last decade, there has been a growing interest in the use of cognitive–behavioural approaches and the use of self-management or self-control procedures by people with intellectual disabilities (Kroese, 1998; Kroese, Dagnan & Loumidis, 1997). Korinek (1991) argues that the benefits of self-management include its short-term efficacy, effective maintenance and generalization, increased independence, reduced need for supervision and enhanced motivation. However, the use of self-management procedures by people with intellectual disabilities has received relatively little attention (cf. Gardner & Cole, 1989; Jones, Williams & Lowe, 1993; Korinek, 1991). This is particularly so with regard to the self-management of challenging behaviour among people with severe intellectual disabilities.

Studies involving people with mild/moderate intellectual disabilities (mild or moderate mental retardation) have indicated that:

- people can reliably self-report on internal states and cognitions (Lindsay et al., 1994);
- self-monitoring alone may reduce self-injury, aggressive and stereotypic behaviour (Pope & Jones, 1996; Reese, Sherman & Sheldon, 1984; Rudrud, Ziarnik & Coleman, 1984; Zeigob, Klukas & Junginger, 1978); and
- more complex self-management procedures including anger management training and social problem-solving skills may reduce aggressive, disruptive, stereotypic and self-injurious behaviour (Benson, Rice & Miranti, 1986; Black, Cullen & Novaco, 1997; Cole, Gardner & Karan, 1985; Gardner, Clees & Cole, 1983; Gardner et al., 1983; Grace et al., 1988; Koegel et al., 1992; Loumidis & Hill, 1997; Rose, 1996; Rose & West, in press; Rose, West & Clifford, in press; Rosine & Martin, 1983).

At present, the applicability of such procedures to people with more severe disabilities is unclear; of particular importance is the relationship between the development of language and the emergence of rule-governed behaviour, of which self-management or self-regulation is an example (Hayes, 1989; Jones et al., 1993; Whitman, 1990).

However, the results of studies investigating self-management among young children with autism suggest that such approaches may be more applicable to people with severe disabilities than is commonly thought. Koegel and Koegel (1990) investigated the applicability of self-management procedures in the reduction of stereotypic behaviours shown by four children with autism. The childrens' mental ages ranged from 2 years 9 months to 5 years 11 months, while their chronological age ranged from 9 to 14 years. Each child displayed between three and six distinct forms of stereotypic behaviour. Implementation of an externally reinforced self-monitoring procedure was associated with highly significant reductions in stereotypy for three of the children. The fourth child, who had the highest mental age, showed consistent, but less pronounced, reductions in stereotypy. Pierce and Schreibman (1994) examined the effects of a pictorial self-cueing and self-reinforcement strategy on the independent performance of daily living skills (e.g. setting the table, making lunch, getting dressed). The participants were three children with autism (age range 6–8 years; mental age range 2 years 2 months to 3 years 10 months). Implementation of the self-management package was associated with an increase in independent performance and a decrease in stereotypy (see also, Krantz, MacDuff & McClannahan, 1993; MacDuff, Krantz & McClannahan, 1993; Stahmer & Schreibman, 1992).

## Multicomponent strategies

Much of the research literature has been concerned with determining the efficacy of discrete approaches to intervention. In clinical practice, however, the need to bring about rapid and significant change argues for the use of complex multicomponent intervention strategies (Cameron, Maguire & Maguire, 1998; Carr et al., 1994; Risley, 1996).

Carr and Carlson (1993), for example, employed a complex package involving choice, embedding, functional communication training, building tolerance for delay of reinforcement and the presentation of discriminative stimuli for non-problem behaviours to teach shopping skills to three adolescent boys with autism and severe intellectual disabilities. Following the implementation of the programme, all participants were able to shop in supermarkets and displayed virtually no challenging behaviour during this activity (see also, Carr et al., 1999b; Kemp & Carr, 1995).

Lovaas (1987), Lovaas and Smith (1994), McEachin et al. (1993) and Smith et al. (1997) described the medium and longer term outcomes of an intensive behaviourally orientated educational treatment programme for a group of 19 young children with autism (mean age 32 months at intake). This involved 'two years or more of one-to-one treatment for 40 hours per week in their homes and communities from a treatment team that included families, normal peers, and teachers of normal classes, as well as staff from UCLA [University of California at Los Angeles]' (Lovaas & Smith, 1994, p. 253). Follow-up of this group at age 7 (Lovaas, 1987) and 13 (McEachin et al., 1993) indicated substantial gains in IQ scores, adaptive behaviours and educational achievement in comparison with a quasi-random control group. Lovaas and Smith (1994) also report that 'our preliminary data show that all but 2 of the intensively treated [children] . . . are free of clinically significant problems associated with destructive behaviors. In contrast, the majority of the control [children] are medicated and living in institutional settings, where their self-injurious and assaultive behaviors present major management problems' (Lovaas & Smith, 1994, p. 253). Unfortunately, no data substantiating this claim have been published.

Finally, Saunders and Spradlin (1991) introduced the idea of addressing challenging behaviour through the establishment of *supported routines* (see also Saunders & Saunders, 1998; Saunders et al., 1996). This fundamentally constructional approach involves the development of detailed procedures for the 'comprehensive enablement' of competent performance in situations which may elicit challenging behaviour. Saunders et al. (1996), for example, reported the exhibition of self-injurious behaviour during mealtimes, often in response to staff prompts or interruptions. Intervention consisted of developing a supported routine by eliminating difficult discriminations and minimizing demands and interruptions, thereby simultaneously increasing independent performance and decreasing challenging behaviour.

## Summary

Table 7.1 summarizes some of the main advantages and disadvantages of the approaches to intervention discussed in this chapter. The evidence which has been reviewed in earlier chapters indicated that severely challenging behaviours may be highly persistent. To recapitulate:

- adults who come to the attention of specialized services have commonly shown the same challenging behaviours for a decade or more (Emerson et al., 1988; Murphy et al., 1993);
- the vast majority of people, who show self-injurious behaviour at one point in time, are also likely to do so many years later (Emerson et al., 1996a, in press c; Kiernan et al., 1997; Turner & Sloper, 1996; Windahl, 1988); and
- longer term follow-up studies of 'successful' intervention programmes often

report a very high rate of relapse (Griffin et al., 1986; Murphy & Wilson, 1980; Schroeder & MacLean, 1987) or, alternatively, indicate that challenging behaviours tend to persist, but at a much lower intensity and/or rate (Foxx, 1990; Jensen & Heidorn, 1993).

Attention was also drawn to some of the personal and social consequences which the person may experience as a result of his or her challenging behaviour. These include: physical injury, ill health and the development of secondary sensory or neurological impairments; abuse; inappropriate treatment involving the long-term prescription of neuroleptics; the use of mechanical restraints and protective devices; exposure to unnecessarily degrading or abusive psychological treatments; exclusion from community settings, relationships and services; and social and material deprivation and systematic neglect.

In the light of these observations, it is important to attempt to determine the general effectiveness of behavioural approaches in bringing about socially significant and durable change. Two aspects of the nature of the available evidence militate against being able to provide a clear answer to this important question.

Firstly, a reliance in the research literature on single-subject experimental designs, when combined with the tendency not to report treatment failures, does mean that we know little about the extent to which the results of successful interventions can be generalized across individuals, therapists and settings (Barlow & Hersen, 1984). Thus, while single-subject designs often have a very high internal validity (i.e. they demonstrate that the observed changes are due to a particular intervention), systematic replication is required to determine whether the same results can be obtained with other participants, other therapists and in other settings. Unfortunately, such *systematic* replication is extremely rare in this field. As a result, while we are able to conclude that various behavioural procedures *can* bring about significant change, we cannot predict with any confidence the proportion of 'cases' in which this is likely to be achieved. Similarly, reliance on single-subject designs means that there is only limited knowledge with regards to the characteristics of the behaviour, participants or setting which are likely to influence the impact of an intervention.

The second major limitation in the available evidence concerns restrictions on the range of outcomes evaluated, and aspects of response and stimulus generalization and the length of time over which the durability of intervention gains are assessed. Attention was drawn to the former issue in Chapter 2. The failure to assess the maintenance or durability of treatment effects is highlighted by the observation that, of the 366 outcomes from 109 studies of positive behavioural support reviewed by Carr et al. (1999a), information on maintenance over a period of more than 1 year was available for only 7 (2%) outcomes (see also Dunlap et al., 1999; Scotti et al., 1996).

**Table 7.1.** Summary of behavioural approaches to intervention

| Approach | Constructional? | Functional? | Primary advantages | Primary disadvantages |
|---|---|---|---|---|
| *Modification of bio-behavioural state* | | | | |
| Modification of idiosyncratic establishing operations | No | Yes | Immediate and significant reductions in challenging behaviour<br>Possible ease of implementation | Requires detailed functional assessment |
| *Changing the nature of preceding activities* | | | | |
| Modify idiosyncratic setting events | No | Yes | Immediate and significant reductions in challenging behaviour<br>Possible ease of implementation | Requires detailed functional assessment |
| Noncontingent exercise | No | No | Ease of implementation<br>Broad-based effects<br>Possible positive collateral changes (e.g. sleeping, general health benefits)<br>Possible when maintaining factors unknown | May be ineffective for, or increase, some escape-motivated challenging behaviour<br>Temporary effects |
| Interspersed requests (behavioural momentum) | No | Yes | Immediate and significant reductions in challenging behaviour<br>Ease of implementation | Requires detailed functional assessment |
| Neutralizing routines | No | Yes | Immediate and significant reductions in challenging behaviour<br>Possible ease of implementation | Requires detailed functional assessment |
| *Changing the nature of concurrent activities: curricular design and supported routines* | | | | |
| Schedule activities to avoid antecedents or on basis of preferences | No | Yes | Immediate and significant reductions in challenging behaviour<br>Ease of implementation | May not be feasible to avoid antecedent<br>Antecedents may be important for health or welfare of person<br>Requires detailed functional assessment |

| | | | | |
|---|---|---|---|---|
| Increase task variety | No | Yes | Immediate and significant reductions in challenging behaviour<br>Ease of implementation | Requires detailed functional assessment |
| Increase opportunities for choice making | No | No | Possible broad-based effects<br>Possible positive collateral changes (e.g. reduced stress)<br>Possible when maintaining factors unknown | Unknown effectiveness<br>May be complex to implement |
| Stimulus fading | No | Yes | May help reduce escape-motivated challenging behaviour elicited by conditioned arousal<br>May help re-introduce antecedents important to health/welfare of person | May not be feasible to control access to antecedents<br>Relatively slow acting<br>Requires detailed functional assessment |
| Modify idiosyncratic setting events | No | Yes | Immediate and significant reductions in challenging behaviour<br>Possible ease of implementation | Requires detailed functional assessment |

*Changing the nature of concurrent activities: environmental enrichment and noncontingent reinforcement*

| | | | | |
|---|---|---|---|---|
| Increase level of background stimulation | No | No | Simple to sustain<br>Ease of implementation<br>Broad-based effects<br>Possible positive collateral changes (e.g. wakefulness) | May be ineffective for or increase escape-motivated challenging behaviours<br>May be difficult to implement initially |
| Noncontingent reinforcement and satiation | No | Yes | Immediate and significant reductions in challenging behaviour | Requires detailed functional assessment |

*Embedding*

| | | | | |
|---|---|---|---|---|
| Modify idiosyncratic setting events | No | Yes | Immediate and significant reductions in challenging behaviour<br>Possible ease of implementation | Requires detailed functional assessment |

**Table 7.1** (cont.)

| Approach | Constructional? | Functional? | Primary advantages | Primary disadvantages |
|---|---|---|---|---|
| *Response covariation* | | | | |
| Functional displacement | Yes | Yes | Immediate and significant reductions in challenging behaviour | Requires detailed functional assessment<br>Complex implementation<br>May involve avoidance of activities important for health/welfare of person |
| Differential reinforcement of other behaviour (DRO) | No | No | Possible when maintaining factors unknown | Complex or intensive implementation |
| Differential reinforcement of incompatible (DRI) or alternative (DRA) behaviour | Yes | ? | Possible when maintaining factors unknown | Complex or intensive implementation |
| Supported routines | Yes | Yes | Immediate and significant reductions in challenging behaviour<br>Highly constructional | Requires detailed functional assessment<br>Possibly complex or intensive implementation |
| *Modification of maintaining contingencies* | | | | |
| Extinction | No | Yes | | Requires detailed functional assessment<br>Complex or intensive implementation<br>Temporary increases in rate/variety/intensity of challenging behaviour<br>Slow acting<br>Poor generalization<br>Low procedural acceptability |

*Punishment (default technologies)*

| | | | | |
|---|---|---|---|---|
| Time-out | No | No | | Requires detailed functional assessment complex or intensive implementation<br>Poor generalization<br>Low procedural acceptability |
| Visual screening | No | No | Possible when maintaining factors unknown<br>Immediate and significant reductions in challenging behaviour | Complex or intensive implementation<br>Possibly poor generalization<br>Low procedural acceptability |
| Positive punishment | No | No | Possible when maintaining factors unknown<br>Immediate and significant reductions in challenging behaviour | Complex or intensive implementation<br>Possibly poor generalization<br>Low procedural acceptability |

This means that relatively little is known regarding such factors as: collateral changes or the 'side-effects' of intervention; the contextual control of challenging behaviour and the generalization of the effects of intervention to new settings, behaviours and people; the long-term outcomes of intervention; and the broader social validity of intervention when applied in community-based settings. Nevertheless, the accumulated evidence does indicate that behavioural approaches *can* be effective in bringing about rapid, significant and widespread reductions in severely challenging behaviours and that such changes *may* be associated with a range of positive 'side-effects', *may* generalize to new settings and *may* be maintained over long periods of time (Carr et al., 1999a; Didden et al., 1997).

# 8

# Psychopharmacology

In this chapter, the evidence relating to psychopharmacological approaches to reducing challenging behaviour will be briefly reviewed. It is beyond the scope of the present book to provide a comprehensive review of the area or to provide specific guidelines for the use of such medication – to do so would duplicate existing reviews (e.g. Ellis, Singh & Singh, 1997; Kalachnik et al., 1998; Kennedy & Meyer, 1998b; Reiss & Aman, 1998; Rush & Frances, 2000; Schroeder, 1999; Thompson et al., 1994a; Verhoeven & Tuinier, 1999). The intention of this review is to pay particular attention to approaches based on current understanding of the neurobiological bases of challenging behaviour (see Chapter 4).

The importance of gaining a basic understanding of psychopharmacological approaches is underscored by three factors. Firstly, as was indicated in Chapter 4, there is growing evidence to suggest that alterations in dopaminergic, serotoninergic and opioid neurotransmitter systems may play a role in the aetiology of some forms of challenging behaviour. This recent research opens up the possibility of developing a functionally based approach to psychopharmacological interventions which may complement behavioural approaches. Secondly, an appreciation of the behavioural mechanisms of drug action (Kennedy & Meyer, 1998b; Thompson et al., 1994a) is likely to be of value when developing behavioural approaches for people in receipt of psychoactive medication. Finally, psychopharmacological interventions constitute the most common form of treatment received by people with severe intellectual disabilities and challenging behaviour.

Studies undertaken in North America and the UK suggest that in many localities approximately one in two people with severe intellectual disabilities who show challenging behaviours is prescribed neuroleptic (anti-psychotic) medication (Altmeyer et al., 1987; Davidson et al., 1994; Emerson et al., in press c; Kiernan et al., 1995; Meador & Osborn, 1992; Molyneux, Emerson & Caine, 1999; Oliver et al., 1987; Rinck, 1998; Robertson et al., in press a).

In Chapter 4, some of the evidence was discussed which related to the role of three different classes of neurotransmitters in the aetiology of challenging behaviour: dopamine, serotonin (5-hydroxytryptamine) and the opioid peptides (in particular, β-endorphin). In the sections below, some of the implications of this evidence for psychopharmacological intervention will be considered. The evidence concerning other psychopharmacological agents will then be briefly reviewed. Throughout the discussion, attention will be drawn to the link between neurobiological processes and challenging behaviour and the behavioural mechanism of drug action (Thompson et al., 1994a).

## Dopamine antagonists

As noted in Chapter 4, the dopaminergic system is closely involved in the regulation of motor activity. It contains two main groups of dopamine receptors (D1 and D2), each of which contains further subtypes. Evidence which suggests that abnormalities in the D1 receptor subsystem may be implicated in the development and maintenance of at least some forms of self-injurious behaviour includes:

- the association between Lesch–Nyhan syndrome and injurious self-biting;
- animal studies which have shown that destruction of dopamine pathways is associated with severe self-biting; and
- the association between isolation rearing of rhesus monkeys, self-injurious behaviour and long-term alterations in dopamine receptor sensitivity and destruction of dopaminergic pathways.

Commonly prescribed anti-psychotic medications (e.g. chlorpromazine, thioridazine) are known to suppress dopaminergic activity. Numerous studies have been published evaluating the effects of such agents on challenging behaviours shown by people with intellectual disabilities (Baumeister et al., 1998; Thompson et al., 1991). While there is, not surprisingly, evidence that such agents may reduce challenging behaviour which is associated with an underlying mental illness (e.g. Williams et al., 1993), evidence regarding their general effectiveness is much less clear.

In summarizing the results of their recent review, Thompson et al. (1991) concluded that 'administration of neuroleptic drugs can result in beneficial effects in treating certain behavioral disorders in some people with mental retardation. It is difficult to specify which individuals and which behavioral disorders will benefit from neuroleptic drugs. Previous reviews . . . reached similar conclusions' (Thompson et al., 1991, pp. 396–7). More recently, Baumeister et al. (1998) conclude that the evidence regarding the use of neuroleptics for treating challenging behaviour is 'weak' (Baumeister et al., 1998, p. 147). Finally, a recent Cochrane collaboration review of this area failed to find any evidence to support the use of neuroleptics in the treatment of challenging behaviour. The authors concluded that:

it is debatable whether the use of anti-psychotic medication for certain people with intellectual disability and challenging behaviour is ethical outside of a randomized controlled trial. At
the very least, target symptoms should be identified, reliably measured and recorded as a
baseline before embarking on a therapeutic trial of anti-psychotic medication. Regular
reviews of efficacy and adverse effects should be instigated. If no improvement in challenging
behaviour results, the anti-psychotic medication should be withdrawn. (Brylewski & Duggan,
1999, p. 369).

Such a conclusion is not surprising when we consider the neurobiological and
behavioural bases of action of common anti-psychotics. As has been shown, the
accumulating evidence suggests links between self-injurious behaviour and supersensitivity of D1 receptors, and between stereotypy and D2 receptor activity
(Breese et al., 1995; Cooper & Dourish, 1990; Schroeder & Tessel, 1994; Schroeder
et al., 1995). Commonly prescribed anti-psychotic agents are dopamine antagonists, which are relatively specific to D2 receptor types. They are extremely unlikely,
therefore, to have any *specific* effects on either aggression or self-injurious behaviour. Evidence of a link between stereotypy and D2 pathways, however, does
suggest that such agents may have a more specific effect on stereotyped behaviour.

However, as was indicated in Chapter 4, there is some preliminary evidence to
suggest that D1 antagonists (e.g. clozapine, fluphenazine) may have a more
specific effect on self-injurious behaviour (e.g. Aman & Madrid, 1999; Goldstein et
al., 1985; Gualtieri & Schroeder, 1989; Hammock, Schroeder & Levine, 1995;
Schroeder et al., 1995). Gualtieri and Schroeder (1989), for example, reported
positive outcomes for 10 out of 15 participants with self-injurious behaviour in a
placebo-controlled trial of low-dose fluphenazine. Schroeder et al. (1995) reported that, of three participants with severe intellectual disabilities and severe
persistent self-injury treated with clozapine, one showed dramatic reductions in
self-injury (hourly rates reduced to 14% of baseline levels) and one showed
moderate reductions in self-injury.

Thompson et al. (1991, 1994a) and Kennedy and Meyer (1998b) have reviewed
some of the behavioural effects of anti-psychotics. They pointed to two general
effects of this class of agents. Firstly, they appear to have a general 'ahedonic' effect
involving a reduction in the efficacy of positive reinforcers (Wise, 1982), an effect
which is most marked for behaviours maintained by low rates of reinforcement.
Secondly, anti-psychotics weaken avoidance behaviour at dosage levels which have
no effect on escape. These observations suggest that anti-psychotics may be
expected to have a general effect on challenging behaviour which is maintained by
operant processes. In particular, they may reduce avoidance-maintained behaviours and behaviours maintained by lean schedules of positive reinforcement.
Given the moderating effects of the background rate of reinforcement on the
relationship between the rate of reinforcement and response rate (McDowell,

1982), this effect may be more pronounced in enriched environments. The observations would also suggest, however, that use of these drugs may be expected to have generalized suppressive effects on other learned behaviours, including adaptive behaviours (Thompson et al., 1994a).

It should also be noted that the use of anti-psychotics is known to be associated with a range of serious side-effects. These include sedation, blurred vision, nausea, dizziness, weight gain, opacities of the cornea, grand mal seizures, a range of extra-pyramidal syndromes including parkinsonism, akathisia, acute dystonic reaction and tardive dyskinesia, and death through neuroleptic malignant syndrome (Baumeister et al., 1998; Kennedy & Meyer, 1998b; Thompson et al., 1991).

## Serotonin agonists

The serotoninergic system is closely linked with a number of processes including arousal, appetite control, anxiety and depression. Disturbances in the system have been linked with insomnia, depression, disorders of appetite control and obsessive–compulsive disorders (cf. Bodfish & Madison, 1993). With regard to potential behavioural mechanisms, Thompson et al. (1994a) suggest that serotonin activity may regulate reactivity to aversive stimuli and moderate the effectiveness of punishment on suppressing behaviour. As was discussed in Chapter 4, evidence is accumulating to point to a link between serotonin and aggression, and, perhaps, serotonin and self-injurious behaviour. This evidence includes:

*   animal studies which show that lesions in areas which contain serotoninergic neurones or inhibit serotonin synthesis can lead to an increase in aggression – similarly, interventions which increase serotonin synthesis or administration of serotonin agonists lead to a reduction in aggression; and
*   studies of nondisabled people suggest a negative correlation between levels of serotonin or its metabolites in the cerebral spinal fluid or blood plasma and aggression.

This evidence suggests that serotoninergic agonists (e.g. buspirone) or reuptake inhibitors (e.g. fluoxetine) may have an impact on reducing aggression and, possibly, other forms of challenging behaviour (Aman et al., 1999; Racusin et al., 1999; Sovner et al., 1998). Indeed, some evidence is beginning to accumulate to suggest that fluoxetine may reduce aggression and self-injurious behaviour in people with severe intellectual disabilities (Bodfish & Madison, 1993; Cook et al., 1992; Davanzo et al., 1998; Kirkpatrick-Sanchez et al., 1998; Lewis et al., 1996; Markowitz, 1992; Singh, Kleynhans & Barton, 1998; Sovner et al., 1993; Sovner et al., 1998; Verhoeven et al., 1999). Bodfish and Madison (1993), for example, reported that fluoxetine (at a dosage of 40 mg/day) significantly reduced self-injurious and aggressive behaviours which had a 'compulsive' nature in seven out of ten participants. None of the six participants who showed 'noncompulsive' aggression or self-injury responded positively. These results are particularly interesting in that they appear to point to possible aetiological factors which may discriminate between responders and nonresponders. As noted in Chapter 4, such results suggest that some forms of self-injurious behaviour may, in fact, be examples of obsessive–compulsive disorder (King, 1993). They may be distinguished by the person also showing other compulsive behaviours (e.g. ordering, touching, hoarding) which interfere with ongoing activities and the person being resistant to change. If these preliminary results are replicated, they suggest a means of identifying and treating a functionally distinct class of self-injury which may be maintained more by neurobiological processes than by environmental contingencies.

Reported side-effects of serotonin reuptake inhibitors include headaches, dizziness, nausea, diarrhoea, sedation, insomnia, sweating, tremor, anxiety, restlessness and sexual dysfunction (Sovner et al., 1998).

## β-endorphin antagonists

β-endorphin, one of the opioid peptide neurotransmitters, has significant analgesic and antinocicoptive (blocking of pain receptors) properties, can be associated with a euphoric mood state and may lead to physical dependence (Singh et al., 1993b). Sandman and his colleagues (e.g. Sandman, 1990/1991; Sandman & Hetrick, 1995; Sandman et al., 1999) have proposed two models in which β-endorphin activity may be related to self-injurious behaviour. In the *congenital opioid excess* model, it is proposed that excess opioid activity leads to permanently raised pain thresholds. In the *addiction* hypothesis, it is proposed that self-injurious behaviour leads to the release of β-endorphin which, through its analgesic, antinocicoptive and euphoria-inducing properties, acts as an automatic reinforcer for the self-injury. Over time, it is suggested, physical dependence (with associated withdrawal symptoms) may develop.

There is accumulating evidence to support a link between β-endorphin and self-injurious behaviour. For instance:

* levels of β-endorphin are raised in the blood plasma of people with severe intellectual disabilities who self-injure when compared with appropriate controls (Sandman et al., 1990a);
* levels of β-endorphin are raised in the blood plasma of people with severe intellectual disabilities following an episode of self-injury (Sandman, 1990/91; Sandman et al., 1997);
* the β-endorphin antagonist naltrexone hydrochloride has brought about

significant reductions in self-injury for some people (Sandman et al., 1998, 1999); and

- the effect of naltrexone hydrochloride is associated with the site of injury (Thompson et al., 1995) and the extent to which levels of β-endorphin metabolites are raised in the blood plasma of people with severe intellectual disabilities following an episode of self-injury (Sandman et al., 1997).

The strongest evidence of an association between β-endorphin and self-injurious behaviour comes from experimental and clinical studies which have examined the impact of the endorphin antagonists naloxone hydrochloride and, more recently, naltrexone hydrochloride on self-injurious behaviour shown by people with severe intellectual disabilities (for recent reviews see Sandman et al., 1998, 1999). Numerous studies have now reported significant reductions in self-injurious behaviour associated with the administration of naltrexone hydrochloride (e.g. Barrett, Feinstein & Hole, 1990; Bernstein et al., 1987; Bodfish et al., 1997; Crews et al., 1993, 1999; Herman et al., 1987; Kars et al., 1990; Knabe, Schulz & Richard, 1990; Lienemann & Walker, 1989; Ryan et al., 1989; Sandman, Barron & Coleman, 1990b; Sandman et al., 1997; Symons et al., 1998; Taylor et al., 1991; Thompson et al., 1994b, 1995; Walters et al., 1990). However, it is clear that such positive results are not inevitable as a number of studies have also reported treatment failures, clinically insignificant results or occasional worsening of self-injury (e.g. Barrera et al., 1994; Johnson, Johnson & Sahl, 1994; Kars et al., 1990; Knabe et al., 1990; Luiselli, Beltis & Bass, 1989; Ricketts et al., 1992; Willemsen-Swinkles et al., 1995; Zingarelli et al., 1992). A number of factors may account for these variations in outcome.

- *Dose-dependent effects*, in that a number of studies have reported positive outcomes only for specific dose levels, other dosages having either no effect or leading to an increase in self-injurious behaviour. Unfortunately, the relationships between dosage and outcome have been inconsistent, in that studies have reported greater effects with both lower (e.g. Barrera et al., 1994; Herman et al., 1987; Ricketts et al., 1992; Sandman et al., 1990b) and higher dosages (e.g. Barrera et al., 1994; Bernstein et al., 1987; Knabe et al., 1990; Ryan et al., 1989; Sandman et al., 1990b).
- *Behavioural topography* – Thompson et al. (1994b) presented data to suggest that particular forms of self-injury may respond differently to naltrexone, with hand-to-head hitting, head-to-object hitting and self-biting showing more positive changes than eye, nose and throat poking and face slapping. These relationships held up within individuals, as well as across participants, and may be related to the extent to which injury of specific body sites leads to the release of β-endorphin.
- *Behavioural function* – as we have seen in Chapter 4, there is extensive evidence

to suggest that self-injurious behaviour may be maintained by a variety of factors. It is plausible to propose, therefore, that forms of self-injurious behaviour which are maintained by powerful operant contingencies, and especially those which may be less effective in leading to the release of β-endorphin, may be less likely to be reduced by the administration of naltrexone.

β-endorphin antagonists may also influence the response efficiency of self-injurious behaviour (Oliver, 1993); that is, by blocking the release of β-endorphin, they may increase the 'cost' of responding by making the behaviour more painful. As has been discussed, decreasing response efficiency may lead to a behaviour being replaced by a functionally equivalent response (Horner & Day, 1991). This also points to the potential for integrating psychopharmacological and behavioural approaches, in that decreasing the response efficiency of the challenging behaviour is an important component of intervention based on the notion of functional displacement (cf. Symons et al., 1998).

Very few side-effects have been reported with naltrexone hydrochloride, although there appears to be some risk of hepatic toxicity due to an increase in liver enzymes (Thompson et al., 1994b). Reports of behavioural 'side-effects' include *increased* attention and learning (Sandman et al., 1998).

## Other approaches

A number of studies have examined the effects of other classes of psychoactive agents on the challenging behaviour shown by people with intellectual disabilities (for more detailed reviews see Reiss & Aman, 1998; Schroeder, 1999).

### Anxiolytics and sedatives/hypnotics

There is little evidence to suggest that anxiolytics, such as the benzodiazepines, or sedatives/hypnotics (e.g. chloral hydrate) have any clinically significant effect on challenging behaviour (Werry, 1998, 1999). Indeed, there is growing evidence to suggest that 'paradoxical' responding to these classes of drugs may occur among people with intellectual disabilities who show self-injurious and stereotypic behaviour (Sandman & Barron, 1992; Werry, 1998). Thompson et al. (1991, 1994b) suggested that this may be due to the effects of benzodiazepines and sedative hypnotics in blocking the suppressive effects of punishment contingencies which may be acting to reduce the occurrence of challenging behaviour.

### Anti-manics

Lithium carbonate is commonly used to reduce symptoms of mania in bipolar affective disorder. A number of poorly controlled case studies have reported that reductions in aggressive, disruptive and self-injurious behaviours may be associated with administration of lithium (Hellings, 1999; Poindexter et al., 1998). It is unclear, however, whether these positive results are reflected in the reduction in challenging behaviour specifically associated with mania (e.g. Lowry & Sovner, 1992) or whether they indicate more general effects.

## Stimulants

A few early studies suggested that stimulants (e.g. d-amphetamine, methylphenedate) may have a general effect on reducing hyperactivity and improving intellectual functioning among people with intellectual disabilities (e.g. Bell & Zubek, 1961). While stimulants can be effective in the treatment of attention deficit hyperactivity disorder (ADHD), there is little evidence to suggest that they have any specific effect on challenging behaviour (Arnold et al., 1998; Kennedy & Meyer, 1998b).

## Anticonvulsants

Clearly, anticonvulsants may have an important role to play in situations in which challenging behaviours may be associated with seizure activity (cf. Gedye, 1989a,b). While a small number of often poorly controlled studies have reported reductions in challenging behaviour associated with administration of carbamazepine (e.g. Langee, 1989; Reid, Naylor & Kay, 1981), others have reported significant increases in the occurrence of challenging behaviours (Alvarez et al., 1998; Kennedy & Meyer, 1998b; Thompson et al., 1991).

## Beta-adrenergic blockers

A number of studies, again many poorly controlled, have suggested that beta-blockers may be associated with significant reductions in self-injury and aggressive behaviours (Fraser et al., 1998; Ruedrich & Erhardt, 1999).

# Summary and conclusions

Virtually every review of psychopharmacological approaches to reducing challenging behaviour among people with intellectual disabilities has commented on the methodological inadequacies of the majority of studies which have been conducted in this field (e.g. Baumeister & Sevin, 1990; Gadow & Poling, 1988; Reiss & Aman, 1998; Singh et al., 1992; Sprague & Werry, 1971; Thompson et al., 1991). These methodological flaws make interpretation of much of the data highly problematic. In addition, very few studies have attempted to evaluate the social validity of psychopharmacological intervention (Poling & Erhardt, 1999; Poling & LeSage, 1995; Symons et al., 1999a) beyond the monitoring of side-effects (Kalachnik, 1999).

Nevertheless, a number of promising directions are evident, many of which stem from the integration of neurobiological theorizing and psychopharmacological intervention (Baumeister & Sevin, 1990). Thus, for example, although the data are as yet scarce, D1 antagonists, serotonin reuptake inhibitors and β-endorphin antagonists may all have specific effects which are predictable from neurobiological models of challenging behaviour (Aman & Madrid, 1999).

As was stressed in Chapter 4, however, it is highly likely that the factors underlying challenging behaviours are complex and varied. Thus, for example, it is quite clear that some examples of self-injurious behaviour appear to be primarily maintained by operant processes (which may in themselves be complex). On the other hand, it does appear that β-endorphin release is also implicated in some examples of self-injury (see above). There is also, of course, evidence that both serotoninergic and dopaminergic systems may play a role in the expression of self-injurious behaviour.

In Chapter 5, an argument was made for the adoption of a functional perspective. In the light of the preceding discussion, this would imply that one task of analysis would be to attempt to identify the biological as well as the behavioural processes underlying challenging behaviour. Markers for the operation of biological processes may include such factors as covariation of challenging behaviour with mood state (e.g. Lowry & Sovner, 1992; Sovner et al., 1993), co-occurrence with compulsive behaviours (e.g. Bodfish & Madison, 1993), behavioural topography (Thompson et al., 1994b) and environmental independence. Selection of intervention, whether behavioural, psychopharmacological or combined, could then proceed on the basis of evidence rather than personal preference, availability or fashion. To date, however, such a hope has yet to be realized.

# 9

# Community-based supports

In the previous chapters of this book, we drew attention to the social significance of challenging behaviours. In short, such behaviours are relatively common, highly persistent and may lead to social exclusion, systematic neglect, inappropriate treatment and abuse. We then summarized current knowledge regarding the behavioural, biological and psychiatric processes underlying challenging behaviour before discussing a wide range of potentially effective approaches to intervention.

As was noted in the introductory chapter, much has been written over recent years about issues involved in developing and sustaining community-based supports for people with challenging behaviours (e.g. Allen, Banks & Staite, 1991; Allen & Felce, 1999; Blunden & Allen, 1987; Department of Health, 1989, 1993; Emerson, McGill & Mansell, 1994a; Fleming & Stenfert Kroese, 1993; Kiernan, 1993; Koegel et al., 1996a; Mental Health Foundation, 1997), including descriptions of innovative projects which have helped to demonstrate the viability and benefits of supporting people with severe challenging behaviour in the community (e.g. Cameron et al., 1998; Mansell, McGill & Emerson, in press; McGill, Emerson & Mansell, 1994; Risley, 1996).

Two distinct (though complementary) rationales underlie the development of community-based supports for people with severe challenging behaviour. Firstly, it has been argued that people with severe challenging behaviour have as legitimate an entitlement as all other people with intellectual disabilities to a decent quality of life. From this basis, supports may be developed to maximize quality of life *regardless* of the extent of challenging behaviour shown by the individual (cf. Emerson et al., 1994a). Secondly, developing community-based supports may be considered a 'molar' approach to the antecedent control of challenging behaviour (Carr et al., 1998); that is, it has been suggested that the provision of high-quality community-based supports should be seen as an integral component of effective intervention (Cameron et al., 1998; Risley, 1996).

In the following sections, we will consider issues that are relevant to the effectiveness of implementing and sustaining community-based supports.

## The effectiveness of community-based support

### Living in the community

The majority of people with severe intellectual disabilities and challenging behaviour live either with their families or receive community-based residential supports (Emerson et al., in press c; Felce et al., 1994; Kiernan & Qureshi, 1993; Lowe & de Paiva, 1991; Lowe et al., 1998; Qureshi, 1994; Qureshi & Alborz, 1992). A substantial international literature has consistently reported that, while deinstitutionalization is not necessarily associated with a decrease in challenging behaviour, people living in community-based residential supports, including people with challenging behaviour, experience a better overall quality of life than people supported in either institutional or medium-sized residential provision (Emerson & Hatton, 1994; Emerson et al., 2000b; Kim, Larson & Lakin, in press; Young et al., 1998). There is also evidence to suggest that the presence of challenging behaviour may not have a negative impact on people's quality of life, at least for people supported by 'better' providers.

For example, Emerson et al. (1999a) undertook a series of multivariate analyses to identify those personal and environmental characteristics which were associated with variation in a range of aspects of the quality of life among 281 people receiving community-based residential supports from agencies nominated as providing examples of better practice (see also Robertson et al., in press a,b,c). This series of analyses failed to identify any significant relationship between the severity of challenging behaviour shown by participants and their quality of life in such areas as self-determination, contact with members of their family, social inclusion, employment, physical activity, risk and community participation.

This general literature has also indicated that better outcomes appear to be associated with those services which employ an 'active support' model (Allen & Felce, 1999; Emerson & Hatton, 1994; Felce, 1996; Felce et al., in press; Jones et al., 1999; McGill & Toogood, 1994). The associations between the implementation of 'active support' in the areas of person-centred planning, activity planning and the training and support of staff has been associated with: increased levels of engagement in everyday activities (Felce, 1996; Jones et al., 1999), more effective staff support (Felce et al., in press), more equitable distribution of staff support (Jones et al., 1999), larger and more varied social networks (Robertson et al., in press b), greater environmental opportunities for self-determination (Robertson et al., in press c) and higher levels of expressed satisfaction among residents (Gregory et al., in press). The structural characteristics of settings and the resources available within them provide an opportunity framework. Careful management and organization of those resources is necessary to translate this opportunity into reality for the people supported.

In addition to this general literature, a number of studies have specifically examined the outcomes associated with small community-based residential supports for people with severe challenging behaviour (Allen & Felce, 1999). These studies have demonstrated that: (1) it is possible to establish and maintain such services, even for those people considered to present the greatest challenge to services (Emerson, 1990; Emerson & McGill, 1993; Mansell et al., in press; McGill et al., 1994; McGill & Mansell, 1995; Risley, 1996); and (2) the outcomes associated with such services are superior to those associated with institutional provision (Felce et al., 1998; Golding, Emerson & Scott, in press; Knobbe et al., 1995; Mansell, 1994, 1995). While community-based supports appear to be both viable and effective for people with severe challenging behaviour, there is concern that such services may lack effective managerial and professional support and, as a result, may be susceptible to breakdown in response to short-term crises (Mansell, Hughes & McGill, 1994a; McGill et al., 1994).

## Community-based intervention services

A number of studies have investigated the effectiveness of different approaches to providing short- to medium-term intervention services for people with severe challenging behaviour (Allen & Felce, 1999). A number of general conclusions can be drawn from this literature.

Firstly, as noted above, it is clear that, in the UK at least, the majority of people who show challenging behaviour do not receive effective behavioural support (Emerson et al., in press c; Oliver et al., 1987; Qureshi, 1994; for North American data, see Jacobsen, 1998; Stancliffe, Hayden & Lakin, 1999). Emerson et al. (in press a), for example, investigated treatment and management practices among 265 people with challenging behaviours who were receiving some form of residential support in 1998 from agencies nominated as providing examples of 'better practice'. Only 15% of participants had a written behaviourally oriented treatment programme. Many of these were highly simplistic (e.g. 'reward good behaviour . . . ignore challenging behaviour') and were far from being exemplars of positive behavioural support (Carr et al., 1999a; Koegel et al., 1996a). Indeed, these data highlight a glaring failure in the extent to which current services for people with severe intellectual disability in the UK embody the principle of 'evidence-based practice'.

A range of factors are likely to underlie the widespread failure of current services to provide appropriate levels of access to behavioural supports, including: organizational inefficiency reflected in lack of commitment, lack of leadership and poor management procedures (Department of Health, 1993; Mansell, 1994; Mansell et al., 1994a; McBrien & Candy, 1998); inefficient organization of the care environment (McGill & Toogood, 1994); conflict between service ideologies, personal beliefs and beliefs about the nature of behavioural practice (Albin et al., 1996; Emerson, Hastings & McGill, 1994b; Emerson & McGill, 1989; Hastings, 1995, 1997; Hastings, Reed & Watts, 1997; Hastings & Remington, 1994a,b; Hastings, Remington & Hopper, 1995; McBrien & Candy, 1998; Morgan & Hastings, 1998; Watts, Reed & Hastings, 1997); lack of knowledge about behavioural interventions among service providers, including specialist providers (Anderson et al., 1996; Desrochers et al., 1997; Emerson et al., 1996c; Hastings & Remington, 1993); and insufficient resources, including specialist health-care providers (Bailey & Cooper, 1997).

Secondly, a number of studies have demonstrated that peripatetic community-based intervention services are capable of providing effective behavioural support, through a process of consultation, to community-based services (e.g. Bering, Tupman & Jacques, 1993; Davidson et al., 1995; Davidson, Morris & Cain, 1999; Durand & Kishi, 1987; Emerson et al., 1996c; Forrest et al., 1995; Lowe, Felce & Blackman, 1996; McBrien, 1994; Northup et al., 1994; Rudolph et al., 1998; Scorer et al., 1993; Toogood et al., 1994). The evidence also suggests that such services may be capable of reducing institutional admissions (Allen, 1998; Colond & Wieseler, 1995) and may be more cost-effective than institutional services (Allen & Lowe, 1995; Colond & Wieseler, 1995; Donnellan et al., 1985; Hudson et al., 1995a,b). However, there is also evidence that the input from peripatetic behavioural support teams may be ineffective in a substantial proportion of cases (Emerson et al., 1996c; Forrest et al., 1995; Lowe et al., 1996). Allen and Felce (1999) have suggested that the factors which are likely to enhance the effectiveness of such support include:

- a broad skill base which would enable the team to intervene with challenging behaviours maintained by psychological, neurobiological and psychiatric processes;
- a capacity for providing long-term support;
- a clear conceptual model for intervention which is based on empirically established models and procedures;
- sufficient resources to enable the team to offer support to a high proportion of those in need;
- the ability to support carers and staff in reactive behaviour management strategies (Allen et al., 1997; Harris, 1996);
- an efficient and coherent management structure; and
- the ability to deploy staff to model or establish effective ways of working with people who present severe challenges.

A further competence which may be added to this list is an ability to develop and implement interventions based on a detailed understanding of the 'ecology' of families and community settings (Albin et al., 1996).

## Implementing and sustaining positive behavioural support in community settings

As noted above, the existing evidence suggests that many approaches to intervention may either need to be sustained over considerable periods of time or require permanent changes in patterns of interaction between people with intellectual disabilities and those who support them. This does not mean that significant reductions in challenging behaviour are not possible over the short term. On the contrary, most of the approaches to providing effective behavioural support which were discussed in Chapter 7 have been shown, under certain circumstances, to bring about rapid and socially valid improvements in the situations of people who show severe challenging behaviour. However, maintaining these gains, generalizing them to new settings and achieving broader 'life-style' outcomes are unlikely to occur without sustained support. Indeed, some approaches (e.g. the functional displacement of challenging behaviour through supporting the use of more appropriate communicative acts) require permanent changes in the behaviour of carers and support staff. As Anderson et al. (1993) point out: 'patterns of severe challenging behaviors do not simply "disappear". Long-term support plans must create and maintain settings and programmatic contexts in which these behaviors are made and continue to be ineffective, inefficient, or irrelevant. Only then will near-zero levels of challenging behaviors occur and be maintained in all settings relevant to a person's life' (Anderson et al., 1993, p. 368).

Such a requirement does, of course, pose a major challenge to the organization of support systems. This should not, however, surprise us. The behavioural approach suggests that challenging behaviours have been shaped over time and are currently being maintained by powerful contingencies of reinforcement. We should expect that, unless intervention brings about a *lasting change* in the maintaining contingencies, intervention gains are unlikely to prove durable. As we have seen, establishing alternative behaviours is only likely to be effective if the person's challenging behaviour is made 'ineffective, inefficient or irrelevant'. Intervention needs to be seen as an ongoing process, rather than as a time-limited episode of 'treatment'.

This perspective forces us to consider ways in which intervention can bring about sustained changes in the ways in which carers and care staff interact with people with learning disabilities. It requires us to address the various sources of influences operating on carers and care staff including: the resources available to families or in community settings; competing demands on the time and energy of carers and care staff; the beliefs and attitudes held about the person's challenging behaviours; and the ways in which these beliefs are shaped, supported and translated into action.

**The importance of resources**

A very basic (and obvious) requirement for successfully sustaining positive behavioural supports is that carers and/or care staff possess the resources required by the task in hand. Two aspects of resources will be briefly considered: the skills or competencies required for programme implementation; and the time and energy available for carers and care staff to work with service users.

Obviously, carers and/or care staff will not be able to implement successfully a programme of intervention unless they possess the requisite skills and competencies. Fortunately, a considerable amount is known regarding effective and efficient ways of teaching carers and care staff to use behavioural methods (Anderson et al., 1993, 1996; Baumgart & Ferguson, 1991; Cullen, 1992; Dunlap & Fox, 1996; Evans, 1999; Koegel et al., 1996b; McClannahan & Krantz, 1993; Parsons, Reid & Green, 1993; Reid & Green, 1990; Reid, Parsons & Green, 1989a,b; Shore et al., 1995). However, one consistent conclusion which has been drawn from reviews of this literature is that increasing resources (in this case, skills or knowledge through training) itself has little or no impact on subsequent performance (Cullen, 1992; Reid & Green, 1990; Reid et al., 1989a). This leads us to examine other variables which are likely to determine whether the skills possessed by carers and care staff are appropriately used.

Again, it is obvious that the successful implementation of behavioural approaches is dependent on carers and/or care staff having the necessary time and energy to engage in the required activities with those whom they are supporting. Knowledge which has been derived from three distinct areas of study is relevant here. Firstly, a number of studies have examined the relationship between indicators of resources such as staff : user ratios and what staff actually do in a range of residential settings. This research literature indicates that the relationship between resources and performance is far from straightforward. It suggests, for example, that:

- the amount of contact received by users is largely unrelated to overall staff : user ratios (e.g. Felce et al., 1991; Emerson & Hatton, 1994), although users who are supported in small groups of one to four by one or two staff do receive more contact from staff (e.g. Felce et al., 1991);
- increasing the ratio of staff to users in a setting does not necessarily lead to users receiving more support (e.g. Seys & Duker, 1988); and
- in very highly staffed residential settings for people with challenging behaviour, the majority of staff time is spent on activities not involving direct contact with users (e.g. Emerson et al., 1992).

Secondly, numerous studies have indicated that there is, at best, only a very tenuous relationship between indicators of resource availability (e.g. costs, staffing ratios) and the personal outcomes associated with receiving residential supports (e.g. Emerson & Hatton, 1994; Emerson et al., 1999a; Robertson et al., in press a,b,c). Finally, studies have highlighted the impact of competing demands on parental time on their ability to implement consistently intervention procedures designed by professional staff (e.g. Mental Health Foundation, 1997) and have drawn attention to the impact of more general resource issues, such as adequacy of housing and poverty, on child outcomes (e.g. Turner & Sloper, 1996). Thus, for example, the costs of not icing a birthday cake for the sister of someone with challenging behaviour may far outweigh the benefits of recording the details of an episode of challenging behaviour for a visiting psychologist (cf. Mental Health Foundation, 1997).

These sources of evidence do not, of course, deny the importance of resources. Rather, they point to a reasonably obvious conclusion – due to the inefficiency of many human service organizations, resources are a necessary, but far from sufficient, condition for sustaining appropriate patterns of interaction between people with learning disabilities and those who support them.

### Rules, beliefs, emotions, attitudes and behaviour

The field of organizational behaviour management has repeatedly demonstrated that the quality of people's performance in the workplace can be significantly improved by a combination of changing or clarifying expectations concerning job requirements and by providing feedback to staff in the light of the relationship between expectations and actual performance (see, for example, Cullen, 1992; Reid et al., 1989a,b; and *Journal of Applied Behavior Analysis*, Vol. 25, Issue 3). Techniques based on this framework have been repeatedly employed in demonstration projects to improve significantly the performance of direct-care staff in services for people with severe intellectual disabilities (Cullen, 1992; Felce et al., in press; Jones et al., 1999; Reid et al., 1989a,b).

While clearly effective (at least in the short- to medium-term), the general approach adopted by organizational behaviour management can be criticized due to its failure to address the question of *why* staff (or carers) act the way they do (Hastings & Remington, 1994a); that is, while they have repeatedly shown that new 'bolt-on' contingencies (e.g. public posting of feedback on performance, reinforcement of appropriate staff performance with lottery tickets) can change the way staff act, little has been learned about why staff behave in the way they do in the absence of these artificially imposed contingencies. This is, of course, typical of the 'behaviour modification' approach which dominated work with people with challenging behaviour for so many years. This failure to base intervention on a prior *analysis* of the factors maintaining inappropriate staff performance may, at least in part, explain the field's reliance at times on artificial, hierarchical and bureaucratic procedures for ensuring staff compliance with the organization's aims (Evans, 1999; although see Burgio, Whitman & Reid, 1983; Jones et al., 1999).

A more *analytical* approach to understanding and bringing about change in the way carers and/or care staff interact with people with intellectual disabilities needs to consider the processes maintaining existing behaviour. This would involve a consideration of the influence of challenging behaviours on the behaviour of carers or care staff, the influence exercised by other family members (for carers) or colleagues (for care staff), the impact of factors from outside of the immediate setting (e.g. neighbours, friends and relatives), as well as any control exerted by the management systems operating within services (cf. Allen, 1999).

Three sources of evidence highlight the influence which is likely to be exerted by challenging behaviours on the behaviour of carers or care staff. Firstly, there would appear to be a general relationship between challenging behaviour and levels of stress or strain experienced by carers (Quine & Pahl, 1985, 1991; Qureshi, 1992; Saxby & Morgan, 1993; Sloper et al., 1991; Stores et al., 1998) and care staff (Bersani & Heifetz, 1985; Hatton et al., 1995; Jenkins et al., 1997). Secondly, care staff often report strong emotional reactions to episodes of challenging behaviour (Bromley & Emerson, 1995; Harris et al., 1996; Hastings, 1995; Mitchell & Hastings, 1998), especially if such behaviour is seen by care staff as being within the control of the person with intellectual disabilities (Dagnan, Trower & Smith, 1998). Finally, a series of experimental studies has shown that the behaviour of the person with challenging behaviour may exert a considerable influence over the approach and avoidance behaviour of care staff (Carr et al., 1991; Taylor & Carr, 1993, 1994; Taylor & Romanczyk, 1994). In general, escape-maintained challenging behaviours are likely to elicit avoidance by staff; attention-maintained challenging behaviours are likely to elicit approach by staff.

Furthermore, a range of 'informal' rules and contingencies is likely to exert a powerful influence on the behaviour of carers and care staff. Peer groups within the workplace and other relatives within family settings shape each other's behaviour by defining the nature of the 'problem' and what should be done about it, monitoring each other's performance against these (often implicit or unstated) aims, and providing effective (if not always constructive) feedback. In service settings, it is often possible to identify processes of socialization by which new staff are taught the 'tricks of the trade' by members of the existing staff group. These may involve, for example, making it very clear that it is easier and simpler all round if staff do things for users, rather than support the participation of users in everyday activities. As such, informal rules and contingencies may support practices which are either irrelevant to, or at odds with, the explicit aims of the service or the advice of consulting professional staff (McBrien & Candy, 1998).

As we suggested in Chapters 4 and 7, a behavioural approach to understanding why carers and/or care staff act as they do would focus on issues related to the rule-governed behaviour (Hastings, 1995; Hastings & Remington, 1994a,b). Hastings and Remington (1994a) described some of the sources, forms and characteristics of the rules which may, in part, determine the behaviour of care staff. A very similar framework could be used to understand the behaviour of family members towards a person with challenging behaviour. They suggested that, if staff/carer behaviour is rule governed, it becomes important to determine: (1) the content of the rules which are influencing behaviour; (2) their sources; and (3) the nature of the contingencies maintaining rule following.

With regard to content, rules are likely to vary widely with regard to their specificity, ranging from the type of highly specific performance-related instructions commonly encountered in behavioural teaching programmes, to much more general beliefs about the nature of challenging behaviour which will require considerable 'translation' before they can provide specific guides to action. It is interesting to note, therefore, that many of the more prevalent beliefs held by staff concerning the causes of challenging behaviour appear to relate to either the person's internal psychological state (e.g. frustration, boredom) or to very broad environmental factors (e.g. previous deprivation, lack of staff); that is, to factors which have relatively weak implications for specific staff performances (Allen, 1999; Bromley & Emerson, 1995; Oliver et al., 1996; Qureshi, 1993).

These rules may be either self-generated (i.e. generalized from other areas of life), or externally supplied by managers, professionals or peers (e.g. through formal training or informal induction into the 'canteen culture' of human service settings). Importantly, viewing staff/carer behaviour as potentially rule governed switches attention from the contingencies operating on specific staff behaviours to the contingencies maintaining more general classes of rule following. Thus, rule-governed behaviour is not independent of the environment, although it may be insensitive to momentary changes in the contingencies it describes (Hastings & Remington, 1994a). The contingencies maintaining rule following will be dependent on the nature of the rule, but could include such factors as: positive reinforcement (e.g. praise) *for rule following* from peers, managers and professionals; avoidance of the withdrawal of positive reinforcers (e.g. having pay docked); escape from, or avoidance of, the presentation of punishing stimuli (e.g. peer censure); and 'automatic reinforcement' arising from the confirmation of the rules' predictions.

### 'Contextual fit' and sustainable change

The type of analysis outlined above suggests that sustainable change is more likely when behavioural supports are developed in ways which maximize their 'goodness of fit' with key aspects of the context in which they are to be implemented (Albin

**Table 9.1.** Assessing 'goodness of fit' of behavioural supports

*Goals and process*

Are the goals of the support plan consistent with the hopes, fears and aspirations of
  the person with intellectual disabilities? Their family? Support staff?

Is the logic of the support plan consistent with the beliefs and values of the person
  with intellectual disabilities? Their family? Support staff?

If not, can the gap be reduced by changing the plan (without jeopardizing its
  integrity) or by any appropriate changes to the values and attitudes of participants?

*Skill base*

What skills will be required to implement the intervention?

Do the people who will be carrying out the intervention have the required skills? If
  not, can those skills be taught, generalized and maintained?

*Resource requirements*

What other resources will be required to implement the intervention?

Do the people who will be implementing the intervention have adequate time and
  resources to carry it out effectively?

What other demands on their time are likely to interfere with implementation?

Can the support plan be made more 'user-friendly' by requiring less intensive input
  or by linking in better with existing routines?

Can additional resources be secured and maintained?

*Sustaining implementation*

Are performance expectations clear?

How can compliance with these expectations be monitored in a way which is viable
  and acceptable to all concerned? Are these consistent with the way performance is
  actually monitored within the setting? Can existing practices be improved?

How can feedback on performance and achievements be given in a way which is
  viable and acceptable to all concerned? Are these consistent with the way feedback
  is actually given within the setting? Can existing practices be improved?

What is likely to interfere with sustained implementation (e.g. emotional reactions of
  staff)? Can these threats to the fidelity of programme implementation be addressed
  (e.g. by teaching effective management strategies)?

Will the people responsible for programme implementation receive appropriate levels
  of emotional, informational and practical support? Are these likely to reinforce or
  be in conflict with the programme requirements?

et al., 1996). It has been suggested that this will be more likely if a behavioural
'support plan and its components are consistent with or highly compatible with
the values and skills of key stakeholders and plan implementors; readily sustainable given the resources and constraints of the environments, conditions and

systems where the plan is implemented; and suitable to the unique needs of the person with problem behaviors' (Albin et al., 1996, pp. 82–3). In practice, the idea of 'contextual fit' (which has clear links to ideas of social validity and feasibility analysis) means that ideally:

- the goals of intervention should be developed in partnership with the person with intellectual disabilities and those who are supporting them (Fox et al., 1997; Kincaid, 1996; Vaughn et al., 1997), or should, at the very least, be consistent with their priorities;
- the form of intervention should reflect the culture, values and the skills available or potentially available to the people who will be implementing the intervention plan;
- the detailed activities required for programme implementation should enmesh with existing routines and activity patterns; and
- the requirements of appropriate implementation are feasible within the constraints and competing demands operating on the people who will be responsible for implementation.

A series of questions relating to the potential contextual fit of behavioural supports is presented in Table 9.1.

# 10

# Challenges ahead

In this chapter, we will return to some of the themes which have arisen throughout this book and draw attention to areas of research and practice which need to be explored in greater detail if applied behavioural approaches are to enhance their contribution to the design of effective community-based supports for people with severe intellectual disability and severe challenging behaviour. Three issues will be discussed: the interaction between behavioural and biological processes; early intervention and preventative services; and the changing social context of intervention.

## Exploring the interaction between behavioural and biological processes

The evidence reviewed in Chapter 4 indicated that a wide range of cultural, social, behavioural, biological and psychiatric processes may be involved in the development and maintenance of challenging behaviour. Cultural and social processes are involved in defining behaviour as challenging (Lowe & Felce, 1995a,b) and in shaping people's reactions to those behaviours (Allen, 1999; Dagnan et al., 1998). Behavioural processes are implicated in the maintenance of some examples of challenging behaviour (Iwata et al., 1994a) and may be responsible for shaping the development of these behaviours over time (Guess & Carr, 1991; MacLean et al., 1994). Evidence also suggests that neurobiological mechanisms are involved in the expression of some examples of challenging behaviour (e.g. Sandman et al., 1998, 1999). Finally, circumstantial evidence suggests a link between psychiatric disorders and challenging behaviours (Emerson et al., 1999b). Integrating the evidence from these disparate sources presents some significant challenges with regard to the development of more sophisticated 'integrated' theoretical models and the use of such models to guide practice in the area of analysis and intervention.

**Developing more sophisticated models of the emergence and maintenance of challenging behaviour**

While there may be compelling evidence that both behavioural and biological processes may be involved in the maintenance of challenging behaviour, most theorizing has been restricted in two ways. Firstly, models of the development and maintenance of challenging behaviour have been advanced within, rather than across, these potentially complementary frameworks. Secondly, few links have been drawn between accounts of challenging behaviour shown by people with learning disabilities and challenging behaviours shown by other client groups. More recently, however, a number of researchers have begun to sketch out some of the possible links between cultural, social, behavioural and biological processes (e.g. Baumeister, 1991; Guess & Carr, 1991; Holland, 1999; Murphy, 1994; Oliver, 1993, 1995; Thompson et al., 1994a) and the link of these processes with the literature and models accounting for challenging behaviours shown by people who do not have intellectual disabilities (e.g. Murphy, 1997).

Guess and Carr (1991), for example, presented a three-stage model of the development of stereotypic and self-injurious behaviours among people with intellectual disabilities. They suggested that stereotyped behaviours initially emerge as part of a biologically determined behavioural 'state' which occurs relatively independently of environmental processes (cf. MacLean et al., 1994). Once established, however, they argue that the young child may learn to use stereotyped behaviours to self-regulate levels of arousal (Berkson, 1983). Stereotypies may be used to either increase levels of arousal/stimulation in barren environments (cf. Favell, McGimsey & Schell, 1982) or to dampen down levels of arousal/stimulation in overstimulating environments (cf. Duker & Rasing, 1989; Isaacson & Gispin, 1990). Finally, they suggest that, through the operation of reciprocal behavioural processes (e.g. Oliver, 1993; Taylor & Carr, 1993, 1994), noninjurious stereotypic behaviours may gradually become shaped into more complex and/or intense forms of behaviour, some of which may become injurious. During this final stage of the process, they suggested that the operant properties of the behaviour become dominant. Thus, within the 'natural history' of a person's self-injurious behaviour, they suggest that the maintaining factors may vary from underlying developmental processes, through modulation of internal states to social reinforcement.

This model could be expanded by including consideration of the possible role played by the endogenous opioid system (cf. Oliver, 1993, 1995; Sandman et al., 1997, 1998, 1999; Thompson et al., 1995). Sandman et al. (1999), for example, have suggested that the self-injurious behaviour of certain individuals may be associated with a genetically determined disregulation of proopiomelanocortin metabolism which may result in either a generally reduced sensitivity to pain or to an increased risk of the maintenance of self-injurious behaviour by contingent release of β-endorphin (see also Sandman et al., 1997, 1998; Thompson et al., 1995). Symons and Thompson (1997) have suggested that a link may exist between self-injurious acts directed at acupuncture analgesia sites and endorphin release (see also Thompson et al., 1994b).

These observations suggest that, for certain individuals (with a genetic predisposition) or for certain self-injurious acts (directed at certain body sites), the response effort associated with self-injury may be lessened due to a reduced sensitivity to pain arising from either a generalized elevation in pain thresholds or to the antinociceptive effects arising from β-endorphin release. This reduction in response effort may be important in enabling the emergence of self-injurious acts as operant behaviours (cf. Friman & Poling, 1995). At later stages in the developmental history of self-injury, it is possible that the 'addictive' processes associated with endorphin release may become dominant (cf. Oliver, 1993, 1995).

To date, however, research examining some of the propositions arising from more complex models is scarce. Potentially profitable areas of enquiry are likely to include: studies of the emergence of challenging behaviours (Murphy et al., 1999); the role of biological and psychiatric establishing operations in accounting for the temporal variation of challenging behaviours maintained by operant processes (Carr & Smith, 1995; Emerson et al., 1999b); the interaction between operant behaviour and physiological processes (Freeman et al., 1999; Romanczyk & Matthews, 1998); the role of carer attributions in determining responses to operantly maintained challenging behaviour (Dagnan et al., 1998); and, as noted above, the interaction between operant processes, response topography and endorphin activity in the emergence and maintenance of self-injury (Garcia & Smith, 1999; Thompson et al., 1995).

Garcia and Smith (1999), for example, examined the relationship between behavioural function (as determined through experimental functional analyses) and response to naltrexone by two women with severe intellectual disabilities. The results provided tentative support for the type of interactional model described above for one participant in that administration of naltrexone was associated with moderate decreases in *negatively reinforced* head slapping. Interestingly, naltrexone had no discernible effect on a second form of self-injury (head banging) shown by the same participant. As Garcia and Smith point out, the impact of naltrexone on operant-maintained self-injury may be the result of one of two processes. Firstly, naltrexone administration may increase the response effort of self-injury by bringing self-injurious acts into contact with their painful consequences. Secondly, naltrexone has been shown to have a number of positive effects including increasing alertness and learning (Sandman et al., 1998). It is possible, therefore, that naltrexone administration may 'neutralize' the establishing effects of instructional demands (i.e. naltrexone may make instructional demands less aversive and thus remove the motivational basis for escape behaviour).

In addition to increasing the sophistication of models linking behavioural and biological mechanisms, it will also be important to ensure that behavioural models themselves continue to be refined and developed. Indeed, one of the recurrent criticisms of applied behavioural analysis has been its failing to take account of developments in operant theory (e.g. Michael, 1980; Pierce & Epling, 1980). Recent developments in analysis and intervention studies of challenging behaviour which run counter to this general trend include the growth in applied studies on implications of the matching law (Fisher & Mazur, 1997), the application of the phenomenon of behavioural momentum to intervention (Mace et al., 1988), analyses of the role of schedule induction (Emerson & Howard, 1992: Emerson et al., 1996d; Lerman et al., 1994b), the use of molar equilibrium theory to identify reinforcement contingencies (Aeschleman & Williams, 1989; Diorio & Konarski, 1989; Konarski et al., 1981; Realon & Konarski, 1993) and application of the notion of rule-governed behaviour to the analysis of staff behaviour (Hastings & Remington, 1994a). Nevertheless, there clearly remains considerable scope for integrating these and other factors into applied models and practices.

## Refining assessment procedures

As has been noted, the processes maintaining challenging behaviour may vary across: topographically similar behaviours shown by different people (e.g. Iwata et al., 1994a); different forms of challenging behaviours shown by the same person (e.g. Emerson et al., 1995); and the same behaviour shown by one person over time (e.g. Carr & McDowell, 1980) or in different contexts (e.g. Haring & Kennedy, 1990). It is also possible that challenging behaviours may be multiply controlled, either by different contingencies of extrinsic reinforcement (Day et al., 1994) or by the interaction of behavioural and neurobiological processes (see above). These observations provide strong support in favour of the adoption of a functionally based approach to intervention (see Chapter 5). Indeed, such an approach would appear to be axiomatric to defining 'good practice' in this field (Ball & Bush, 2000; Carr et al., 1999a; Didden et al., 1997; Rush & Frances, 2000).

The adoption of a functional approach does, of course, presuppose the existence of assessment techniques which are capable of identifying the operation of underlying processes. As was shown in Chapter 6, however, existing approaches to functional assessment do have a number of limitations. These include the questionable reliability and validity of approaches based on informant reports and the resource requirements and validity of more complex descriptive and experimental techniques. Acknowledgement of these limitations indicates certain obvious areas for future research and development. So, for example, attention needs to be paid to determining the nature of information and the conditions under which such information can be reliably obtained from third parties and the extent to which this information generalizes across settings, informants, users and forms of challenging behaviours. In addition, much more needs to be known about the validity of experimental and descriptive approaches to functional assessment (cf. Halle & Spradlin, 1993; Iwata et al., 1990b; Mace, 1994b; Oliver, 1991; Sturmey, 1995; Vollmer & Van Camp, 1998; Wacker et al., 1998).

Perhaps the most important challenge, however, lies in broadening the field of functional assessment to include the analysis of establishing operations (Vollmer & Van Camp, 1998; Wacker et al., 1998), physiological variables (Freeman et al., 1999; Romanczyk & Matthews, 1998) and rule-governed behaviour (e.g. Taylor & O'Reilly, 1997). As was indicated in Chapter 6, the technology provided by existing experimental and descriptive approaches to assessment is well suited to addressing some of these issues. Thus, for example, observational and experimental approaches can be used to investigate the impact of contextual variables (e.g. setting, biological state) on behaviour–environment relationships (Vollmer & Van Camp, 1998; Wacker et al., 1998). Indeed, one of the great values of alternating treatment designs, the basis of many experimental approaches, is their sensitivity to contextual factors (Higgins Hains & Baer, 1989).

The analysis of the roles of rules and nonoperant process in the maintenance of challenging behaviours, however, involves technical as well as conceptual challenges. Assessing the content and nature of rules will require the development of valid approaches for interviewing people with severe intellectual disabilities as well as establishing ways of evaluating the actual impact of such rules on behaviour (Taylor & O'Reilly, 1997). Such developments are long overdue – for too long, the individual with intellectual disabilities has been viewed as the passive subject of the assessment and intervention process.

Perhaps most challenging of all, however, will be the development of a means to assess the contribution of biological processes to the maintenance of challenging behaviour. Possible approaches include the assessment of bio-behavioural 'markers' for the operation of neurobiological and behavioural processes (cf. Mace & Mauk, 1995). Possible markers may include: the environmental dependence/independence of challenging behaviour (cf. Iwata et al., 1994a); the site of self-injury (Symons & Thompson, 1997; Thompson et al., 1994b); 'paradoxical' responses to sedatives/hypnotics (Sandman & Barron, 1992); controlled trials of mechanism-specific medication (e.g. naltrexone hydrochloride); variation in plasma levels of β-endorphin following self-injury (Sandman et al., 1997, 1999); and co-occurrence of ritualistic or compulsive behaviours, self-restraint and distress on interruption of self-injury (e.g. Bodfish & Madison, 1993). Clearly, much more needs to be learned about the role of neurobiological processes and their interaction with operant processes before routine practice could incorporate such methods with any degree of confidence.

## Early intervention and preventative services

In Chapter 3 we drew attention to the early onset and apparent high degree of persistence of severely challenging behaviours. These observations point to the potential value of developing preventative interventions and ensuring that appropriate and intensive behavioural supports are provided as early as possible once challenging behaviours have begun to emerge (Dunlap & Fox, 1996; Dunlap, Johnson & Robbins, 1990; Koegel et al., 1996b; Schroeder, Bickel & Richmond, 1986).

### Prevention

To date, there is no direct evidence to suggest that the development of challenging behaviours can be prevented. There are, however, strong arguments and some circumstantial evidence to suggest that the possibility of prevention is worthy of serious consideration. As has been shown, many examples of challenging behaviour appear to be maintained by operant processes and can be reduced by interventions which either undercut the motivational basis for such behaviours or support the emergence of alternative functionally equivalent behaviours. This suggests that preventative approaches based on either (1) reducing exposure to potentially eliciting conditions or (2) ensuring that more efficient functional equivalent behaviours already exist in the person's repertoire *may* act to reduce the incidence of challenging behaviour.

Examples of the former approach would include reducing exposure to conditions of sensory, material and social deprivation, high levels of unpredictable stressors, repeated illnesses, abuse, repeated changes of carers and rigid external controls (McGill et al., 1996; Schroeder et al., 1986). Examples of the latter approach would involve the use of intensive behavioural supports to develop socially appropriate ways of expressing choice and controlling access to, and escape from, potentially salient events through the use of assistive devices (e.g. Wacker et al., 1988) and general approaches to language and social development (cf. Dunlap et al., 1991). Knowledge concerning 'risk factors' associated with variations in the prevalence of challenging behaviour as a result of either genetic predisposition or environmental factors could enable such preventative interventions to be targeted at those children and families in greatest need.

Unfortunately, while there has been much general interest in the impact of broad-based early intervention programmes over the last three decades, no data are available to determine whether such programmes have reduced the incidence of challenging behaviours among children with severe intellectual disabilities. There is some evidence, however, to suggest that these programmes may be effective in accelerating language development in the short term, improving social performance and reducing delinquency later in life among children who have mild intellectual disabilities or are socially disadvantaged (Guralnick, 1997, 1998).

There is also some anecdotal evidence to suggest that children with autism who have received highly intensive early intervention services show significantly less challenging behaviour on follow-up than similar children who did not receive such services (Lovaas & Smith, 1994); what is not known, however, is whether this is due to a reduction in the incidence of challenging behaviour or effective treatment of challenging behaviours as they emerged (i.e. reduced persistence). These studies will be considered in the section below.

## Early intervention

Dunlap et al. (1991) reviewed the evidence and arguments in support of the proposition that intervention is more likely to be effective if it occurs as soon as possible during the emergence of challenging behaviour. These arguments include:

- increased receptivity to behaviour change;
- increased commitment among carers and care staff; and
- the potentially greater ease of physically managing the behaviour, given that challenging behaviours may begin to develop in early childhood when the individual is still physically maturing.

Evidence to support these propositions is extremely limited, being based on a small number of studies which report negative correlations between the success of, often broadly-based, intervention programmes and the child's age at point of entry (cf. Dunlap et al., 1991; Westlake & Kaiser, 1991). So, for example, Fenske et al. (1985) reported that positive outcomes in a specialized programme for children with autism were achieved for six of the nine children who entered before 5 years of age, but for only one of the nine who entered after this age.

As noted above, the *potential* benefits of intensive home-based early intervention are illustrated by the results of a long-term follow-up of 19 autistic children reported by Lovaas and his colleagues (Lovaas, 1987; Lovaas & Smith, 1994; McEachin et al., 1993; Smith et al., 1993b, 1997). At the time of entry of the programme (before 46 months of age), most children were demonstrating severe tantrums and all showed 'extensive ritualistic and stereotyped behavior'. The programme involved 40 or more hours per week of one-to-one behavioural treatment for 2 or more years (McEachin et al., 1993, p. 361). A comparison group of 19 autistic children received less intensive support. At the time of the follow-up, the children in the experimental group were between 9 and 19 years of age. At that time, they were showing significant gains over the comparison groups with respect to IQ and adaptive and challenging behaviour. Lovaas and Smith (1994) report that

our preliminary data shows that all but 2 of the intensively treated experimental subjects . . . are free from clinically significant problems associated with destructive behaviors. In contrast, the majority of the control group subjects are medicated and living in institutional settings, where their self-injurious and assaultive behaviors present major management problems. Should these initial observations be substantiated in further follow-ups, it may mean that permanent reductions in destructive behaviors displayed by autistic children may come only from intensive home- and community-based intervention, with a comprehensive focus, administered while the children are in their pre-school years' (Lovaas & Smith, 1994).

Unfortunately, no data substantiating these claims have been published. Indeed, the only relevant published data suggest that, while children with severe intellectual disabilities may make significant gains in IQ and expressive communication, intensive early intervention had no beneficial effects on challenging behaviour when compared with less intense support (Smith et al., 1997). It should be noted, however, that the measure of challenging behaviour employed within this study consisted of a simple rating derived from case notes of the presence/absence of tantrums or aggression.

## Facilitating the widespread implementation of behavioural supports

The widespread adoption and consistent implementation of positive behavioural supports could significantly improve the quality of life of many people with severe intellectual disabilities and severe challenging behaviour. To achieve this constitutes, perhaps, the single greatest challenge for this area of applied behaviour analysis. There exists an enormous gap between our knowledge concerning effective approaches and the routine availability of such approaches in our education, health and social services (Department of Health, 1993). Even among people receiving residential supports from 'better' providers in the UK, those who show challenging behaviour are unlikely to receive effective behavioural support (Emerson et al., in press a).

Such concerns are not, however, specific to this field. Stolz (1981), for example, has questioned why behavioural technologies in general, which have been shown to be effective in addressing socially important problems, 'mostly lie unnoticed in our ever-proliferating professional journals' (Stolz, 1981, p. 492). The answers to such questions undoubtably lie in broader analyses of the role of social research in the processes of policy making and implementation (e.g. Bulmer, 1982, 1986; Weiss & Bucuvalas, 1980). The concerns expressed by behaviour analysts, as well as their proposed solutions, often appear to reflect a belief in what have been termed knowledge-driven or problem-solving (Weiss, 1979), engineering (Bulmer, 1982, 1986) or instrumental (Beyer & Trice, 1982) approaches to policy making and implementation. These essentially rationalist approaches suggest that a logical flow should exist from basic research, through applied research and development, to application (the knowledge-driven model), or that those involved in making or implementing policy engage in rational searches for scientific information when confronted with a social problem (the problem-solving model). Neither model, of course, reflects the reality of the policy making and implementation process. Rather, such processes may be more accurately characterized as involving a process of 'partisan mutual adjustment' (Bulmer, 1986), as accommodations are made between key stakeholders. If this analysis is correct, it has a number of implications for the dissemination and adoption of behavioural approaches.

Firstly, recognition needs to be given to the potentially important role of behavioural concepts (rather than technologies) in shaping the grounds of the debate surrounding policy formulation and implementation. Indeed, most commentators in this area have suggested that ideas or concepts derived from social research may have a significantly greater impact than either data or technologies (e.g. Beyer & Trice, 1982; Bulmer, 1982, 1986; Weiss, 1979; Weiss & Bucuvalas, 1980). Thus, for example, the concept of 'institutionalization' appears to have had an effect on policy debates far in excess of that justified by the data on which the idea was based. This suggests that, in order to maximize the impact of behavioural approaches, the behavioural community will need to become more proficient at communicating ideas and concepts, rather than assuming that data will 'speak for itself'.

Secondly, recognition of the inherently 'political' nature of the process of policy making and implementation indicates the importance of identifying, influencing and building alliances with key stakeholders or interest groups (e.g. managers and administrators, political groups, advocacy organizations, professional associations). Here, influence is likely to be maximized if, for example, information is transmitted in the preferred medium and terminology, and addresses key issues of concern for that group (e.g. personal contact, written and visual information, visits to model programmes); the 'evidence' proffered in support of behavioural approaches is seen as credible by the main stakeholder groups; and the stakeholder(s) perceive there to be a pressing problem whose potential solutions fall within the range of behavioural technologies (cf. Fixsen & Blase, 1993; Stolz, 1981).

Responding to these requirements is likely to mean that behavioural ideas of what constitutes a 'believable demonstration' of the efficacy of behavioural interventions will be challenged on two counts. Firstly, many stakeholder groups are likely to respond more positively to rounded 'qualitative' accounts of the impact of interventions (e.g. Fox et al., 1997; Lucyshyn et al., 1995; Scotti & Meyer, 1999) than to the types of graphical displays of changes in behavioural rate beloved of the leading journals in the field. This is, of course, consistent with the arguments which have been advanced to suggest that the applied behavioural community needs to attend much more seriously to evaluating the social validity of its practices (Meyer & Evans, 1993a,b; Meyer & Janney, 1989; Schwartz & Baer, 1991; Symons et al., 1999a; Wolf, 1978) and to maximizing the 'contextual fit' of behaviour support plans (Albin et al., 1996).

Secondly, the advent of 'managed care' and 'evidence-based practice' has been accompanied by an increasing reliance on randomized controlled trials as providing the 'gold standard' against which other forms of evidence are to be compared. While not without their problems, such methods are useful for addressing some of the issues which will be of concern to those responsible for commissioning intervention services. Thus, while the behavioural literature has demonstrated, through hundreds of sophisticated case studies, that the implementation of behavioural procedures *can* bring about clinically and socially significant reductions in challenging behaviour, many questions relevant to the implementation of health policy remain unanswered. These include:

- What proportion of people with particular forms of challenging behaviour is likely to benefit from behavioural intervention?
- What would be the economic and social benefits associated with achieving this level of reductions in challenging behaviour?
- What resource requirements would be associated with providing behavioural supports to that segment of the population?

Providing credible answers to these questions may significantly improve the prospects for the more widespread implementation of behavioural supports for people with severe challenging behaviours in the twenty-first century.

# References

Adelinis, J.D., Piazza, C.C., Fisher, W.W., & Hanley, G.P. (1997). The establishing effects of client location on self-injurious behavior. *Research in Developmental Disabilities* **18**, 383–91.

Aeschleman, S.R., & Williams, M.L. (1989). A test of the response deprivation hypothesis in a multiple-response context. *American Journal on Mental Retardation* **93**, 345–53.

Ahmed, Z., Fraser, W.I., Kerr, M., Kiernan, C. et al. (2000). The effects of reducing antipsychotic medication in people with a learning disability. *British Journal of Psychiatry* **176**, 42–6.

Akande, A. (1998). Some South African evidence on the inter-rater reliability of the Motivation Assessment Scale. *Educational Psychology* **18**, 111–15.

Albin, R.W., Lucyshyn, J.M., Horner, R.H., & Flannery, K.B. (1996). Contextual fit for behavior support plans: a model of 'goodness of fit'. In L.K. Koegel, R.L. Koegel & G. Dunlap (Eds.). *Positive Behavioral Support: Including People With Difficult Behavior in the Community*, pp. 81–98. Baltimore: Paul H. Brookes.

Allen, D. (1998). Changes in admissions to a hospital for people with intellectual disabilities following the development of alternative community services. *Journal of Applied Research in Intellectual Disabilities* **11**, 156–65.

Allen, D. (1999). Mediator analysis: an overview of recent research on carers supporting people with intellectual disability and challenging behaviour. *Journal of Intellectual Disability Research* **43**, 325–39.

Allen, D., Banks, R., & Staite, S. (1991). *Meeting the Challenge: Some Perspectives On Community Services for People with Learning Difficulties and Learning Disabilities*. London: King's Fund.

Allen, D., & Felce, D. (1999). Service responses to challenging behaviour. In N. Bouras (Ed.). *Psychiatric and Behavioural Disorders in Developmental Disabilities and Mental Retardation*, pp. 279–94. Cambridge: Cambridge University Press.

Allen, D., & Lowe, K. (1995). Providing intensive community support to people with learning disabilities and challenging behaviour: a preliminary analysis of outcomes and costs. *Journal of Intellectual Disability Research* **39**, 67–82.

Allen, D., McDonald, L., Dunn, C., & Doyle, T. (1997). Changing care staff approaches to the prevention and management of aggressive behavior in a residential treatment unit for persons with mental retardation and challenging behavior. *Research in Developmental Disabilities* **18**, 101–12.

Altmeyer, B.K., Locke, B.J., Griffin, J.C. et al. (1987). Treatment strategies for self-injurious behavior in a large service delivery network. *American Journal on Mental Deficiency* **91**, 333–40.

Altmeyer, B.K., Williams, D.E., & Sams, V. (1985). Treatment of severe self-injurious and aggressive biting. *Journal of Behavior Therapy and Experimental Psychiatry* **16**, 159–67.

Alvarez, N., Kern, R.A., Cain, N.N., Coulter, D.L., Iivanainen, M., & Plummer, A.T. (1998). Antiepileptics. In S. Reiss & M.G. Aman (Eds.). *Psychotropic Medication and Developmental Disabilities: The International Consensus Handbook*, pp. 151–78. Ohio: Nisonger Center, Ohio State University.

Aman, M.G., Arnold, L.E., & Armstrong, S.C. (1999). Review of serotonergic agents and perseverative behavior in patients with developmental disabilities. *Mental Retardation and Developmental Disabilities Research Reviews* **5**, 279–89.

Aman, M.G., & Madrid, A. (1999). Atypical antipsychotics in persons with developmental disabilities. *Mental Retardation and Developmental Disabilities Research Reviews* **5**, 253–63.

Anderson, J.L., Albin, R.W., Mesaros, R.A., Dunlap, G., & Morelli-Robbins, M. (1993). Issues in providing training to achieve comprehensive behavioral support. In J. Reichle & D.P. Wacker (Eds.). *Communicative Alternatives to Challenging Behavior*, pp. 317–42. Baltimore: P.H. Brookes.

Anderson, J.L., Russo, A., Dunlap, G., & Albin, R.W. (1996). A team training model for building the capacity to provide positive behavioral supports in inclusive settings. In L.K. Koegel, R.L. Koegel & G. Dunlap (Eds.). *Positive Behavioral Support: Including People With Difficult Behavior in the Community*, pp. 467–90. Baltimore: Paul H. Brookes.

Anderson, D.J., Lakin, K.C., Hill, B.K., & Chen, T.H. (1992). Social integration of older persons with Mental Retardation in residential facilities. *American Journal on Mental Retardation* **96**, 488–501.

Anderson, L.T., & Ernst, M. (1994). Self-injury in Lesch Nyhan disease. *Journal of Autism and Developmental Disorders* **24**, 67–81.

Ando, H., & Yoshimura, I. (1978). Prevalence of maladaptive behavior in retarded children as a function of IQ and age. *Journal of Abnormal Child Psychology* **6**, 345–9.

Arnold, L.E., Gadow, K.D., Pearson, D.A., & Varley, C.K. (1998). Stimulants. In S. Reiss & M.G. Aman (Eds.). *Psychotropic Medication and Developmental Disabilities: The International Consensus Handbook*, pp. 229–58. Ohio: Nisonger Center, Ohio State University.

Axelrod, S. (1987). Functional and structural analyses of behavior: approaches leading to the reduced use of punishment procedures? *Research in Developmental Disabilities* **8**, 165–78.

Axelrod, S., & Apsche, J. (1983). *The Effects of Punishment on Human Behavior*. New York: Academic Press.

Azrin, N.H., Besalal, V.A., Jamner, J.P., & Caputo, J.N. (1988). Comparative study of behavioral methods of treating severe self-injury. *Behavioral Residential Treatment* **3**, 119–52.

Azrin, N.H., & Foxx, R.M. (1971). A rapid method of toilet training the institutionalized retarded. *Journal of Applied Behavior Analysis* **4**, 89–99.

Bachman, J.E., & Fuqua, R.W. (1983). Management of inappropriate behaviors of trainable mentally impaired students using antecedent exercise. *Journal of Applied Behavior Analysis* **16**, 477–84.

Bachman, J.E., & Sluyter, D. (1988). Reducing inappropriate behaviors of developmentally disabled adults using antecedent aerobic dance exercises. *Research in Developmental Disabilities* **9**, 73–83.

Baer, D.M. (1993). To disagree with Meyer and Evans is to debate a cost–benefit ratio. *Journal of the Association for Persons with Severe Handicaps* **18**, 235–6.

Baer, D.M., Wolf, M.M., & Risley, T.R. (1968). Some current dimensions of applied behavior analysis. *Journal of Applied Behavior Analysis* **1**, 91–7.

Baer, D.M., Wolf, M.M., & Risley, T.R. (1987). Some still-current dimensions of applied behavior analysis. *Journal of Applied Behavior Analysis* **20**, 313–27.

Bailey, J.S., & Meyerson, L. (1969). Vibration as a reinforcer with a profoundly retarded child. *Journal of Applied Behavior Analysis* **2**, 135–7.

Bailey, J.S., Shook, G.L., Iwata, B.A., Reid, D.H., & Repp, A.C. (1987). *Behavior Analysis in Developmental Disabilities 1968–1985*. Lawrence, KS: Society for the Experimental Analysis of Behavior.

Bailey, N.M., & Cooper, S-A. (1997). The current provision of specialist health services to people with learning disabilities in England and Wales. *Journal of Intellectual Disability Research* **41**, 52–9.

Ball, T., & Bush, A. (2000). *Clinical Practice Guidelines: Psychological Interventions For Severely Challenging Behaviours in People With Learning Disabilities*. Leicester: British Psychological Society.

Balsam, P.D., & Bondy, A.S. (1983). The negative side effects of reward. *Journal of Applied Behavior Analysis* **16**, 283–96.

Bambara, L.M., Ager, C., & Koger, F. (1994). The effects of choice and task preference on the work performance of adults with severe disabilities. *Journal of Applied Behavior Analysis* **27**, 555–6.

Bannerman, D.J., Sheldon, J.B., Sherman, J.A., & Harchik, A.E. (1990). Balancing the right to habilitation with the right to personal liberties: the rights of people with developmental disabilities to eat too many doughnuts and take a nap. *Journal of Applied Behavior Analysis* **23**, 79–89.

Barlow, D.H., & Hersen, M. (1984). *Single Case Experimental Designs*. Oxford: Pergamon.

Barrera, F.J., Teodoro, J.M., Selmeci, T., & Madappuli, A. (1994). Self-injury, pain and the endorphin theory. *Journal of Developmental and Physical Disabilities* **6**, 169–92.

Barrett, R.P, Feinstein, C, & Hole, W.T. (1989). Effects of Naloxone and Naltrexone on self-injury: a double blind, placebo-controlled analysis. *American Journal on Mental Retardation* **93**, 644–51.

Baumeister, A.A. (1991). Expanded theories of stereotypy and self-injurious responding: commentary on 'Emergence and maintenance of stereotypy and self-injury'. *American Journal on Mental Retardation* **96**, 321–3.

Baumeister, A.A., & MacLean, W.E. (1984). Deceleration of self-injurious and stereotypic responding by exercise. *Applied Research in Mental Retardation* **5**, 385–93.

Baumeister, A.A., MacLean, W.E., Kelly, J., & Kasari, C. (1980). Observational studies of retarded children with multiple stereotyped movements. *Journal of Abnormal Child Psychology* **8**, 501–21.

Baumeister, A.A., & Sevin, J.A. (1990). Pharmacologic control of aberrant behavior in the mentally retarded: toward a more rational approach. *Neuroscience and Biobehavioral Reviews* **14**, 253–62.

Baumeister, A.A., Sevin, J.A., & King, B.H. (1998). Neuroleptic medications. In S. Reiss & M.G. Aman (Eds.). *Psychotropic Medication and Developmental Disabilities: The International Consensus Handbook*, pp. 133–50. Ohio: Nisonger Center, Ohio State University.

Baumgart, D., & Ferguson, D.L. (1991). Personnel preparation: directions for the next decade. In L.H. Meyer, C.A. Peck, & L. Brown (Eds.). *Critical Issues in the Lives of People with Severe Disabilities.* Baltimore: Paul H. Brookes.

Beecham, J., & Knapp, M.R.J. (1992). Costing psychiatric interventions. In G.J. Thornicroft, C.R. Brewin & J.K. Wing (Eds). Measuring Mental Health Needs. London: Gaskell.

Bell, A., & Zubek, J.P. (1961). Effects of Deanol on the intellectual performance of mental retardates. *Canadian Journal of Psychology* **15**, 172–5.

Bellamy, G.T., Horner, R.H., & Inman, D. (1979). *Vocational Habilitation of Severely Retarded Adults: A Direct Service Technology.* Baltimore: University Park Press.

Benson, B.A. (1990). Emotional Problems I: anxiety and Depression. In J.L. Matson (Ed.). *Handbook of Behavior Modification with the Mentally Retarded.* New York: Plenum.

Benson, B.A., Rice, C.J., & Miranti, S.V. (1986). Effects of anger management training with mentally retarded adults in group treatment. *Journal of Counselling and Clinical Psychology* **54**, 728–9.

Bentall, R.P., Lowe, C.F., & Beasty, A. (1985). The role of verbal behavior in human learning: II. Developmental differences. *Journal of the Experimental Analysis of Behavior* **43**, 165–81.

Bering, S., Tupman, C., & Jacques, R. (1993). The Liverpool specialist support service: meeting challenging needs in practice. In I. Fleming & B. Kroese (Eds.). *People With Learning Disability and Severe Challenging Behaviour: New Developments in Services and Therapy.* Manchester: Manchester University Press.

Berkson, G. (1983). Repetitive stereotyped behaviors. *American Journal of Mental Deficiency* **88**, 239–46.

Bernstein, G.A., Hughes, J.R., Mitchell, J.E., & Thompson, T. (1987). Effects of narcotic antagonists on self-injurious behavior: a single case study. *Journal of the American Academy of Child and Adolescent Psychiatry* **26**, 886–9.

Bersani, H.A., & Heifetz, L.J. (1985). Perceived stress and satisfaction of direct-care staff members in community residences for mentally retarded adults. *American Journal of Mental Deficiency* **90**, 289–95.

Beyer, J.M. & Trice, H.M. (1982). The utilization process: a conceptual framework and synthesis of empirical findings. *Administrative Science Quarterly* **27**, 591–622.

Bihm, E.M., Kienlen, T.L., Ness, M.E., & Poindexter, A.R. (1991). Factor structure of the Motivation Assessment Scale for persons with mental retardation. *Psychological Reports* **68**, 1235–8.

Bijou, S.W. (1966). A functional analysis of retarded development. In N. Ellis (Ed.). *International Review of Research in Mental Retardation* (Volume 1). New York: Academic Press.

Bijou, S.W., & Baer, D.M. (1978). *Behavior Analysis of Child Development.* Englewood Cliffs, NJ: Prentice-Hall.

Bijou, S.W., Peterson, R.F., & Ault, M.H. (1968). A method to integrate descriptive and experimental field studies at the level of data and empirical concepts. *Journal of Applied Behavior Analysis* **1**, 175–91.

Bird, F., Dores, P.A., Moniz, D., & Robinson, J. (1989). Reducing severe aggressive and self-injurious behaviours with functional communication training. *American Journal on Mental Retardation* **94**, 37–48.

Black, L., Cullen, C., & Novaco, R. (1997). Anger assessment for people with mild intellectual disabilities in secure settings. In B. Kroese, D. Dagnan & K. Loumidis (Eds.). *Cognitive Behaviour Therapy for People with Intellectual Disabilities*, pp. 33–52. London: Routledge.

Blunden, R., & Allen, D. (1987). *Facing the Challenge: An Ordinary Life for People with Learning Difficulties and Challenging Behaviours.* London: King's Fund.

Bodfish, J.W., Crawford, T.W., Powell, S.B., Parker, D.E., Golden, R.N., & Lewis, M.H. (1995). Compulsions in adults with mental retardation: prevalence, phenomenology, and co-morbidity with stereotypy and self-injury. *American Journal of Mental Retardation* **100**, 183–92.

Bodfish, J.W., & Madison, J.T. (1993). Diagnosis and fluoxetine treatment of compulsive behavior disorder of adults with mental retardation. *American Journal on Mental Retardation* **98**, 360–7.

Bodfish, J.W., McCuller, W.R., Madison, J.M., Register, M., Mailman, R.B., & Lewis, M.H. (1997). Placebo, double-blind evaluation of long-term naltrexone treatment effects for adults with mental retardation and self-injury. *Journal of Developmental and Physical Disabilities* **9**, 135–52.

Borghgraef, M., Fryns, J.P., Van den Bergh, R., Ryck, K., & Van den Berghe, H. (1990). The post-pubertal Fra (X) male: a study of the intelligence and the psychological profile of 17 Fra (X) boys. In W.I. Fraser (Ed.). *Key Issues in Mental Retardation Research*, pp. 94–105. London: Routledge.

Borthwick-Duffy, S.A. (1994). Prevalence of destructive behaviors. In T. Thompson & D.B. Gray (Eds.). *Destructive Behavior in Developmental Disabilities: Diagnosis and Treatment*, pp. 3–23. Thousand Oaks: Sage.

Borthwick-Duffy, S.A., Eyman, R.K., & White, J.F. (1987). Client characteristics and residential placement patterns. *American Journal of Mental Deficiency* **92**, 24–30.

Bosch, J., Van Dyke, D.C., Smith, S.M., & Poulton, S. (1997). Role of medical conditions in the exacerbation of self-injurious behavior: an exploratory study. *Mental Retardation* **35**, 124–30.

Bott, C., Farmer, R., & Rhode, J. (1997). Behaviour problems associated with lack of speech in people with learning disabilities. *Journal of Intellectual Disability Research* **41**, 3–7.

Bouras, N. (1999). *Psychiatric and Behavioural Disorders in Developmental Disabilities and Mental Retardation.* Cambridge: Cambridge University Press.

Bowman, L.G., Fisher, W.W., Thompson, R.H., & Piazza, C.C. (1997). On the relation of mands and the function of destructive behavior. *Journal of Applied Behavior Analysis* **30**, 251–65.

Breese, G.R., Criswell, H.E., Duncan, G.E. et al. (1995). Model for reduced brain dopamine in Lesch–Nyhan syndrome and the mentally retarded: neurobiology of neonatal-6-hydroxydopamine-lesioned rats. *Mental Retardation and Developmental Disabilities Research Reviews* **1**, 111–19.

Bromley, J., & Emerson, E. (1995). Beliefs and emotional reactions of care staff working with people with challenging behaviour. *Journal of Intellectual Disability Research* **39**, 341–52.

Browder, D.M. (1991). *Assessment of Individuals with Severe Disabilities.* Baltimore: Paul H. Brookes.

Bruininks, R.H., Olsen, K.M., Larson, S.A., & Lakin, K.C. (1994). Challenging behaviors among persons with mental retardation in residential settings. In T. Thompson & D.B. Gray (Eds.). *Destructive Behavior in Developmental Disabilities: Diagnosis and Treatment,* pp. 24–48. Thousand Oaks: Sage.

Brylewski, J., & Duggan, L. (1999). Antipsychotic medication for challenging behaviour in people with intellectual disability: a systematic review of randomized controlled trials. *Journal of Intellectual Disability Research* **43**, 360–71.

Brylewski, J., & Wiggs, L. (1999). Sleep problems and daytime challenging behaviour in a community-based sample of adults with intellectual disability. *Journal of Intellectual Disability Research* **43**, 504–12.

Bull, M., & Vecchio, F. (1978). Behavior therapy for a child with Lesch–Nyhan syndrome. *Developmental Medicine and Child Neurology* **20**, 368–75.

Bulmer, M. (1982). *The Uses of Social Research.* London: Allen and Unwin.

Bulmer, M. (1986). *Social Science and Social Policy.* London: Allen and Unwin.

Burgio, L.D., Whitman, T.L., & Reid, D.H. (1983). A participative management approach for improving direct care staff performance in an institutional setting. *Journal of Applied Behavior Analysis* **16**, 37–53.

Bzoch, K.R., & League, R. (1991). *Receptive–Expressive Emergent Language Scale* (2nd Edition). Austin, TX: Pro-Ed.

Cameron, M.J., Maguire, R.W., & Maguire, M. (1998). Lifeway influences on challenging behaviors. In J.K. Luiselli & M.J. Cameron (Eds.). *Antecedent Control: Innovative Approaches to Behavioral Support,* pp. 273–88. Baltimore: Paul H. Brookes.

Campbell, R.V., & Lutzker, J.R. (1993). Using functional equivalence training to reduce severe challenging behavior: a case study. *Journal of Developmental and Physical Disabilities* **5**, 203–16.

Carr, E.G. (1977). The motivation of self-injurious behavior: a review of some hypotheses. *Psychological Bulletin* **84**, 800–16.

Carr, E.G. (1988). Functional equivalence as a mechanism of response generalization. In R.H. Horner, G. Dunlap & R.L. Koegel (Eds.). *Generalization and Maintenance: Life Style Changes in Applied Settings.* Baltimore: P.H. Brookes.

Carr, E.G. (1994). Emerging themes in the functional analysis of problem behavior. *Journal of Applied Behavior Analysis* **27**, 393–9.

Carr, E.G., & Carlson, J.I. (1993). Reduction of severe behavior problems in the community using a multicomponent treatment approach. *Journal of Applied Behavior Analysis* **26**, 157–72.

Carr, E.G., Carlson, J.I., Langdon, N.A., Magito-McLaughlin, D., & Yarbrough, S.C. (1998). Two perspectives on antecedent control: molecular and molar. In J.K. Luiselli & M.J. Cameron (Eds.). *Antecedent Control: Innovative Approaches to Behavioral Support,* pp. 3–28. Baltimore: Paul H. Brookes.

Carr, E.G., & Durand, V.M. (1985a). Reducing behavior problems through functional communication training. *Journal of Applied Behavior Analysis* **18**, 111–26.

Carr, E.G., & Durand, V.M. (1985b). The social–communicative basis of severe behavior problems in children. In S. Reiss & R.R. Bootzin (Eds.). *Theoretical Issues in Behavior Therapy*. New York: Academic Press.

Carr, E.G., Horner, R.H., Turnbull, A.P. et al. (1999a). *Positive Behavior Support For People with Developmental Disabilities*. Washington, DC: American Association on Mental Retardation.

Carr, E.G., Levin, L., McConnachie, G., Carlson, J.I., Kemp, D.C., & Smith, C.E. (1994). *Communication-Based Intervention for Problem Behavior: A User's Guide for Producing Positive Change*. Baltimore: P.H. Brookes.

Carr, E.G., Levin, L., McConnachie, G. et al. (1999b). Comprehensive multisituational intervention for problem behavior in the community: long-term maintenance and social validation. *Journal of Positive Behavior Interventions* **1**, 5–25.

Carr, E.G., & Lovaas, O.I. (1983). Contingent electric shock as a treatment for severe behavior problems. In S. Axelrod & J. Apsche (Eds.). *The Effects of Punishment on Human Behavior*. New York: Academic Press.

Carr, E.G., & McDowell, J.J. (1980). Social control of self-injurious behavior of organic etiology. *Behavior Therapy* **11**, 402–9.

Carr, E.G., & Newsom, C.D. (1985). Demand-related tantrums: conceptualization and treatment. *Behavior Modification* **9**, 403–26.

Carr, E.G., Newsom, C.D., & Binkoff, J.A. (1976). Stimulus control of self-destructive behavior in a psychotic child. *Journal of Abnormal Child Psychology* **4**, 139–53.

Carr, E.G., Newsom, C.D., & Binkoff, J.A. (1980). Escape as a factor in the aggressive behavior of two retarded children. *Journal of Applied Behavior Analysis* **13**, 101–17.

Carr, E.G., Reeve, C.E., & Magito-McLaughlin, D. (1996). Contextual influences on problem behavior in people with developmental disabilities. In L.K. Koegel, R.L. Koegel & G. Dunlap (Eds.). *Positive Behavioral Support: Including People With Difficult Behavior in the Community*, pp. 403–24. Baltimore: Paul H. Brookes.

Carr, E.G., Robinson, S., & Palumbo, L.W. (1990a). The wrong issue: aversive versus nonaversive treatment. The right issue: functional versus nonfunctional treatment. In A.C. Repp & N. Singh (Eds.). *Current Perspectives in the Use of Nonaversive and Aversive Interventions with Developmentally Disabled Persons*. Sycamore, IL: Sycamore Press.

Carr, E.G., Robinson, S., Taylor, J.C., & Carlson, J.I. (1990b). *Positive Approaches to the Treatment of Severe Behavior Problems in Persons with Developmental Disabilities*. Seattle: The Association for Persons with Severe Handicaps.

Carr, E.G., & Smith, C.E. (1995). Biological setting events for self-injury. *Mental Retardation and Developmental Disabilities Research Reviews* **1**, 94–8.

Carr, E.G., Taylor, J.C., & Robinson, S. (1991). The effects of severe behavior problems in children on the teaching behavior of adults. *Journal of Applied Behavior Analysis* **24**, 523–35.

Carr, E.G., Yarbrough, S.C., & Langdon, N.A. (1997). Effects of idiosyncratic stimulus variables on functional analysis outcomes. *Journal of Applied Behavior Analysis* **30**, 673–86.

Cataldo, M.F. (1991). The effects of punishment and other behavior reducing procedures on the destructive behaviors of persons with developmental disabilities. In National Institute of Health (Ed.). *Treatment of Destructive Behaviors in Persons with Developmental Disabilities*. Department of Health and Human Services: Washington.

Cataldo, M.F., & Harris, C.J. (1982). The biological basis for self-injury in the mentally retarded.

*Analysis and Intervention in Developmental Disabilities* **2**, 21–39.

Charlop, M.H., Kurtz, P.F., & Casey, F.G. (1990). Using aberrant behaviors as reinforcers for autistic children. *Journal of Applied Behavior Analysis* **23**, 163–81.

Cipani, E., & Spooner, F. (1997). Treating problem behaviors maintained by negative reinforcement. *Research in Developmental Disabilities* **18**, 329–42.

Clarke, D.J., & Boer, H. (1998). Problem behaviors associated with deletion Prader–Willi, Smith–Magenis, and Cri Du Chat syndromes. *American Journal of Mental Retardation* **103**, 264–71.

Clarke, D.J., Boer, H., Chung, M.C., Sturmey, P., & Webb, T. (1996). Maladaptive behaviour in Prader–Willi syndrome in adult life. *Journal of Intellectual Disability Research* **40**, 159–65.

Cole, C.L., Gardner, W.I., & Karan, O.C. (1985). Self management training of mentally retarded adults presenting severe conduct difficulties. *Applied Research in Mental Retardation* **6**, 337–47.

Colond, J., & Wieseler, N.A. (1995). Preventing restrictive placements through community support services. *American Journal of Mental Retardation* **100**, 201–6.

Conroy, M., Fox, J., Crain, L., & Jenkins, A. (1996). Evaluating the social and ecological validity of analog assessment procedures for challenging behaviors in young children. *Education and Treatment of Children* **19**, 233–56.

Conway, J.B., & Butcher, B.D. (1974). Soap in the mouth as an aversive consequence. *Behavior Therapy* **5**, 154–6.

Cook, E.H., Randall, R., Jaselskis, C., & Leventhal, B.L. (1992). Fluoxetine treatment of children and adults with autistic disorder and mental retardation. *Journal of the American Academy of Child and Adolescent Psychiatry* **31**, 739–45.

Cooper, L.J., Wacker, D.P., Thursby, D. et al. (1992). Analysis of the effects of task preferences, task demands and adult attention on child behavior in outpatient and classroom settings. *Journal of Applied Behavior Analysis* **25**, 823–40.

Cooper, S.J., & Dourish, C.T. (1990). *Neurobiology of Stereotyped Behaviour*. Oxford: Oxford University Press.

Corbett, J.A., & Campbell, H.J. (1980). Causes of self-injurious behavior. In P. Mitler & J.M. de Jong (Eds.). *Frontiers of Knowledge in Mental Retardation Volume II – Biomedical Aspects*, pp. 285–92. Baltimore: University Park Press.

Crawford, J., Brockel, B., Schauss, S. & Miltenberger, R.G. (1992). A comparison of methods for the functional assessment of stereotypic behavior. *Journal of the Association for Persons with Severe Handicaps* **17**, 77–86.

Crews, W.D., Bonaventura, S., Rowe, F.B., & Bonsie, D. (1993). Cessation of long-term naltrexone therapy and self-injury: a case study. *Research in Developmental Disabilities* **14**, 331–40.

Crews, W.D., Rhodes, R.D., Bonaventura, S.H., Rowe, F.B., & Goering, A.M. (1999). Cessation of long-term naltrexone administration: longitudinal follow-ups. *Research in Developmental Disabilities* **20**, 23–30.

Cullen, C. (1992). Staff training and management for intellectual disability services. In N. Bray (Ed.). *International Review of Research in Mental Retardation* (Volume 18), pp. 225–45. New York: Academic Press.

Cullen, C., Burton, M., Watts, S., & Thomas, M. (1983). A preliminary report on the nature of interactions in a mental handicap institution. *Behaviour Research and Therapy* **21**, 579–83.

Cullen, C., Hattersley, J., & Tennant, L. (1981). Establishing behaviour: the constructional approach. In G. Davey (Ed.). *Applications of Conditioning Theory*. London: Methuen.

Dagnan, D., Trower, P., & Smith, R. (1998). Care staff responses to people with learning disabilities and challenging behaviour: a cognitive behavioural analysis. *British Journal of Clinical Psychology* **37**, 59–68.

Darcheville, J.C., Rivière, V., & Wearden, J.H. (1993). Fixed-interval performance and self-control in infants. *Journal of the Experimental Analysis of Behavior* **60**, 239–54.

Davanzo, P.A., Belin, T.R., Widawski, M.H., & King, B.H. (1998). Paroxetine treatment of aggression and self-injury in persons with mental retardation. *American Journal of Mental Retardation* **102**, 427–37.

Davidson, P.W., Cain, N.N., Sloane-Reeves, J.E. et al. (1995). Crisis intervention for community-based individuals with developmental disabilities and behavioral and psychiatric disorders. *Mental Retardation* **33**, 21–30.

Davidson, P.W., Cain, N.N., Sloane-Reeves, J.E. et al. (1994). Characteristics of community-based individuals with mental retardation and aggressive behavioral disorders. *American Journal on Mental Retardation* **98**, 704–16.

Davidson, P.W., Jacobsen, J., Cain, N.N. et al. (1996). Characteristics of children and adolescents with mental retardation and frequent outwardly directed aggressive behavior. *American Journal of Mental Retardation* **101**, 244–55.

Davidson, P.W., Morris, D., & Cain, N.N. (1999). Community services for people with developmental disabilities and psychiatric or severe behaviour disorders. In N. Bouras (Ed.). *Psychiatric and Behavioural Disorders in Developmental Disabilities and Mental Retardation*. Cambridge: Cambridge University Press.

Davis, C.A., Brady, M.P., Williams, R.E., & Hamilton, R. (1992). Effects of high-probability requests on the acquisition and generalization and responses to requests in young children with behavior disorders. *Journal of Applied Behavior Analysis* **25**, 905–16.

Davis, S., Wehmeyer, M.L., Board, J.P., Fox, S., Maher, F., & Roberts, B. (1998). Interdisciplinary teams. In S. Reiss & M.G. Aman (Eds.). *Psychotropic Medication and Developmental Disabilities: The International Consensus Handbook*, pp. 73–84. Ohio: Nisonger Center, Ohio State University.

Davison, M., & McCarthy, D. (1988). *The Matching Law: A Research Review*. Hillsdale, NJ: Lawrence Erlbaum and Associates.

Day, R.M., Johnson, W.L., & Schussler, N.G. (1986). Determining the communicative properties of self-injury: research, assessment and treatment implications. In K.D. Gadow (Ed.). *Advances in Learning and Behavioral Disabilities* (Volume 5). London: JAI Press.

Day, R.M., Horner, R.H., & O'Neill, R.E. (1994). Multiple functions of problem behaviors: assessment and intervention. *Journal of Applied Behavior Analysis* **27**, 279–89.

Day, R.M., Rea, J.A., Schussler, N.G., Larsen, S.E. & Johnson, W.L. (1988). A functionally based approach to the treatment of self-injurious behavior. *Behavior Modification* **12**, 565–89.

de Lissovoy, V. (1962). Head banging in early childhood. *Child Development* **33**, 43–56.

de Lissovoy, V. (1963). Head banging in early childhood: a suggested cause. *Journal of Genetic*

*Psychology* **102**, 109–14.

DeLeon, I.G., & Iwata, B.A. (1996). Evaluation of a multiple stimulus presentation format for assessing reinforcer preferences. *Journal of Applied Behavior Analysis* **29**, 519–33.

Demchak, M.A., & Bossert, K.W. (1996). *Assessing Problem Behaviours*. Washington, DC: American Association on Mental Retardation.

Department of Health (1989). *Needs and Responses*. Stanmore: Department of Health Leaflets Unit.

Department of Health (1993). *Services for People with Learning Disabilities and Challenging Behaviour or Mental Health Needs*. London: HMSO.

Derby, K.M., Fisher, W.W., Piazza, C.C., & Wilke, A.E. (1998). The effects of noncontingent and contingent attention for self-injury, manding and collateral responses. *Behavior Modification* **22**, 474–84.

Derby, K.M., Wacker, D.P., Berg, W. et al. (1997). The long-term effects of functional communication training in home settings. *Journal of Applied Behavior Analysis* **30**, 507–31.

Derby, K.M., Wacker, D.P., Peck, S. et al. (1994). Functional analysis of separate topographies of aberrant behavior. *Journal of Applied Behavior Analysis* **27**, 267–78.

Derby, K.M., Wacker, D.P., Sasso, G. et al. (1992). Brief functional assessment techniques to evaluate aberrant behavior in an outpatient setting: a summary of 79 cases. *Journal of Applied Behavior Analysis* **25**, 713–21.

Desrochers, M.N., Hile, M.G., & Williams-Moseley, T.L. (1997). Survey of functional assessment procedures used with individuals who display mental retardation and severe problem behaviors. *American Journal of Mental Retardation* **101**, 535–46.

Di Terlizzi, M., Cambridge, P., & Maras, P. (1999). Gender, ethnicity and challenging behaviour: a literature review and exploratory study. *Tizard Learning Disability Review* **4**, 33–44.

Didden, R., Duker, P.C., & Korzilius, H. (1997). Meta-analytic study on treatment effectiveness for problem behaviors with individuals who have mental retardation. *American Journal of Mental Retardation* **101**, 387–99.

Diorio, M.S., & Konarski, E.A. (1989). Effects of a freely available response on the schedule performance of mentally retarded persons. *American Journal on Mental Retardation* **93**, 373–9.

Donnellan, A.M., LaVigna, G.W., Negri-Shoultz, N., & Fassbender, L.L. (1988). *Progress Without Punishment: Effective Approaches for Learners with Behavior Problems*. New York: Teachers College Press.

Donnellan, A.M., LaVigna, G.W., Zambito, J., & Thvedt, J. (1985). A time-limited intensive intervention program model to support community placement for persons with severe behaviour problems. *Journal of the Association For Persons with Severe Handicaps* **10**, 123–31.

Donnellan, A.M., Mirenda, P., Mesaros, R., & Fassbender, L. (1984). Analyzing the communicative functions of aberrant behavior. *Journal of the Association for Persons with Severe Handicaps* **9**, 201–12.

Dossetor, D.R., Couryer, S., & Nicol, A.R. (1991). Massage for very severe self-injurious behaviour in a girl with Cornelia de Lange syndrome. *Developmental Medicine and Child Neurology* **33**, 636–44.

Duker, P.C. (1999). The Verbal Behavior Assessment Scale (VerBAS): construct validity, reliability and internal consistency. *Research in Developmental Disabilities* **20**, 347–53.

Duker, P.C., Jol, K., & Palmen, A. (1991). The collateral decrease of self-injurious behavior with teaching communicative gestures to individuals who are mentally retarded. *Behavioral Residential Treatment* **6**, 183–96.

Duker, P.C., & Rasing, E. (1989). Effects of redesigning the physical environment on self-stimulation and on-task behavior in three autistic-type developmentally disabled individuals. *Journal of Autism and Developmental Disorders* **19**, 449–60.

Duker, P.C., & Seys, D.M. (1996). Long-term use of electrical aversion treatment with self-injurious behavior. *Research in Developmental Disabilities* **17**, 293–301.

Duker, P.C., & Sigafoos, J. (1998). The Motivation Assessment Scale: reliability and construct validity across three topographies of behavior. *Research in Developmental Disabilities* **19**, 131–41.

Duncan, D., Matson, J.L., Bamburg, J.W., Cherry, K.E., & Buckley, T. (1999). The relationship of self-injurious behavior and aggression to social skills in persons with severe and profound learning disability. *Research in Developmental Disabilities* **20**, 441–8.

Dunlap, G., Clarke, S., & Steiner, M. (1999). Intervention research in behavioral and developmental disabilities: 1980–1997. *Journal of Positive Behavior Interventions* **1**, 170–80.

Dunlap, G., dePerczel, M., Clarke, S. et al. (1994). Choice making to promote adaptive behavior for students with emotional and behavioral challenges. *Journal of Applied Behavior Analysis* **27**, 505–18.

Dunlap, G., Foster-Johnson, L., Clarke, S., Kern, L., & Childs, K.E. (1995). Modifying activities to produce functional outcomes: effects on the problem behaviors of students with disabilities. *Journal of the Association For Persons With Severe Handicaps* **20**, 248–58.

Dunlap, G., & Fox, L. (1996). Early intervention and serious problem behaviors: a comprehensive approach. In L.K. Koegel, R.L. Koegel & G. Dunlap (Eds.). *Positive Behavioral Support: Including People With Difficult Behavior in the Community*, pp. 31–50. Baltimore: Paul H. Brookes.

Dunlap, G., Johnson, L.F., & Robbins, F.R. (1990). Preventing serious behavior problems through skill development and early interventions. In A.C. Repp & N.N. Singh (Eds.). *Perspectives on the Use of Nonaversive and Aversive Interventions for Persons with Developmental Disabilities.* Sycamore, IL: Sycamore Publishing Company.

Dunlap, G., Kern, L., dePerczel, M. et al. (1993). Functional analysis of classroom responding for students with emotional and behavioral disorders. *Behavioral Disorders* **18**, 275–91.

Dunlap, G., Kern-Dunlap, L., Clarke, S., & Robbins, F.R. (1991). Functional assessment, curricular revision and severe behavior problems. *Journal of Applied Behavior Analysis* **24**, 387–97.

Dura, J. (1997). Expressive communication ability, symptoms of mental illness and aggressive behavior. *Journal of Clinical Psychology* **53**, 307–18.

Durand, V.M. (1986). Self-injurious behavior as intentional communication. In K.D. Gadow (Ed.). *Advances in Learning and Behavioral Disabilities* (Volume 5). London: JAI Press.

Durand, V.M. (1990). *Severe Behavior Problems: A Functional Communication Training Approach.* New York: Guilford Press.

Durand, V.M. (1993). Functional communication training using assistive devices: effects on challenging behavior and affect. *AAC: Augmentative and Alternative Communication* **9**, 168–76.

Durand, V.M. (1999). Functional communication training using assistive devices: recruiting natural communities of reinforcement. *Journal of Applied Behavior Analysis* **32**, 247–67.

Durand, V.M., Berotti, D., & Weiner, J.S. (1993). Functional communication training: factors affecting effectiveness, generalization and maintenance. In J. Reichle & D.P. Wacker (Eds.). *Communicative Alternatives to Challenging Behavior*, pp. 317–42. Baltimore: P.H. Brookes.

Durand, V.M., & Carr, E.G., (1987). Social influences on 'self-stimulatory' behavior: analysis and treatment implications. *Journal of Applied Behavior Analysis* **20**, 119–32.

Durand, V.M., & Carr, E.G., (1991). Functional communication training to reduce challenging behavior: maintenance and application in new settings. *Journal of Applied Behavior Analysis* **24**, 251–64.

Durand, V.M., & Carr. E.G. (1992). An analysis of maintenance following functional communication training. *Journal of Applied Behavior Analysis* **25**, 777–94.

Durand, V.M., & Crimmins, D.B. (1988). Identifying the variables maintaining self-injurious behavior. *Journal of Autism and Developmental Disorders* **18**, 99–115.

Durand, V.M., & Crimmins, D.B. (1992). *The Motivation Assessment Scale.* Topkepa, KS: Monaco & Associates.

Durand, V.M., Crimmins, D., Caulfield, M., & Taylor, J. (1989). Reinforcer assessment I: using problem behavior to select reinforcers. *Journal of the Association for Persons with Severe Handicaps* **14**, 113–26.

Durand, V.M., Gernert-Dott, P., & Mapstone, E. (1996). Treatment of sleep disorders in children with developmental disabilities. *Journal of the Association For Persons With Severe Handicaps* **21**, 114–22.

Durand, V.M., & Kishi, G. (1987). Reducing severe behavior problems among persons with dual sensory impairments: an evaluation of a technical assistance model. *Journal of the Association for Persons with Severe Handicaps* **12**, 2–10.

Durand, V.M., & Mapstone, E. (1998). Influence of 'mood inducing' music on challenging behavior. *American Journal of Mental Retardation* **102**, 367–78.

Dyer, K. (1987). The competition of autistic stereotyped behavior with usual and specially assessed reinforcers. *Research in Developmental Disabilities* **8**, 607–26.

Dyer, K., Dunlap, G., & Winterling, V. (1990). Effects of choice making on the serious problem behaviors of students with severe handicaps. *Journal of Applied Behavior Analysis* **23**, 515–24.

Dyer, K. & Larsson, E.V. (1997). Developing functional communication skills: alternatives to severe behavior disorders. In N.N. Singh (Ed.). *Prevention and Treatment of Severe Behavior Problems: Models and Methods in Developmental Disabilities.* Baltimore: Paul H. Brookes.

Dykens, E. (1995). Measuring behavioral phenotypes: provocations from the 'New Genetics'. *American Journal of Mental Retardation* **99**, 522–32.

Dykens, E.M., Cassidy, S.B., & King, B.H. (1999). Maladaptive behavior differences in Prader–Willi syndrome due to paternal deletion versus maternal uniparental disomy. *American Journal of Mental Retardation* **104**, 67–77.

Dykens, E.M., & Hodapp, R.M., (1999). Behavioural phenotypes: towards new understandings of people with developmental disabilities. In N. Bouras (Ed.). *Psychiatric and Behavioural*

*Disorders in Developmental Disabilities and Mental Retardation,* pp. 96–108. Cambridge: Cambridge University Press.

Dykens, E.M., & Kasari, C. (1997). Maladaptive behavior in children with Prader–Willi syndrome, Down syndrome and non-specific mental retardation. *American Journal of Mental Retardation* **102**, 228–37.

Dykens, E.M., & Smith, A.C. (1998). Distinctiveness and correlates of maladaptive behaviour in children and adolescents with Smith–Magenis syndrome. *Journal of Intellectual Disability Research* **42**, 481–9.

Edelson, S.M., Taubman, M.T., & Lovaas, O.I. (1983). Some social contexts of self-destructive behavior. *Journal of Abnormal Child Psychology* **11**, 299–312.

Einfeld, S., Tonge, B., Turner, G., Parmenter, T., & Smith, A. (1999). Longitudinal course of behavioural and emotional problems of young persons with Prader–Willi, Fragile X, Williams and Down syndromes. *Journal of Intellectual and Developmental Disabilities* **24**, 349–54.

Ellis, C.R., Singh, N.N., & Ruane, A.L. (1999). Nutritional, dietary, and hormonal treatments for individuals with mental retardation and developmental disabilities. *Mental Retardation and Developmental Disabilities Research Reviews* **5**, 335–41.

Ellis, C.R., Singh, Y.N., & Singh, N.N. (1997). Use of behavior-modifying drugs. In N.N. Singh (Ed.). *Prevention and Treatment of Severe Behavior Problems: Models and Methods in Developmental Disabilities,* pp. 149–178. Pacific Grove: Brooks/Cole.

Emerson, E. (1990). Designing individualised community based placements as alternatives to institutions for people with a severe mental handicap and severe problem behaviour. In W. Fraser (Eds.). *Key Issues in Mental Retardation.* London: Routledge.

Emerson, E. (1992). Self-injurious behaviour: an overview of recent developments in epidemiological and behavioural research. *Mental Handicap Research* **4**, 49–81.

Emerson, E. (1993). Severe learning disabilities and challenging behaviour: developments in behavioural analysis and intervention. *Behavioural and Cognitive Psychotherapy* **21**, 171–98.

Emerson, E. (1995). *Challenging Behaviour: Analysis and Intervention in People With Learning Disabilities.* Cambridge: Cambridge University Press.

Emerson, E. (1998). Working with people with challenging behaviour. In E. Emerson, C. Hatton, J. Bromley & A. Caine (Eds.). *Clinical Psychology and People With Intellectual Disabilities.* Chichester: Wiley.

Emerson, E., Alborz, A., Kiernan, C. et al. (in press c). Predicting the persistence of severe self-injurious behavior. *Research in Developmental Disabilities.*

Emerson, E., Beasley, F., Offord, G., & Mansell, J. (1992). Specialised housing for people with seriously challenging behaviours. *Journal of Mental Deficiency Research* **36**, 291–307.

Emerson, E., & Bromley, J. (1995). The form and function of challenging behaviours. *Journal of Intellectual Disability Research* **39**, 388–98.

Emerson, E., Cambridge, P., & Harris, P. (1991). *Evaluating the Challenge: A Guide to Evaluating Services for People with Learning Difficulties and Challenging Behaviour.* London: King's Fund.

Emerson, E., Cummings, R., Barrett, S., Hughes, H., McCool, C., Toogood, A. (1988). Challenging behaviour and community services: 2. Who are the people who challenge services? *Mental Handicap* **16**, 16–19.

Emerson, E., Forrest, J., Cambridge, P., & Mansell, J. (1996c). Community support teams for people with learning disabilities and challenging behaviour: results of a National survey. *Journal of Mental Health* **5**, 395–406.

Emerson, E., Hastings, R., & McGill, P. (1994b). Values, attitudes and service ideology. In E. Emerson, P. McGill & J. Mansell (Eds.). *Severe Learning Disabilities and Challenging Behaviours: Designing High Quality Services*. London: Chapman & Hall.

Emerson, E., & Hatton, C. (1994). *Moving Out: The Effect of the Move from Hospital to Community on the Quality of Life of People with Learning Disabilities*. London: HMSO.

Emerson, E., Hatton, C., Robertson, J., Henderson, D., & Cooper, J. (1999c). A descriptive analysis of the relationships between social context, engagement and stereotypy in residential services for people with severe and complex disabilities. *Journal of Applied Research in Intellectual Disabilities* **12**, 11–29.

Emerson, E., & Howard, D. (1992). Schedule induced stereotypy. *Research in Developmental Disabilities* **13**, 335–61.

Emerson, E., Kiernan, C., Alborz, A. et al. (in press b). The prevalence of challenging behaviors: a total population study. *Research in Developmental Disabilities*.

Emerson, E., & McGill, P. (1989). Normalisation and applied behaviour analysis: values and technology in services for people with learning difficulties. *Behavioural Psychotherapy* **17**, 101–17.

Emerson, E., & McGill, P. (1993). Developing services for people with severe learning difficulties and seriously challenging behaviours: six years experience from the South East Thames Regional Health Authority. In *People with Learning Disability and Severe Challenging Behaviours: New Developments in Services and Therapy*. (Eds. I. Fleming & B. Kroese). Manchester: Manchester University Press.

Emerson, E., McGill, P., & Mansell, J. (1994a). *Severe Learning Disabilities and Challenging Behaviours: Designing High Quality Services*. London: Chapman & Hall.

Emerson, E., Moss, S., & Kiernan, C. (1999b). The relationship between challenging behaviour and psychiatric disorder in people with severe developmental disabilities. In N. Bouras (Ed.). *Psychiatric and Behavioural Disorders in Developmental Disabilities and Mental Retardation*. Cambridge: Cambridge University Press.

Emerson, E., Reeves, D., & Felce, D. (2000). Palm-top computer technologies for behavioral observation research. In T. Thompson, D. Felce & F. Symons (Eds.). *Computer Assisted Behavioral Observation Methods for Developmental Disabilities*. Baltimore: Paul H. Brookes.

Emerson, E., Reeves, D., Thompson, S., Henderson, D., & Robertson, J. (1996b). Time-based lag sequential analysis in the functional assessment of severe challenging behaviour. *Journal of Intellectual Disability Research* **40**, 260–74.

Emerson, E., Robertson, J., Gregory, N. et al. (in press a). The treatment and management of challenging behaviours in residential settings. *Journal of Applied Research in Intellectual Disabilities*.

Emerson, E., Robertson, J., Gregory, N. et al. (2000b). The quality and costs of village communities, residential campuses and community-based residential supports in the UK. *American Journal of Mental Retardation*, **105**, 81–102.

Emerson, E., Robertson, J., Hatton, C. et al. (1999a). *Quality and Costs of Residential Supports for People With Learning Disabilities: Predicting Variation in Quality and Costs*. Manchester:

Hester Adrian Research Centre, University of Manchester.

Emerson, E., Robertson, J., Letchford, S., Fowler, S., & Jones, M. (1996a). The long-term effects of behavioural residential special education on children with severely challenging behaviours: changes in behaviour and skills. *Journal of Applied Research in Intellectual Disabilities* **9**, 240–55.

Emerson, E., Thompson, S., Reeves, D., Henderson, D., & Robertson, J. (1995). Descriptive analysis of multiple response topographies of challenging behavior. *Research in Developmental Disabilities* **16**, 301–29.

Emerson, E., Thompson, S., Robertson, J., & Henderson, D. (1996d). Schedule-induced challenging behavior. *Journal of Developmental and Physical Disabilities* **8**, 89–103.

Endicott, O. (1988). This may hurt a bit. In G. Allen Roeher Institute (Ed.). *The Language of Pain: Perspectives on Behavior Modification.* Downsview, Ont: G. Allan Roeher Institute.

Epling, W.F., & Pierce, W.D. (1983). Applied behavior analysis: new directions from the laboratory. *The Behavior Analyst* **6**, 27–37.

Espie, C. (1992). Optimal sleep-wake scheduling and profound mental handicap: potential benefits. *Mental Handicap* **20**, 102–7.

Etzel, B.C., Hineline, P.N., Iwata, B.A. et al. (1987). The ABA humanitarian awards for outstanding achievement in pursuit of the right to effective treatment. *The Behavior Analyst* **10**, 235–7.

Evans, I.M. (1999). Staff development, caring and community. In J.R. Scotti & L.H. Meyer (Eds.). *Behavioral Intervention: Principles, Models and Practices.* Baltimore: Paul H. Brookes.

Evans, I.M., & Meyer, L.M. (1985). *An Educative Approach to Behavior Problems.* Baltimore: P.H. Brookes.

Evans, I.M., & Meyer, L.H. (1990). Toward a science in support of meaningful outcomes: a response to Horner et al. *Journal of the Association for Persons with Severe Handicaps* **15**, 133–5.

Evans, I.M., & Meyer, L. (1993). One more with feeling: on the importance of moving forward. *Journal of the Association for Persons with Severe Handicaps* **18**, 249–52.

Evans, I.M., Meyer, L.H., Kurkjian, J.A., & Kishi, G.S. (1988). An evaluation of behavioral interrelationships in child behavior therapy. In J.C. Witt, S.N. Elliott & F.N. Gresham (Eds.). *Handbook of Behavior Therapy in Education*, pp. 189–216. New York: Plenum.

Ewen, D. (1988). Aversive therapy. In G. Allen Roeher Institute (Ed.). *The Language of Pain: Perspectives on Behavior Modification.* Downsview, Ont: G. Allen Roeher Institute.

Eyman, R.K., Borthwick, S.A., & Miller, C. (1981). Trends in maladaptive behavior of mentally retarded persons placed in community and institutional settings. *American Journal of Mental Deficiency* **85**, 473–7.

Eyman, R.K., & Call, T. (1977). Maladaptive behavior and community placement of mentally retarded persons. *American Journal of Mental Deficiency* **82**, 137–44.

Favell, J.E., McGimsey, J.F., Jones, M.L., & Cannon, P.R. (1981). Physical restraint as positive reinforcement. *American Journal of Mental Deficiency* **85**, 425–32.

Favell, J.E., McGimsey, J.F., & Schell, R.M. (1982). Treatment of self-injury by providing alternate sensory activities. *Analysis and Intervention in Developmental Disabilities* **2**, 83–104.

Fee, V.E., & Matson, J.L. (1992). Definition, classification and taxonomy. In J.K. Luiselli, J.L.

Matson & N.N. Singh (Eds.). *Self-Injurious Behavior: Analysis, Assessment and Treatment*, pp. 3–20. New York: Springer-Verlag.

Felce, D. (1996). The quality of support for ordinary living: staff:resident interactions and resident activity. In J. Mansell & K. Ericsson (Eds.). *Deinstitutionalization and Community Living: Intellectual Disability Services in Britain, Scandinavia and the USA*. London: Chapman & Hall.

Felce, D., Bowley, C., Baxter, H., Jones, E., Lowe, C., & Emerson, E. (in press). The effectiveness of staff support: evaluating Active Support Training using a conditional probability approach. *Research in Developmental Disabilities*.

Felce, D., & Emerson, E., (2000). Observational methods in the assessment of quality of life. In T. Thompson, D. Felce & F. Symons (Eds.) *Computer Assisted Behavioral Observation Methods for Developmental Disabilities*. Baltimore: Paul H. Brookes.

Felce, D., Lowe, K. & de Paiva, S. (1994). Ordinary housing for people with severe learning disabilities and challenging behaviours. In E. Emerson, P. McGill & J. Mansell (Eds.). *Severe Learning Disabilities and Challenging Behaviours: Designing High Quality Services*, pp. 97–118. London: Chapman and Hall.

Felce, D., Lowe, K., Perry, J. et al. (1998). Service support to people in Wales with severe intellectual disability and the most severe challenging behaviours: processes, outcomes and costs. *Journal of Intellectual Disability Research* **42**, 390–408.

Felce, D., Repp, A., Thomas, M., Ager, A., & Blunden, R. (1991). The relationship of staff:client ratios, interactions, and residential placement. *Research in Developmental Disabilities* **12**, 315–31.

Felce, D., Saxby, H., de Kock, U., Repp, A., Ager, A., & Blunden, R. (1987). To what behaviors do attending adults respond? A replication. *American Journal of Mental Deficiency* **91**, 496–504.

Feldman, M.A., & Griffiths, D. (1997). Comprehensive assessment of severe behavior problems. In N.N. Singh (Ed.). *Prevention and Treatment of Severe Behavior Problems: Models and Methods in Developmental Disabilities*, pp. 23–48. Pacific Grove: Brooks/Cole.

Fenske, E.C., Zalenski, S., Krantz, P.J., & McClannahan, L.E. (1985). Age at intervention and treatment outcome for autistic children in a comprehensive intervention programme. *Analysis and Intervention in Developmental Disabilities* **5**, 49–58.

Ferguson, D.L., & Ferguson, P.M. (1993). Postmodern vexations: a reply to Meyer and Evans. *Journal of the Association for Persons with Severe Handicaps* **18**, 237–9.

Ferro, J., Foster-Johnson, L., & Dunlap, G. (1996). Relation between curricular activities and problem behaviors of students with mental retardation. *American Journal of Mental Retardation* **101**, 184–94.

Finney, J., Russo, D., & Cataldo, M. (1982). Reduction of pica in young children with lead poisoning. *Journal of Paediatric Psychology* **7**, 197–207.

Fischer, S.M., Iwata, B.A., & Mazaleski, J.L. (1997). Noncontingent delivery of arbitrary reinforcers as treatment for self-injurious behavior. *Journal of Applied Behavior Analysis* **30**, 239–49.

Fisher, W.W., Adelinis, J.D., Thompson, R.H., Worsdell, A.S., & Zarcone, J.R. (1998a). Functional analysis and treatment of destructive behavior maintained by termination of 'don't' (and symmetrical 'do') requests. *Journal of Applied Behavior Analysis* **31**, 339–56.

Fisher, W.W., Kuhn, D.E., & Thompson, R.H. (1998b). Establishing discriminative control of responding using functional and alternative reinforcers during functional communication training. *Journal of Applied Behavior Analysis* **31**, 543–60.

Fisher, W.W., & Mazur, J.E. (1997). Basic and applied research on choice responding. *Journal of Applied Behavior Analysis* **30**, 387–410.

Fisher, W., Piazza, C.C., Bowman, L.G., Hagopian, L.P., Owens, J.C., & Slevin, I. (1992). A comparison of two approaches for identifying reinforcers for persons with severe and profound disabilities. *Journal of Applied Behavior Analysis* **25**, 491–8.

Fisher, W., Piazza, C., Cataldo, M., Harrell, R., Jefferson, G., & Conner, R. (1993). Functional communication training with and without extinction & punishment. *Journal of Applied Behavior Analysis* **26**, 23–36.

Fisher, W.W., Piazza, C.C., & Chiang, C.L. (1996). Effects of equal and unequal reinforcer duration during functional analysis. *Journal of Applied Behavior Analysis* **29**, 117–20.

Fixsen, D.L, & Blase, K.A. (1993). Creating new realities: program development and dissemination. *Journal of Applied Behavior Analysis* **26**, 597–615.

Fleming, I., & Stenfert Kroese, B. (1993). *People with Leaning Disability and Severe Challenging Behaviour: New Developments in Services and Therapy*. Manchester: Manchester University Press.

Forehand, R., & Baumeister, A.A. (1970). The effect of auditory and visual stimulation on stereotyped rocking behavior and general activity of severe retardates. *Journal of Clinical Psychology* **26**, 426–9.

Forrest, J., Cambridge, P., Emerson, E., Mansell, J., Ashbury, M., & Beecham, J. (1995). Community support teams for people with learning disabilities and challenging behaviour. In A Wertheimer (Ed.). *Challenging Behaviour: What We Know*. London: Mental Health Foundation.

Foster-Johnson, L., Ferro, J., & Dunlap, G. (1994). Preferred curricular activities and reduced problem behaviors in students with intellectual disabilities. *Journal of Applied Behavior Analysis* **27**, 493–504.

Fox, L., Vaughn, B.J., Dunlap, G., & Bucy, M. (1997). Parent–professional partnership in behavioral support: a qualitative analysis of one family's experience. *Journal of the Association For Persons With Severe Handicaps* **22**, 198–207.

Fox, P., & Emerson, E. (in press). Socially valid outcomes of intervention for people with mental retardation and challenging behavior: a preliminary descriptive analysis of the views of different stakeholders. *Journal of Positive Behavior Interventions*.

Foxx, R.M. (1990). 'Harry': a ten year follow-up of the successful treatment of a self-injurious man. *Research in Developmental Disabilities* **11**, 67–76.

Foxx, R.M., & Dufrense, D. (1984). 'Harry': the use of physical restraint as a reinforcer, time-out from restraint, and fading restraint in treating a self-injurious man. *Analysis and Intervention in Developmental Disabilities* **4**, 1–14.

Foxx, R.M., & Shapiro, S.T. (1978). The time-out ribbon: a nonexclusionary time-out procedure. *Journal of Applied Behavior Analysis* **11**, 125–36.

Fraser, W.I., Ruedrich, S., Kerr, M., & Levitas, A. (1998). Beta-adrenergic blockers. In S. Reiss & M.G. Aman (Eds.). *Psychotropic Medication and Developmental Disabilities: The International Consensus Handbook*, pp. 133–50. Ohio: Nisonger Center, Ohio State University.

Frea, W.D., & Hughes, C.H. (1997). Functional analysis and treatment of social-communicative behavior of adolescents with developmental disabilities. *Journal of Applied Behavior Analysis* **30**, 701–4.

Freagon, S. (1990). One educator's perspective on the use of punishment or aversives: advocating for supportive and protective systems. In A.C. Repp & N.N. Singh (Eds.). *Perspectives on the Use of Nonaversive and Aversive Interventions for Persons with Developmental Disabilities*, pp. 145–55. Sycamore, IL: Sycamore.

Freeman, R.L., Horner, R.H., & Reichle, J. (1999). Relation between heart rate and problem behaviors. *American Journal of Mental Retardation* **104**, 330–45.

Friman, P.C., & Poling, A. (1995). Making life easier with effort: basic findings and applied research on response effort. *Journal of Applied Behavior Analysis* **28**, 583–90.

G. Allan Roeher Institute (1988). *The Language of Pain: Perspectives on Behavior Management.* Downsview, Ont: G. Allan Roeher Institute.

Gadow, K.D., & Poling, A.G. (1988). *Pharmacotherapy and Mental Retardation.* Boston: Little, Brown & Co.

Garcia, D., & Smith, R.G. (1999). Using analog baselines to assess the effects of naltrexone on self-injurious behavior. *Research in Developmental Disabilities* **20**, 1–21.

Gardner, W.I., Clees, T.J., & Cole, C.L. (1983). Self-management of disruptive verbal ruminations by a mentally retarded adult. *Applied Research in Mental Retardation* **4**, 41–58.

Gardner, W.I., & Cole, C.L. (1989). Self-management approaches. In E. Cipani (Ed.). *The Treatment of Severe Behavior Disorders: Behavior Analysis Approaches.* Washington, DC: American Association on Mental Retardation.

Gardner, W.I., Cole, C.L., Berry, D.L., & Nowinski, J.M. (1983). Reduction of disruptive behaviors in mentally retarded adults: a self-management approach. *Behavior Modification* **7**, 76–96.

Gardner, W.I., Cole, C.L., Davidson, D.P., & Karan, O.C. (1986). Reducing aggression in individuals with developmental disabilities: an expanded stimulus control, assessment, and intervention model. *Education and Training of the Mentally Retarded* **21**, 3–12.

Gardner, W.I., Karan, O.C., & Cole, C.L. (1984). Assessment of setting events influencing functional capacities of mentally retarded adults with behavior difficulties. In A.S. Halpern & M.J. Fuhrer (Eds.). *Functional Assessment in Rehabilitation*, pp. 171–85. Baltimore: Paul H. Brookes.

Gardner, W.I., & Whalen, J.P. (1996). A multimodal behavior analytic model for evaluating the effects of medical problems on nonspecific behavioral symptoms in persons with developmental disabilities. *Behavioral Interventions* **11**, 147–61.

Gary, L.A., Tallon, R.J., & Stangl, J.M. (1980). Environmental influences on self-stimulatory behavior. *American Journal of Mental Deficiency* **85**, 171–5.

Gaylord-Ross, R., Weeks, M., & Lipner, C. (1980). An analysis of antecedent, response and consequence events in the treatment of self-injurious behavior. *Education and Training of the Mentally Retarded* **15**, 35–42.

Gedye, A. (1989a). Extreme self-injury attributed to frontal lobe seizures. *American Journal on Mental Retardation* **94**, 20–6.

Gedye, A. (1989b). Episodic rage and aggression attributed to frontal lobe seizures. *Journal of*

*Mental Deficiency Research* **33**, 369–79.

Gedye, A. (1990). Dietary increase in serotonin reduces self-injurious behaviour in a Down's syndrome adult. *Journal of Mental Deficiency Research* **34**, 195–203.

Gedye, A. (1991). Buspirone alone or with serotonergic diet reduced aggression in a developmentally disabled adult. *Biological Psychiatry* **30**, 88–91.

Gedye, A. (1993). Evidence of serotonergic reduction of self-injurious movements. *Habilitative Mental Health Newsletter* **12**, 53–6.

Goh, H.L., Iwata, B.A., & Kahng, S.W. (1999). Multicomponent assessment and treatment of cigarette pica. *Journal of Applied Behavior Analysis* **32**, 297–316.

Goh, H.L., Iwata, B.A., Shore, B.A. et al. (1995). An analysis of the reinforcing properties of hand mouthing. *Journal of Applied Behavior Analysis* **28**, 269–84.

Gold, M.W. (1980). *Try Another Way: Training Manual.* Champaign, IL: Research Press.

Goldiamond, I. (1974). Toward a constructional approach to social problems: ethical and constitutional issues raised by applied behavior analysis. *Behaviorism* **2**, 1–84.

Golding, L., Emerson, E., & Scott, A. (in press). An evaluation of specialised community-based residential supports for people with challenging behaviour. *Journal of Applied Research in Intellectual Disabilities.*

Goldstein, M., Anderson, L.T., Reuben, R., & Dancis, J. (1985). Self-mutilation in Lesch–Nyhan disease is caused by dopaminergic denervation. *Lancet* **1**, 338–9.

Grace, N., Cowart, C., & Matson, J. (1988). Reinforcement and self-control for treating a chronic case of self-injury in Lesch–Nyhan syndrome. *Journal of the Multihandicapped Person* **1**, 53–9.

Grant, G.W. & Moores, B. (1977). Resident characteristics and staff behavior in two hospitals for mentally retarded adults. *American Journal of Mental Deficiency* **82**, 259–65.

Green, C.W., Gardner, S.M., Canipe, V.S., & Reid, D.H. (1994). Analyzing alertness among people with profound multiple disabilities: implications for provision of training. *Journal of Applied Behavior Analysis* **27**, 519–31.

Green, C.W., Gardner, S.M., & Reid, D.M. (1997). Increasing indices of happiness among people with profound multiple disabilities: a program replication and component analysis. *Journal of Applied Behavior Analysis* **30**, 217–28.

Green, C.W., Reid, D.H., Canipe, V.S., & Gardner, S.M. (1991). A comprehensive evaluation of reinforcer identification processes for persons with profound multiple handicaps. *Journal of Applied Behavior Analysis* **24**, 537–52.

Green, C.W., Reid, D.H., White, L.K., Halford, R.C., Brittain, D.P., & Gardner, S.M. (1988). Identifying reinforcers for persons with profound handicaps: staff opinion versus systematic assessment of preferences. *Journal of Applied Behavior Analysis* **21**, 31–43.

Gregory, N., Robertson, J., Kessissoglou, S., Emerson, E., & Hatton, C. (in press). Predictors of expressed satisfaction among people with intellectual disabilities receiving residential supports. *Journal of Intellectual Disability Research.*

Griffin, J.C., Paisey, T.J., Stark, M.T., & Emerson, J.H. (1988). B. F. Skinner's position on aversive treatment. *American Journal on Mental Retardation* **93**, 104–5.

Griffin, J.C., Ricketts, R.W., & Williams, D.E. (1986). Reaction to Richmond et al.: propriety of mechanical restraint and protective devices as tertiary techniques. In K.D. Gadow (Ed.).

*Advances in Learning and Behavioural Disabilities* (Volume 5). London: JAI Press.

Griffin, J.C., Ricketts, R.W., Williams, D.E., Locke, B.J., Altmeyer, B.K., & Stark, M.T. (1987). A community survey of self-injurious behavior among developmentally disabled children and adolescents. *Hospital and Community Psychiatry* **38**, 959–63.

Griffin, J.C., Williams, D.E., Stark, M.T., Altmeyer, B.K., & Mason, M. (1986). Self-injurious behavior: a state-wide prevalence survey of the extent and circumstances. *Applied Research in Mental Retardation* **7**, 105–16.

Grossman, H.J., Begab, M.J., Cantwell, D.P. et al. (1983). *Classification in Mental Retardation.* Washington, DC: American Association on Mental Deficiency.

Gualtieri, C.T., & Schroeder, S.R. (1989). Pharmacotherapy of self-injurious behavior: preliminary tests of the D1 hypothesis. *Psychopharmacology Bulletin* **25**, 364–71.

Guess, D., & Carr, E.G. (1991). Emergence and maintenance of stereotypy and self-injury. *American Journal on Mental Retardation* **96**, 299–319.

Guess, D., Helmstetter, H., Turnbull, H.R., & Knowlton, S. (1987). *Use of Aversive Procedures with Persons who are Disabled: An Historical Review and Critical Analysis.* Seattle, WA: The Association for Persons with Severe Handicaps.

Guess, D., Roberts, S., Siegel-Causey, E., et al. (1993). Analysis of behavior state conditions and associated variables among students with profound handicaps. *American Journal on Mental Retardation* **97**, 634–53.

Guess, D., Siegel-Causey, E., Roberts, S., Rues, J., Thompson, B., & Siegel-Causey, D. (1990). Assessment and analysis of behavior state and related variables among students with profoundly handicapping conditions. *Journal of the Association for Persons with Severe Handicaps* **15**, 211–30.

Guralnick, M.J. (1997). *The Effectiveness of Early Intervention.* Baltimore: Paul H. Brookes.

Guralnick, M.J. (1998). Effectiveness of early intervention for vulnerable children: a developmental perspective. *American Journal of Mental Retardation* **102**, 319–45.

Hagopian, L.P., Fisher, W.W., & Legacy, S.M. (1994). Schedule effects of noncontingent reinforcement on attention-maintained destructive behavior in identical quadruplets. *Journal of Applied Behavior Analysis* **27**, 317–25.

Hagopian, L.P., Fisher, W.W., Sullivan, M.T., Acquisto, J., & LeBlanc, L.A. (1998). Effectiveness of functional communication training with and without extinction and punishment: a summary of 21 inpatient cases. *Journal of Applied Behavior Analysis* **31**, 211–35.

Hagopian, L.P., Fisher, W.W., Thompson, R.H., Owen-DeSchryver, J., Iwata, B.A., & Wacker, D.P. (1997). Toward the development of structured criteria for interpretation of functional analysis data. *Journal of Applied Behavior Analysis* **30**, 313–26.

Hall, A.M., Neuharth-Pritchett, S., & Belfiore, P.J. (1997). Reduction of aggressive behaviors with changes in activity: linking descriptive and experimental analyses. *Education and Training in Mental Retardation and Developmental Disabilities* **32**, 331–9.

Hall, S. & Oliver, C. (1992). Differential effects of severe self-injurious behaviour on the behaviour of others. *Behavioural Psychotherapy* **20**, 355–65.

Hall, S. & Oliver, C. (2000). An alternative approach to the sequential analysis of behavioral interactions. In T. Thompson, D. Felce & F. Symons (Eds.). *Computer Assisted Behavioral Observation Methods for Developmental Disabilities.* Baltimore: Paul H. Brookes.

Halle, J.W., & Spradlin, J.E. (1993). Identifying stimulus control of challenging behavior. In J. Reichle & D.P. Wacker (Eds.). *Communicative Alternatives to Challenging Behavior*, pp. 83–112. Baltimore: Paul H. Brookes.

Hammock, R.G., Schroeder, S.R., & Levine, W.R. (1995). The effects of clozapine on self-injurious behavior. *Journal of Autism and Developmental Disorders* **25**, 611–26.

Hanley, G.P., Piazza, C.C., & Fisher, W.W. (1997). Noncontingent presentation of attention and alternative stimuli in the treatment of attention-maintained destructive behavior. *Journal of Applied Behavior Analysis* **30**, 229–37.

Hanley, G.P., Piazza, C.C., Fisher, W.W., Contrucci, S.A., & Maglieri, K.A. (1997). Evaluation of client preference for function-based treatment packages. *Journal of Applied Behavior Analysis* **30**, 459–73.

Hanley, G.P., Piazza, C.C., Keeney, K.M., Blakeley-Smith, A.B., & Worsdell, A.S. (1998). Effects of wrist weights on self-injurious and adaptive behaviors. *Journal of Applied Behavior Analysis* **31**, 307–10.

Harchik, A.E., & Putzier, V.S. (1990). The use of high-probability requests to increase compliance with instructions to take medication. *Journal of the Association for Persons with Severe Handicaps* **15**, 40–3.

Haring, T.G., & Kennedy, C.H. (1990). Contextual control of problem behaviors in students with severe disabilities. *Journal of Applied Behavior Analysis* **23**, 235–43.

Harris, J.C. (1992). Neurobiological factors in self-injurious behavior. In J.K. Luiselli, J.L. Matson & N.N. Singh (Eds.). *Self-Injurious Behavior: Analysis, Assessment and Treatment*, pp. 59–92. New York: Springer-Verlag.

Harris, P. (1993). The nature and extent of aggressive behaviour among people with learning difficulties (mental handicap) in a single health district. *Journal of Intellectual Disability Research* **37**, 221–42.

Harris, J. (1996). Physical restraint procedures for managing challenging behaviors presented by mentally retarded adults and children. *Research in Developmental Disabilities* **17**, 99–134.

Harris, J., Cook, M., & Upton, G. (1996). *Pupils with Severe Learning Disabilities Who Present Challenging Behaviour*. Clevedon: BILD Publications.

Hastings, R.P. (1995). Understanding factors that influence staff responses to challenging behaviour. *Mental Handicap Research* **8**, 296–320.

Hastings, R.P. (1996). Staff strategies and explanations for intervening with challenging behaviour. *Journal of Intellectual Disability Research* **40**, 166–75.

Hastings, R.P. (1997). Measuring staff perceptions of challenging behaviour: the Challenging Behaviour Attributions Scale (CHABA). *Journal of Intellectual Disability Research* **41**, 495–501.

Hastings, R.P., Reed, T.R., & Watts, M.J. (1997). Community staff causal attributions about challenging behaviour in people with intellectual disabilities. *Journal of Applied Research in Intellectual Disabilities* **10**, 238–49.

Hastings, R., & Remington, B. (1993). 'Is there anything on . . . Why "good" behavioural programmes fail?': a brief review. *Clinical Psychology Forum* **55**, 9–11.

Hastings, R., & Remington, B. (1994a). Rules of engagement: toward an analysis of staff responses to challenging behaviour. *Research in Developmental Disabilities* **15**, 279–98.

Hastings, R., & Remington, B. (1994b). Staff behaviour and its implications for people with learning disabilities and challenging behaviour. *British Journal of Clinical Psychology* **33**, 423–38.

Hastings, R.P., Remington, B., & Hopper, G.M. (1995). Experienced and inexperienced health case workers' beliefs about challenging behaviour. *Journal of Intellectual Disability Research* **39**, 474–83.

Hatton, C. (1998). Epidemiology. In E. Emerson, C. Hatton, J. Bromley & A. Caine (Eds.). *Clinical Psychology and People With Intellectual Disabilities*. Chichester: Wiley.

Hatton, C., Brown, R., Caine, A., & Emerson, E. (1995). Stressors, coping strategies and stress-related outcomes among direct care staff in staffed houses for people with learning disabilities. *Mental Handicap Research* **8**, 252–71.

Hayes, S.C. (1989). *Rule-Governed Behavior: Cognition, Contingencies and Instructional Control*. New York: Plenum.

Heal, L.W., Harner, C.J., Novak Amado, A.R., & Chadsey-Rusch, J. (1993). *Lifestyle Satisfaction Scale*. Worthington, OH: IDS.

Heidorn, S.D., & Jensen, C.C. (1984). Generalization and maintenance of the reduction of self-injurious behavior maintained by two types of reinforcement. *Behaviour Research and Therapy* **22**, 581–6.

Hellings, J.A. (1999). Psychopharmacology of mood disorders in persons with mental retardation and autism. *Mental Retardation and Developmental Disabilities Research Reviews* **5**, 270–8.

Herman, B.H., Hammock, M.K., Arthur-Smith, A. et al. (1987). Naltrexone decreases self-injurious behavior. *Annals of Neurology* **22**, 550–2.

Higgins Hains, A., & Baer, D.M. (1989). Interaction effects in multielement designs: inevitable, desirable, and ignorable. *Journal of Applied Behavior Analysis* **22**, 57–69.

Hile, M.G., & Vatterott, M.K. (1991). Two decades of treatment for self-injurious biting in individuals with mental retardation or developmental disabilities: a treatment focussed review of the literature. *Journal of Developmental and Physical Disabilities* **3**, 81–113.

Hill, B.K., & Bruininks, R.H. (1984). Maladaptive behavior of mentally retarded individuals in residential facilities. *American Journal of Mental Deficiency* **88**, 380–7.

Hillery, J., & Mulcahy, M. (1997). Self-injurious behavior in persons with a mental handicap: an epidemiological study in an Irish population. *Irish Journal of Psychological Medicine* **14**, 12–15.

Hobbs, S.A., & Forehand, R. (1977). Important parameters in the use of time-out with children: a re-examination. *Journal of Behavior Therapy and Experimental Psychiatry* **8**, 365–70.

Hodapp, R.M. (1997). Direct and indirect behavioral effects of different genetic disorders of mental retardation. *American Journal of Mental Retardation* **102**, 67–79.

Holland, A.J. (1999). Understanding the eating disorder affecting people with Prader–Willi syndrome. *Journal of Applied Research in Intellectual Disabilities* **11**, 192–206.

Horner, R.D. (1980). The effects of an environmental 'enrichment' program on the behavior of institutionalized profoundly retarded children. *Journal of Applied Behavior Analysis* **13**, 473–91.

Horner, R.H. (1991). The future of applied behavior analysis for people with severe disabilities:

commentary I. In L.H. Meyer, C.A. Peck, & L. Brown (Eds.). *Critical Issues in the Lives of People with Severe Disabilities*, pp. 601–6. Baltimore: Paul H. Brookes.

Horner, R.H., & Budd, C.M. (1985). Acquisition of manual sign use: collateral reduction in maladaptive behavior and factors limiting generalisation. *Education and Training of the Mentally Retarded* **20**, 39–47.

Horner, R.H., & Day, H.M. (1991). The effects of response efficiency on functionally equivalent competing behaviors. *Journal of Applied Behavior Analysis* **24**, 719–32.

Horner, R.H., Day, H.M., & Day, J.R. (1997). Using neutralizing routines to reduce problem behaviors. *Journal of Applied Behavior Analysis* **30**, 601–14.

Horner, R.H., Day, H.M., Sprague, J.R., O'Brien, M., & Heathfield, L.T. (1991). Interspersed requests: a nonaversive procedure for reducing aggression and self-injury during instruction. *Journal of Applied Behavior Analysis* **24**, 265–78.

Horner, R.H., Sprague, J.R., O'Brien, M., & Heathfield, L.T. (1990). The role of response efficiency in the reduction of problem behaviors through functional equivalence training: a case study. *Journal of the Association for Persons with Severe Handicaps* **15**, 91–7.

Horner, R.H., Vaughn, B.J., Day, H.M., & Ard, W.R. (1996). The relationship between setting events and problem behaviour: expanding our understanding of behavioral support. In L.K. Koegel, R.L. Koegel & G. Dunlap (Eds.). *Positive Behavioral Support: Including People With Difficult Behavior in the Community*, pp. 381–402. Baltimore: Paul H. Brookes.

Howlin, P., Davies, M., & Udwin, O. (1998). Syndrome specific characteristics in Williams syndrome: to what extent do early behavioural patterns persist into adult life. *Journal of Applied Research in Intellectual Disabilities* **11**, 207–26.

Hudson, A., Jauernig, R., Wilken, P., & Radler, G. (1995a). Behavioural treatment of challenging behaviour: a cost-benefit analysis of a service delivery model. *Behaviour Change* **12**, 216–26.

Hudson, A., Wilken, P., Jauernig, R., & Radler, G. (1995b). Regionally based teams for the treatment of challenging behaviour: a three-year outcome study. *Behaviour Change* **12**, 209–15.

Hutchinson, R.R. (1977). By-products of aversive control. In W.K. Honig & J.E.R. Staddon (Eds.). *Handbook of Operant Behavior*. Prentice- Hall: Englewood-Cliffs, NJ.

Intagliata, J., & Willer, B. (1982). Reinstitutionalization of mentally retarded persons successfully placed into family care and group homes. *American Journal of Mental Deficiency* **87**, 34–9.

Irvin, D.S., Thompson, T.J., Turner, W.D., & Williams, D.E. (1998). Utilizing increased response effort to reduce chronic hand mouthing. *Journal of Applied Behavior Analysis* **31**, 375–85.

Isaacson, R.L., & Gispin, W.H. (1990). Neuropeptides and the issue of stereotypy in behaviour. In S.J. Cooper & C.T. Dourish (Eds.). *Neurobiology of Stereotyped Behaviour*. Oxford: Oxford University Press.

Iversen, I.H., & Lattal, K.A. (1991a). *Experimental Analysis of Behavior: Part 1*. Amsterdam: Elsevier.

Iversen, I.H., & Lattal, K.A. (1991b). *Experimental Analysis of Behavior: Part 2*. Amsterdam: Elsevier.

Iwata, B.A. (1988). The development and adoption of controversial default technologies. *The*

*Behavior Analyst* **11**, 149–57.

Iwata, B.A., Dorsey, M.F., Slifer, K.J., Bauman, K.E., & Richman, G.S. (1982). Toward a functional analysis of self-injury. *Analysis and Intervention in Developmental Disabilities* **2**, 3–20.

Iwata, B.A., Pace, G.M., Cowdery, G.E., & Miltenberger, R.G. (1994b). What makes extinction work: an analysis of procedural form and function. *Journal of Applied Behavior Analysis* **27**, 131–44.

Iwata, B., Pace, G.M., Dorsey, M.F. et al. (1994a). The functions of self-injurious behavior: an experimental–epidemiological study. *Journal of Applied Behavior Analysis* **27**, 215–40.

Iwata, B.A., Pace, G.M., Kalsher, M.J., Cowdery, G.E., & Cataldo, M.F. (1990a). Experimental analysis and extinction of self-injurious escape behavior. *Journal of Applied Behavior Analysis* **23**, 11–27.

Iwata, B.A., Pace, G.M., Kissel, R.C., Nau, P.A., & Farber, J.M. (1990c). The Self-Injury Trauma (SIT) Scale: a method for quantifying surface tissue damage caused by self-injurious behavior. *Journal of Applied Behavior Analysis* **23**, 99–110.

Iwata, B.A., Vollmer, T.R., & Zarcone, J.R. (1990b). The experimental (functional) analysis of behavior disorders: methodology, applications, and limitations. In A.C. Repp & N.N. Singh (Eds.). *Perspectives on the Use of Nonaversive and Aversive Interventions for Persons with Developmental Disabilities*. Sycamore, IL: Sycamore Publishing Company.

Jacobsen, J.W. (1998). Psychological services utilization: relationship to severity of behaviour problems in intellectual disability services. *Journal of Intellectual Disability Research* **42**, 307–15.

Jacobsen, J.W., Silver, E.J., & Schwartz, A.A. (1984). Service provision in New York's group homes. *Mental Retardation* **22**, 231–9.

Jansma, P., & Combs, C.S. (1987). The effects of fitness training and reinforcement on maladaptive behaviors of institutionalized adults classified as mentally retarded/emotionally disturbed. *Education and Training of the Mentally Retarded* **22**, 268–79.

Jenkins, R., Rose, J., & Lovell, C. (1997). Psychological well-being of staff working with people who have challenging behaviour. *Journal of Intellectual Disability Research* **41**, 502–11.

Jensen, C.C., & Heidorn, S.D. (1993). Ten-year follow-up of a successful treatment of self-injurious behavior. *Behavioral Residential Treatment* **8**, 263–80.

Johnson, K., Johnson, C.R., & Sahl, R.A. (1994). Behavioral and naltrexone treatment of self-injurious behavior. *Journal of Developmental and Physical Disabilities* **6**, 193–202.

Johnson, W.L., & Day, R.M. (1992). The incidence and prevalence of self-injurious behavior. In J.K. Luiselli, J.L. Matson & N.N. Singh (Eds.). *Self-Injurious Behavior: Analysis, Assessment and Treatment*, pp. 21–58. New York: Springer-Verlag.

Jones, E., Perry, J., Lowe, K. et al. (1999). Opportunity and the promotion of activity among adults with severe intellectual disability living in community residences: the impact of training in active support. *Journal of Intellectual Disability Research* **43**, 164–78.

Jones, R.S.P. (1991). Reducing inappropriate behaviour using non-aversive procedures: evaluating differential reinforcement schedules. In B. Remington (Ed.). *The Challenge of Severe Mental Handicap: A Behaviour Analytic Approach*. Chichester: Wiley.

Jones, R.S.P., Williams, H., & Lowe, F. (1993). Verbal self-regulation. In I. Fleming & B. Stenfert

Kroese (Eds.). *People with Learning Disability and Severe Challenging Behaviour: New Developments in Services and Therapy.* Manchester: Manchester University Press.

Jones, R.S.P., Wint, D., & Ellis, N.C. (1990). The social effects of stereotyped behaviour. *Journal of Mental Deficiency Research* **34**, 261–8.

Jordan, J., Singh, N.N., & Repp, A.C. (1989). An evaluation of gentle teaching and visual screening in the reduction of stereotypy. *Journal of Applied Behavior Analysis* **22**, 9–22.

Kahng, S.W., & Iwata, B.A. (1999). Correspondence between outcomes of brief and extended functional analyses. *Journal of Applied Behavior Analysis* **32**, 149–59.

Kahng, S.W., Iwata, B.A., DeLeon, I.G., & Worsdell, A.S. (1997). Evaluation of the 'control over reinforcement' component in functional communication training. *Journal of Applied Behavior Analysis* **30**, 267–77.

Kahng, S.W., Iwata, B.A., Fischer, S.M., Page, T.J., Treadwell, K.R.H., Williams, D.E., & Smith, R.G. (1998). Temporal distributions of problem behavior based on scatter plot analysis. *Journal of Applied Behavior Analysis* **31**, 593–604.

Kaiser, A.P. (1993). Understanding human behavior: problems of science and practice. *Journal of the Association for Persons with Severe Handicaps* **18**, 240–2.

Kalachnik, J.E., (1999). Measuring side-effects of psychopharmacologic medication in individuals with mental retardation and developmental disabilities. *Mental Retardation and Developmental Disabilities Research Reviews* **5**, 348–59.

Kalachnik, J.E., Hanzel, T.E., Harder, S.R., Bauernfeind, J.D., & Engstrom, E.A. (1995). Antiepileptic drug behavioral side effects in individuals with mental retardation and the use of behavioral measurement techniques. *Mental Retardation* **33**, 374–82.

Kalachnik, J.E., Leventhal, B.L., James, D.J. et al. (1998). Guidelines for the use of psychotropic medication. In S. Reiss & M.G. Aman (Eds.). *Psychotropic Medication and Developmental Disabilities: The International Consensus Handbook,* pp. 45–72. Ohio: Nisonger Center, Ohio State University.

Kantor, J.R. (1959). *Interbehavioral Psychology.* Chicago: Principa Press.

Kars, H., Broekema, W., Glaudemans-van Gelderen, I., Verhoeven, W.M.A., & van Ree, J.M. (1990). Naltrexone attenuates self-injurious behavior in mentally retarded subjects. *Biological Psychiatry* **27**, 741–6.

Kazdin, A.E., & Matson, J.L. (1981). Social validation in mental retardation. *Applied Research in Mental Retardation* **2**, 39–53.

Kearney, C.A. (1994). Interrater reliability of the Motivation Assessment Scale: another, closer look. *Journal of the Association for Persons with Severe Handicaps* **19**, 139–42.

Kemp, D.C., & Carr, E.G. (1995). Reduction of severe problem behavior in community employment using an hypothesis-driven multi-component intervention approach. *Journal of the Association for Persons with Severe Handicaps* **20**, 229–47.

Kennedy, C.H. (1994a). Automatic reinforcement: oxymoron or hypothetical construct? *Journal of Behavioral Education* **4**, 387–95.

Kennedy, C.H. (1994b). Manipulating antecedent conditions to alter the stimulus control of problem behavior. *Journal of Applied Behavior Analysis* **27**, 161–70.

Kennedy, C.H., & Itkonen, T. (1993). Effects of setting events on the problem behavior of students with severe disabilities. *Journal of Applied Behavior Analysis* **26**, 321–7.

Kennedy, C.H., Itkonen, T., & Lindquist, K. (1995). Comparing interspersed requests and social comments as antecedents for increasing student compliance. *Journal of Applied Behavior Analysis* **28**, 97–8.

Kennedy, C.H., & Meyer, K.A. (1996). Sleep deprivation, allergy symptoms, and negatively reinforced problem behavior. *Journal of Applied Behavior Analysis* **29**, 133–5.

Kennedy, C.H., & Meyer, K.A. (1998a). Establishing operations and the motivation of challenging behavior. In J.K. Luiselli & M.J. Cameron (Eds.). *Antecedent Control: Innovative Approaches to Behavioral Support*, pp. 329–46. Baltimore: Paul H. Brookes.

Kennedy, C.H., & Meyer, K.A. (1998b). The use of psychotropic medication for people with severe disabilities and challenging behavior: current status and future directions. *Journal of the Association For Persons With Severe Handicaps* **23**, 83–97.

Kern, L., Carberry, N., & Haidara, C. (1997). Analysis and intervention with two topographies of challenging behavior exhibited by a young woman with autism. *Research in Developmental Disabilities* **18**, 275–87.

Kern, L., & Dunlap, G. (1998). Curricular modifications to promote desirable classroom behavior. In J.K. Luiselli & M.J. Cameron (Eds.). *Antecedent Control: Innovative Approaches to Behavioral Support*, pp. 289–308. Baltimore: Paul H. Brookes.

Kern, L., Koegel, R.L., & Dunlap, G. (1984). The influence of vigorous versus mild exercise on autistic stereotyped behaviors. *Journal of Autism and Developmental Disorders* **14**, 57–67.

Kern, L., Koegel, R.L., Dyer, K., Blew, P.A., & Fenton, L.R. (1982). The effects of physical exercise on self-stimulation and appropriate responding in autistic children. *Journal of Autism and Developmental Disorders* **12**, 399–419.

Kern, L., Mauk, J.E., Marder, T.J., & Mace, F.C. (1995). Functional analysis and intervention for breath holding. *Journal of Applied Behavior Analysis* **28**, 339–40.

Kiely, M., & Lubin, R.A. (1991). Epidemiological methods. In J.L. Matson & J.A. Mulick (Eds.). *Handbook of Mental Retardation*, pp. 586–602. New York: Pergamon.

Kiernan, C. (1991). Professional ethics: behaviour analysis and normalization. In B. Remington (Ed.). *The Challenge of Severe Mental Handicap: A Behaviour Analytic Approach*. Chichester: Wiley.

Kiernan, C. (1993). *Research Into Practice? Implications of Research on the Challenging Behaviour of People with Learning Disabilities*. Kidderminster: British Institute on Learning Disabilities.

Kiernan, C., & Alborz, A. (1994). *Parents Caring for Young Adults with Challenging Behaviours*. Manchester: Hester Adrian Research Centre, University of Manchester.

Kiernan, C., & Alborz, A. (1996). Persistence and change in challenging and problem behaviours of young adults with learning disability living in the family home. *Journal of Applied Research in Intellectual Disability* **9**, 181–93.

Kiernan, C., & Kiernan, D. (1994). Challenging behaviour in schools for pupils with severe learning difficulties. *Mental Handicap Research* **7**, 117–201.

Kiernan, C., & Qureshi, H. (1993). Challenging behaviour. In C. Kiernan (Ed.). *Research to Practice? Implications of Research on the Challenging Behaviour of People with Learning Disabilities*, pp. 53–87. Kidderminster: British Institute of Learning Disabilities.

Kiernan, C., Reeves, D., Hatton, C. et al. (1997). *The HARC Challenging Behaviour Project. Report 1: Persistence and Change in the Challenging Behaviour of People with Learning*

*Disability*. Manchester: Hester Adrian Research Centre, University of Manchester.

Kiernan, C., Reeves, D., & Alborz, A. (1995). The use of anti-psychotic drugs with adults with learning disabilities and challenging behaviour. *Journal of Intellectual Disability Research* **39**, 263–74.

Kim, S., Larson, S.A., & Lakin, K.C. (in press). Behavioral outcomes of deinstitutionalization for people with intellectual disabilities: a review of studies conducted between 1980 and 1999. *Journal of Intellectual and Developmental Disabilities*

Kincaid, D. (1996). Person-centred planning. In L.K. Koegel, R.L. Koegel & G. Dunlap (Eds.). *Positive Behavioral Support: Including People With Difficult Behavior in the Community*, pp. 425–38. Baltimore: Paul H. Brookes.

King, B.H. (1993). Self-injury by people with mental retardation: a compulsive behavior hypothesis. *American Journal on Mental Retardation* **98**, 93–112.

Kirkpatrick-Sanchez, S., Williams, D.E., Gualtieri, C.T., & Raichman, J.A. (1998). The effects of serotonergic reuptake inhibitors combined with behavioral treatment on self-injury associated with Lesch–Nyhan syndrome. *Journal of Developmental and Physical Disabilities* **10**, 283–90.

Knabe, R., Schulz, P., & Richard, J. (1990). Initial aggravation of self-injurious behavior in autistic patients receiving naltrexone treatment. *Journal of Autism and Developmental Disorders* **20**, 591–2.

Knobbe, C.A., Carey, S.P., Rhodes, L., & Horner, R.H. (1995). Benefit-cost analysis of community residential versus institutional services for adults with severe mental retardation and challenging behaviors. *American Journal of Mental Retardation* **99**, 533–41.

Koegel, R.L., & Frea, W.D. (1993). Treatment of social behavior in autism through the modification of pivotal social skills. *Journal of Applied Behavior Analysis* **26**, 369–77.

Koegel, R.L., & Koegel, L.K. (1988). Generalized responsivity and pivotal behaviors. In R.H. Horner, G. Dunlap & R.L. Koegel (Eds.). *Generalization and Maintenance: Life-Style Changes in Applied Settings*. Baltimore: Paul H. Brookes.

Koegel, R.L., & Koegel, L.K. (1990). Extended reductions in stereotypic behavior of students with autism through a self-management treatment package. *Journal of Applied Behavior Analysis* **23**, 119–27.

Koegel, L.K., Koegel, R.L., & Dunlap, G. (1996a). *Positive Behavioral Support: Including People With Difficult Behavior in the Community*. Baltimore: Paul H. Brookes.

Koegel, L.K., Koegel, R.L., Hurley, C., & Frea, W.D. (1992). Improving social skills and disruptive behavior in children with autism through self-management. *Journal of Applied Behavior Analysis* **25**, 341–53.

Koegel, L.K., Koegel, R.L., Kellegrew, D., & Mullen, K. (1996b). Parent education for prevention and reduction of severe problem behaviors. In L.K. Koegel, R.L. Koegel & G. Dunlap (Eds.). *Positive Behavioral Support: Including People With Difficult Behavior in the Community*, pp. 3–30. Baltimore: Paul H. Brookes.

Konarski, E.A., Favell, J.E., & Favell, J.E. (1992). *Manual for the Assessment and Treatment of the Behavior Disorders of People with Mental Retardation*. Morganton, NC: Western Carolina Centre Foundation.

Konarski, E.A., Johnson, M.R., Crowell, C.R., & Whitman, T.L. (1981). An alternative approach to reinforcement for applied researchers: response deprivation. *Behavior Therapy* **12**, 653–66.

Konarski, E.A., Sutton, K., & Huffman, A. (1997). Personal characteristics associated with episodes of injury in a residential facility. *American Journal of Mental Retardation* **102**, 37–44.

Korinek, L. (1991). Self management for the mentally retarded. In R.A. Gable (Ed.). *Advances in Mental Retardation and Developmental Disabilities* (Volume 4). London: Jessica Kingsley.

Kraemer, G.W., & Clarke, H.S. (1990). The behavioral neurobiology of self-injurious behavior in rhesus monkeys. *Progress in Neuropsychopharmacology and Biological Psychiatry* **14**, 141–68.

Krantz, P.J., MacDuff, M.T., & McClannahan, L.E. (1993). Programming participation in family activities for children with autism: parents' use of photographic activity schedules. *Journal of Applied Behavior Analysis* **26**, 137–8.

Krantz, P., & Risley, T.R. (1977). Behavioral ecology in the classroom. In S.G. O'Leary & K.D. O'Leary (Eds.). *Classroom Management: The Successful Use of Behavior Modification*. New York: Pergamon.

Kratochwill, T.R., & Levin, J.R. (1992). *Single-Case Research Design and Analysis: New Directions for Psychology and Education*. Hillsdale, NJ: Lawrence Erlbaum Associates.

Kroese, B.S. (1998). Cognitive–behavioural therapy for people with learning disabilities. *Behavioural and Cognitive Psychotherapy* **26**, 315–22.

Kroese, B., Dagnan, D., & Loumidis, K. (1997). *Cognitive Behaviour Therapy for People with Intellectual Disabilities*. London: Routledge.

Kuhn, D.E., DeLeon, I.G., Fisher, W.W., & Wilke, A.E. (1999). Clarifying an ambiguous functional analysis with matched and mismatched extinction procedures. *Journal of Applied Behavior Analysis* **32**, 99–102.

Lachiewicz, A.M., Spiridigliozzi, G.A., Gullion, C.M., Ransford, S.N., & Rao, K. (1994). Aberrant behaviors of young boys with Fragile X syndrome. *American Journal on Mental Retardation* **98**, 657–79.

Lader. M., & Herrington, R. (1996). *Biological Treatments in Psychiatry* (2nd Edition). Oxford: Oxford University Press.

LaGrow, S.J., & Repp, A.C. (1984). Stereotypic responding: a review of intervention research. *American Journal of Mental Deficiency* **88**, 595–609.

Lakin, K.C., Hill, B.K., Hauber, F.A., Bruininks, R.H., & Heal, L.W. (1983). New admissions and readmissions to a national sample of public residential facilities. *American Journal of Mental Deficiency* **88**, 13–20.

Lalli, J.S., Browder, D.M., Mace, F.C., & Brown, D.K. (1993). Teacher use of descriptive analysis data to implement interventions to decrease students' problem behaviors. *Journal of Applied Behavior Analysis* **26**, 227–38.

Lalli, J.S., & Casey, S.D. (1996). Treatment of multiply controlled problem behavior. *Journal of Applied Behavior Analysis* **29**, 391–5.

Lalli, J.S., Casey, S., & Kates, K. (1995). Reducing escape behavior and increasing task compliance with functional communication training, extinction and response chaining. *Journal of Applied Behavior Analysis* **28**, 261–8.

Lalli, J.S., Casey, S.D., & Kates, K. (1997). Noncontingent reinforcement as treatment for severe problem behavior: some procedural variations. *Journal of Applied Behavior Analysis* **30**, 127–37.

Lalli, J.S., & Goh, H-L. (1993). Natural observations in community settings. In J. Reichle & D.P. Wacker (Eds.). *Communicative Alternatives to Challenging Behavior*, pp. 11–40. Baltimore: Paul H. Brookes.

Lalli, J.S., & Kates, K. (1998). The effect of reinforcer preference on functional analysis outcomes. *Journal of Applied Behavior Analysis* **31**, 79–90.

Lalli, J.S., Kates, K., & Casey, S.D. (1999). Response covariation: the relationship between correct academic responding and problem behavior. *Behavior Modification* **23**, 339–57.

Lalli, J.S., Mace, F.C., Wohn, T., & Livezey, K. (1995). Identification and modification of a response-class hierarchy. *Journal of Applied Behavior Analysis* **28**, 551–9.

Lalli, J.S., Vollmer, T.R., Progar, P.R. et al. (1999). Competition between positive and negative reinforcement in the treatment of escape behavior. *Journal of Applied Behavior Analysis* **32**, 285–96.

Lancioni, G.E., & Hoogeveen, F.R. (1990). Non-aversive and mildly aversive procedures for reducing problem behaviours in people with developmental disorders: a review. *Mental Handicap Research* **3**, 137–60.

Lancioni, G.E., & O'Reilly, M.F. (1998). A review of research on physical exercise with people with severe and profound developmental disabilities. *Research in Developmental Disabilities* **19**, 477–92.

Lancioni, G.E., O'Reilly, M.F., & Basili, G. (1999). Review of strategies for treating sleep problems in persons with severe or profound mental retardation or multiple handicaps. *American Journal of Mental Retardation* **104**, 170–86.

Lancioni, G., O'Reilly, M.F., Campodonico, F., & Mantini, M. (1998). Task variation versus task repetition for people with profound developmental disabilities: an assessment of preferences. *Research in Developmental Disabilities* **19**, 189–99.

Lancioni, G., O'Reilly, M., & Emerson, E. (1996). A review of choice research with people with severe and profound developmental disabilities. *Research in Developmental Disabilities* **17**, 391–11.

Lancioni, G.E., Smeets, P.M., Ceccarani, P.S., Capodaglio, L., & Campanari, G. (1984). Effects of gross motor activities on the severe self-injurious tantrums of multihandicapped individuals. *Applied Research in Mental Retardation* **5**, 471–82.

Langee, H.R. (1989). A retrospective study of mentally retarded patients with behavioral disorders who were treated with carbamazepine. *American Journal of Mental Deficiency* **93**, 389–91.

Larson, J.L., & Miltenberger, R.G. (1992). The influence of antecedent exercise on problem behaviors in persons with mental retardation: a failure to replicate. *Journal of the Association for Persons with Severe Handicaps* **17**, 40–6.

Larson, S.A., & Lakin, K.C. (1989). Deinstitutionalization of persons with mental retardation: behavioral outcomes. *Journal of the Association for Persons with Severe Handicaps* **14**, 324–32.

Lattal, K.A., & Neef, N.A. (1996). Recent reinforcement-schedule research and applied behavior analysis. *Journal of Applied Behavior Analysis* **29**, 213–30.

LaVigna, G.W., & Donnellan, A.M. (1986). *Alternatives to Punishment: Solving Behavior Prob-*

*lems with Non-Aversive Strategies*. New York: Irvington.

Lehr, D.H., & Brown, F. (1996). *People With Disabilities Who Challenge the System*. Baltimore: Paul H. Brookes.

Lennox, D.B., Miltenberger, R.G., Spengler, P., & Erfanian, N. (1988). Decelerative treatment practices with persons who have mental retardation: a review of five years of the literature. *American Journal on Mental Retardation* **92**, 492–501.

Lerman, D.C., & Iwata, B.A. (1993). Descriptive and experimental analysis of variables maintaining self-injurious behaviour. *Journal of Applied Behavior Analysis* **26**, 293–319.

Lerman, D.C., & Iwata, B.A. (1995). Prevalence of the extinction burst and its attenuation during treatment. *Journal of Applied Behavior Analysis* **28**, 93–4.

Lerman, D.C. & Iwata, B.A. (1996). Developing a technology for the use of operant extinction in clinical settings: an examination of basic and applied research. *Journal of Applied Behavior Analysis* **29**, 345–82.

Lerman, D.C., Iwata, B.A., Smith, R.G., Zarcone, J.R., & Vollmer, T. (1994a). Transfer of behavioral function as a contributing factor in treatment relapse. *Journal of Applied Behavior Analysis* **27**, 357–70.

Lerman, D.C., Iwata, B.A., Zarcone, J.R., & Ringdahl, J. (1994b). Assessment of stereotypic and self-injurious behavior as adjunctive responses. *Journal of Applied Behavior Analysis* **27**, 715–28.

Leudar, I., Fraser, W.I., & Jeeves, M.A. (1984). Behaviour disturbance and mental handicap: typology and longitudinal trends. *Psychological Medicine* **14**, 923–35.

Lewis, M. (1992). Neurobiological basis of stereotyped behavior: non-human primate and clinical studies. Paper presented at the *Gatlinburg Conference on Research and Theory in Mental Retardation and Developmental Disabilities*, Gatlinburg TN.

Lewis, M.H., & Baumeister, A.A. (1982). Stereotyped mannerisms in mentally retarded persons: animal models and theoretical analyses. In *International Review of Research in Mental Retardation* (Ed. N.R. Ellis). Academic Press: New York.

Lewis, M.H., & Bodfish, J.W. (1998). Repetitive behavior disorders in autism. *Mental Retardation and Developmental Disabilities Research Reviews* **4**, 80–9.

Lewis, M.H., Bodfish, J.W., Powell, S.B., Parker, D.E., & Golden, R.N. (1996). Clomipramine treatment for self-injurious behavior of individuals with mental retardation: a double-blind comparison with placebo. *American Journal of Mental Retardation* **100**, 654–65.

Lewis, M.H., Silva, J.R., & Silva, S.G. (1995). Cyclicity of aggression and self-injurious behavior in individuals with mental retardation. *American Journal of Mental Retardation* **99**, 436–44.

Lienemann, J., & Walker, F.D. (1989). Naltrexone for treatment of self-injury. *American Journal of Psychiatry* **146**, 1639–40.

Lindauer, S.E., DeLeon, I.G., & Fisher, W.W. (1999). Decreasing signs of negative affect and correlated self-injury in an individual with mental retardation and mood disturbances. *Journal of Applied Behavior Analysis* **32**, 103–6.

Lindberg, J.S., Iwata, B.A., Kahng, S.W., & DeLeon, I.G. (1999). DRO contingencies: an analysis of variable–momentary schedules. *Journal of Applied Behavior Analysis* **32**, 123–36.

Lindsay, W.R., Michie, A.M., Baty, F.J., Smith, A.H., & Miller, S. (1994). The consistency of reports about feelings and emotions from people with intellectual disability. *Journal of*

*Intellectual Disability Research* **38**, 61–6.

Linscheid, T.R. (1992). Aversive stimulation. In J.K. Luiselli, J.L. Matson & N.N. Singh (Eds.). *Self-Injurious Behavior: Analysis, Assessment and Treatment.* New York: Springer-Verlag.

Linscheid, T.R., Iwata, B.A., Ricketts, R.W., Williams, D.E., & Griffin, J.C. (1990). Clinical evaluation of the Self-Injurious Behavior Inhibiting System (SIBIS). *Journal of Applied Behavior Analysis* **23**, 53–78.

Linscheid, T.R., Pejeau, C., Cohen, S., & Footo-Lenz, M. (1994). Positive side-effects in the treatment of SIB using the Self- Injurious Behavior Inhibiting System (SIBIS): implications for operant and biochemical explanations of SIB. *Research in Developmental Disabilities* **15**, 81–90.

Lohrmann-O'Rourke, S., & Browder, D. (1998). Empirically-based methods to assess the preferences of individuals with severe disabilities. *American Journal of Mental Retardation* **103**, 146–61.

Loumidis, K.S., & Hill, A. (1997). Training social problem-solving skill to reduce maladaptive behaviors in intellectual disability groups: the influence of individual difference factors. *Journal of Applied Research in Intellectual Disabilities* **10**, 217–37.

Lovaas, O.I. (1982). Comments on self-destructive behaviors. *Analysis and Intervention in Developmental Disabilities* **2**, 115–24.

Lovaas, O.I. (1987). Behavioral treatment and normal educational and intellectual functioning in young autistic children. *Journal of Consulting and Clinical Psychology* **55**, 3–9.

Lovaas, O.I., Freitag, G., Gold, V.J., & Kassorla, I.C. (1965). Experimental studies in childhood schitzophrenia: analysis of self-destructive behavior. *Journal of Experimental Child Psychology* **2**, 67–84.

Lovaas, O.I., Newsom, C., & Hickman, C. (1987). Self-stimulatory behavior and perceptual reinforcement. *Journal of Applied Behavior Analysis* **20**, 45–68.

Lovaas, O.I., & Simmons, J.Q. (1969). Manipulation of self-destructive behavior in three retarded children. *Journal of Applied Behavior Analysis* **2**, 143–57.

Lovaas, O.I., & Smith, T. (1994). Intensive and long-term treatments for clients with destructive behaviors. In T. Thompson & D.B. Gray (Eds.). *Destructive Behavior in Developmental Disabilities: Diagnosis and Treatment,* pp. 68–79. Thousand Oaks: Sage.

Lowe, C.F. (1979). Determinants of human operant behavior. In M.D. Zeilor & P. Harjem (Eds.). *Reinforcement and the Organization of Behavior.* Chichester: Wiley.

Lowe, K., & de Paiva, S. (1991). *NIMROD – An Overview.* London: HMSO.

Lowe, K., & Felce, D. (1995a). How do carers assess the severity of challenging behaviour? A total population study. *Journal of Intellectual Disability Research* **39**, 117–28.

Lowe, K., & Felce, D. (1995b). The definition of challenging behaviour in practice. *British Journal of Learning Disabilities* **23**, 118–23.

Lowe, K., Felce, D., & Blackman, D. (1996). Challenging behaviour: the effectiveness of specialist support teams. *Journal of Intellectual Disability Research* **40**, 336–47.

Lowe, K., Felce, D., Perry, J., Baxter, H., & Jones, E. (1998). The characteristics and residential situations of people with severe intellectual disability and the most severe challenging behaviour in Wales. *Journal of Intellectual Disability Research* **42**, 375–89.

Lowry, M.A., & Sovner, R. (1992). Severe behavior problems associated with rapid cycling bipolar disorder in two adults with profound mental retardation. *Journal of Intellectual Disability Research* **36**, 269–81.

Luckasson, R., Coulter, D.L., Polloway, E.A. et al. (1992). *Mental Retardation: Definition, Classification, and Systems of Supports.* Washington, DC: American Association on Mental Retardation.

Lucyshyn, J.M., Olson, D., & Horner, R.H. (1995). Building an ecology of support: a case study of one young woman with severe problem behaviors living in the community. *Journal of the Association For Persons With Severe Handicaps* **20**, 16–30.

Luiselli, J.K. (1992a). Protective equipment. In J.K. Luiselli, J.L. Matson & N.N. Singh (Eds.). *Self-Injurious Behavior: Analysis, Assessment and Treatment.* New York: Springer-Verlag.

Luiselli, J.K. (1992b). Assessment and treatment of self-injury in a deaf-blind child. *Journal of Developmental and Physical Disabilities* **4**, 219–26.

Luiselli, J.K., Beltis, J.A., & Bass, J. (1989). Clinical analysis of naltrexone in the treatment of self-injurious behavior. *Journal of the Multihandicapped Person* **2**, 43–50.

Luiselli, J.K., & Cameron, M.J. (1998). *Antecedent Control: Innovative Approaches to Behavioral Support.* Baltimore: Paul H. Brookes.

Luiselli, J.K., Matson, J.L., & Singh, N.N. (1992). *Self-Injurious Behavior: Analysis, Assessment and Treatment.* New York: Springer-Verlag.

Luiselli, J.K., Myles, E., Evans, T.P., & Boyce, D.A. (1985). Reinforcement control of severe dysfunctional behavior of blind, multihandicapped students. *American Journal of Mental Deficiency* **90**, 328–34.

Lundervold, D., & Bourland, G. (1988). Quantitative analysis of treatment of aggression, self-injury, and property destruction. *Behavior Modification* **12**, 590–617.

Lutzker, J.R. (1978). Reducing self-injurious behavior by facial screening. *American Journal of Mental Deficiency* **82**, 510–13.

MacDuff, G.S., Krantz, P.J., & McClannahan, L.E. (1993). Teaching children with autism to use photographic activity schedules: maintenance and generalisation of complex response chains. *Journal of Applied Behavior Analysis* **26**, 89–97.

Mace, F.C. (1994a). Basic research needed for stimulating the development of behavioral technologies. *Journal of the Experimental Analysis of Behavior* **61**, 529–50.

Mace, F.C. (1994b). The significance and future of functional analysis methodologies. *Journal of Applied Behavior Analysis* **27**, 385–92.

Mace, F.C., & Belfiore, P. (1990). Behavioral momentum in the treatment of escape-motivated stereotypy. *Journal of Applied Behavior Analysis* **23**, 507–14.

Mace, F.C., Hock, M.L., Lalli, J.S. et al. (1988). Behavioral momentum in the treatment of noncompliance. *Journal of Applied Behavior Analysis* **21**, 123–41.

Mace, F.C., & Knight, D. (1986). Functional analysis and treatment of severe pica. *Journal of Applied Behavior Analysis* **19**, 411–16.

Mace, F.C., & Lalli, J.S. (1991). Linking descriptive and experimental analyses in the treatment of bizarre speech. *Journal of Applied Behavior Analysis* **24**, 553–62.

Mace, F.C., Lalli, J.S., & Lalli, E.P. (1991). Functional analysis and treatment of aberrant behavior. *Research in Developmental Disabilities* **12**, 155–80.

Mace, F.C., Lalli, J.S., & Shea, M.C. (1992). Functional analysis and treatment of self-injury. In J.K. Luiselli, J.L. Matson & N.N. Singh (Eds.). *Self-Injurious Behavior: Analysis, Assessment and Treatment*, pp. 122–54. New York: Springer-Verlag.

Mace, F.C., & Mauk, J.E. (1995). Bio-behavioral diagnosis and treatment of self-injury. *Mental Retardation and Developmental Disabilities Research Reviews* **1**, 104–10.

Mace, F.C., Page, T.J., Ivancic, M.T., & O'Brien, S. (1986). Analysis of environmental determinants of aggression and disruption in mentally retarded children. *Applied Research in Mental Retardation* **7**, 203–21.

Mace, F.C., & Roberts, M.L. (1993). Factors affecting selection of behavioral interventions. In J. Reichle & D.P. Wacker (Eds.). *Communicative Alternatives to Challenging Behavior*, pp. 113–33. Baltimore: Paul H. Brookes.

Mace, F.C., Yankanich, M.A., & West, B. (1989). Toward a methodology of experimental analysis and treatment of aberrant classroom behaviors. *Special Services in the School* **4**, 71–88.

MacLean, W.E., Stone, W.L., & Brown, W.H. (1994). Developmental psychopathology of destructive behavior. In T. Thompson & D.B. Gray (Eds.). *Destructive Behavior in Developmental Disabilities: Diagnosis and Treatment*, pp. 68–79. Thousand Oaks: Sage.

Maisto, C.R., Baumeister, A.A., & Maisto, A.A. (1978). An analysis of variables related to self-injurious behavior among institutionalised retarded persons. *Journal of Mental Deficiency Research* **22**, 27–36.

Mansell, J. (1994). Specialized group homes for persons with severe or profound mental retardation and serious behavior problems in England. *Research in Developmental Disabilities* **15**, 371–88.

Mansell, J. (1995). Staffing and staff performance in services for people with severe or profound learning disability and seriously challenging behaviour. *Journal of Intellectual Disability Research* **39**, 3–14.

Mansell, J., Hughes, H., & McGill, P. (1994a). Maintaining local residential placements. In E. Emerson, P. McGill & J. Mansell (Eds.). *Severe Learning Disabilities and Challenging Behaviours: Designing High Quality Services*. London: Chapman & Hall.

Mansell, J., McGill, P., & Emerson, E. (1994b). Conceptualising service provision. In E. Emerson, P. McGill & J. Mansell (Eds.). *Severe Learning Disabilities and Challenging Behaviours: Designing High Quality Services*. London: Chapman & Hall.

Mansell, J., McGill, P., & Emerson, E. (in press). Innovative services for people with severe or profound intellectual disability and serious challenging behaviour in south-east England. In L.M. Glidden (Ed.). *International Review of Research in Mental Retardation*. New York: Academic Press.

Marcus, B.A., & Vollmer, T.R. (1996). Combining noncontingent reinforcement and differential reinforcement schedules as treatment for aberrant behavior. *Journal of Applied Behavior Analysis* **29**, 43–51.

Markowitz, P. (1992). Effect of fluoxetine on self-injurious behavior in the developmentally disabled: a preliminary study. *Journal of Clinical Psychopharmacology* **12**, 27–31.

Marks, I.M. (1987). *Fears, Phobias and Rituals*. Oxford: Oxford University Press.

Martens, B.K., & Houk, J.L. (1989). The application of Herrnstein's Law of Effect to disruptive and on-task behavior of a retarded adolescent girl. *Journal of the Experimental Analysis of Behavior* **51**, 17–27.

Martens, B.K., Lochner, D.G., & Kelly, S.Q. (1992). The effects of variable-interval reinforcement on academic engagement: a demonstration of matching theory. *Journal of Applied*

*Behavior Analysis* **25**, 143–51.

Martin, N.T., Gaffan, E.A., & Williams, T. (1999). Experimental functional analyses for challenging behavior: a study of validity and reliability. *Research in Developmental Disabilities* **20**, 125–46.

Matson, J.L. (1990). *Handbook of Behavior Modification with the Mentally Retarded*. New York: Plenum.

Matson, J.L., Bamburg, J.W., Cherry, K.E., & Paclawskyj, T.R. (1999). A validity study on the Questions About Behavioral Function (QABF) scale: predicting treatment success for self-injury, aggression and stereotypies. *Research in Developmental Disabilities* **20**, 163–76.

Matson, J.L., Benavidez, D.A., Compton, L.S., Paclawskyj, T., & Baglio, C. (1996). Behavioral treatment of autistic persons: a review of research from 1980 to the present. *Research in Developmental Disabilities* **17**, 433–65.

Maurice, P., & Trudel, G. (1982). Self-injurious behavior: prevalence and relationships to environmental events. In J.H. Hollis & C.E. Meyers (Eds.). *Life-Threatening Behavior: Analysis and Intervention*. Washington, DC: American Association on Mental Deficiency.

Mazaleski, J.L., Iwata, B.A., Rodgers, T.A., Vollmer, T.R., & Zarcone, J.R. (1994). Protective equipment as treatment for stereotypic hand mouthing: sensory extinction or punishment effects? *Journal of Applied Behavior Analysis* **27**, 345–55.

McAfee, J.K. (1987). Classroom density and the aggressive behavior of handicapped children. *Education and Treatment of Children* **10**, 134–45.

McBrien, J. (1994). The Behavioural Services Team for people with learning disabilities. In E. Emerson, P. McGill & J. Mansell (Eds.). *Severe Learning Disabilities and Challenging Behaviours: Designing High Quality Services*. London: Chapman and Hall.

McBrien, J., & Candy, S. (1998). Working with organisations, or: why won't they follow my advice? In E. Emerson, C. Hatton, J. Bromley & A. Caine (Eds.). *Clinical Psychology and People With Intellectual Disabilities*. Chichester: Wiley.

McBrien, J., & Felce, D. (1994). *Working with People Who Have Severe Learning Difficulty and Challenging Behaviour*. Clevedon: BILD Publications.

McClannahan, L.E., & Krantz, P.J. (1993). On systems-analysis in autism intervention programs. *Journal of Applied Behavior Analysis* **26**, 589–96.

McDowell, J.J. (1982). The importance of Herrnstein's mathematical statement of the law of effect for behavior therapy. *American Psychologist* **37**, 771–9.

McEachin, J.J., Smith, T., & Lovaas, O.I. (1993). Long-term outcome for children with autism who received early intensive behavioral treatment. *American Journal on Mental Retardation* **97**, 359–72.

McGee, J.J., Menolascino, F.J., Hobbs, D.C., & Menousek, P.E. (1987). *Gentle Teaching: A Non-Aversive Approach to Helping Persons with Mental Retardation*. New York: Human Sciences Press.

McGill, P. (1999). Establishing operations: implications for the assessment, treatment and prevention of problem behavior. *Journal of Applied Behavior Analysis* **32**, 393–418.

McGill, P., Clare, I., & Murphy, G. (1996). Understanding and responding to challenging behaviour: from theory to practice. *Tizard Learning Disability Review* **1**, 9–17.

McGill, P., Emerson, E., & Mansell, J. (1994). Individually designed residential provision for people with seriously challenging behaviours. In E. Emerson, P. McGill & J. Mansell (Eds.).

*Severe Learning Disabilities and Challenging Behaviours: Designing High Quality Services.* London: Chapman and Hall.

McGill, P, & Mansell, J. (1995). Community placements for people with severe and profound learning disabilities and seriously challenging behaviour: individual illustrations of issues and problems. *Journal of Mental Health* **4**, 183–98.

McGill, P., & Toogood, S. (1994). Organising community placements. In E. Emerson, P. McGill & J. Mansell (Eds.). *Severe Learning Disabilities and Challenging Behaviours: Designing High Quality Services*, pp. 119–56. London: Chapman and Hall.

McGimsey, J.F., & Favell, J.E. (1988). The effects of increased physical exercise on disruptive behavior in retarded persons. *Journal of Autism and Developmental Disorders* **18**, 167–79.

McGlynn, A.P., & Locke, B.J. (1997). A 25 year follow-up of a punishment program for severe self-injury. *Behavioral Interventions* **12**, 203–7.

Meador, D.M., & Osborn, R.G. (1992). Prevalence of severe behavior disorders in persons with mental retardation and treatment procedures used in community and institutional settings. *Behavioral Residential Treatment* **4**, 299–314.

Meinhold, P.M., & Mulick, J.A. (1990). Risks, choices and behavioral treatment. *Behavioral Residential Treatment* **5**, 29–44.

Meins, W., (1995). Symptoms of major depression in mentally retarded adults. *Journal of Intellectual Disability Research* **39**, 41–5.

Mental Health Foundation (1997). *Don't Forget Us: Children With Learning Disabilities and Severe Challenging Behaviour.* London: Mental Health Foundation.

Meyer, L.H., & Evans, I.M. (1989). *Nonaversive Interventions for Behavior Problems: A Manual for Home and Community.* New York: Teachers College Press.

Meyer, L.H., & Evans, I.M. (1993a). Meaningful outcomes in behavioral intervention: evaluating positive approaches to the remediation of challenging behaviors. In J. Reichle & D.P. Wacker (Eds.). *Communicative Alternatives to Challenging Behavior*, pp. 407–28. Baltimore: Paul H. Brookes.

Meyer, L.H., & Evans, I.M. (1993b). Science and practice in behavioral intervention: meaningful outcomes, research validity, and usable knowledge. *Journal of the Association for Persons with Severe Handicaps* **18**, 224–34.

Meyer, L.H., & Janney, R. (1989). User-friendly measures of meaningful outcomes: evaluating behavioral interventions. *Journal of the Association for Persons with Severe Handicaps* **14**, 262–70.

Michael, J.L. (1980). Flight from behavior analysis. *The Behavior Analyst* **3**, 1–21.

Michael, J. (1982). Distinguishing between discriminative and motivational functions of stimuli. *Journal of the Experimental Analysis of Behavior* **37**, 149–55.

Michael, J. (1993). Establishing operations. *The Behavior Analyst* **16**, 191–206.

Miltenberger, R.G. (1998). Methods for assessing antecedent influences on challenging behaviors. In J.K. Luiselli & M.J. Cameron (Eds.). *Antecedent Control: Innovative Approaches to Behavioral Support*, pp. 47–66. Baltimore: Paul H. Brookes.

Mitchell, G., & Hastings, R.P. (1998). Learning disability care staff's emotional reactions to aggressive challenging behaviour: development of a measurement tool. *British Journal of Clinical Psychology* **37**, 441–9.

Mithaug, D.E., & Mar, D.K. (1980). The relation between choosing and working prevocational tasks in two severely retarded young adults. *Journal of Applied Behavior Analysis* **13**, 177–82.

Molyneux, P., Emerson, E., & Caine, A. (1999). Prescription of psychotropic medication to people with intellectual disabilities in primary health care settings. *Journal of Applied Research in Intellectual Disabilities* **12**, 46–57.

Morgan, G.M., & Hastings, R.P. (1998). Special educators' understanding of challenging behaviour in children with learning disabilities: sensitivity to information about behavioural function. *Behavioural and Cognitive Psychotherapy* **26**, 43–52.

Morris, E.K. (1993). Revise and resubmit. *Journal of the Association for Persons with Severe Handicaps* **18**, 242–8.

Morris, E.K., & Midgley, B.D. (1990). Some historical and conceptual foundations of ecobehavioral analysis. In S.R. Schroeder (Ed.). *Ecobehavioral Analysis and Developmental Disabilities.* New York: Springer-Verlag.

Mulick, J.A. (1990). The ideology and science of punishment in mental retardation. *American Journal on Mental Retardation* **95**, 142–56.

Murphy, G.H. (1982). Sensory reinforcement in the mentally handicapped and autistic child: a review. *Journal of Autism and Developmental Disorders* **12**, 265–78.

Murphy, G.H. (1993). The use of aversive stimuli in treatment: the issue of consent. *Journal of Intellectual Disability Research* **37**, 211–19.

Murphy, G.H. (1994). Understanding challenging behaviour. In E. Emerson, P. McGill & J. Mansell (Eds.). *Severe Learning Disabilities and Challenging Behaviours: Designing High Quality Services*, pp. 37–68. London: Chapman and Hall.

Murphy, G.H. (1996). Self-injurious behaviour: what do we know and where are we going? *Tizard Learning Disability Review* **4**, 5–12.

Murphy, G. (1997). Understanding aggression in people with intellectual disabilities: lessons from other populations. *International Review of Research in Mental Retardation*, **21**, 33–67.

Murphy, G.H., Hall, S., Oliver, C., & Kissi-Debra, R. (1999). Identification of early self-injurious behaviour in young children with intellectual disability. *Journal of Intellectual Disability Research* **43**, 149–63.

Murphy, G.H., & Oliver, C. (1987). Decreasing undesirable behaviours. In W. Yule & J. Carr (Eds.). *Behaviour Modification for People with Mental Handicaps* (2nd Edition). London: Croom Helm.

Murphy, G.H., Oliver, C., Corbett, J. et al. (1993). Epidemiology of self-injury, characteristics of people with severe self-injury and initial treatment outcome. In C. Kiernan (Ed.). *Research to Practice? Implications of Research on the Challenging Behaviour of People with Learning Disabilities*, pp. 1–35. Kidderminster: BILD.

Murphy, G.H., & Wilson, B. (1980). Long-term outcome of contingent shock treatment for self-injurious behavior. In P. Mitler & J.M. de Jong (Eds.). *Frontiers of Knowledge in Mental Retardation, Vol II – Biomedical Aspects.* Baltimore: University Park Press.

Neef, N.A., Mace, F.C., Shea, M., & Shade, D.B. (1992). Effects of reinforcer rate and reinforcer quality on time allocation: extension of matching theory to educational settings. *Journal of Applied Behavior Analysis* **25**, 691–9.

Neef, N.A., Mace, F.C., & Shade, D. (1993). Impulsivity in students with serious emotional disturbance: the interactive effects of reinforcer rate, delay and quality. *Journal of Applied*

*Behavior Analysis* **26**, 37–52.

Neri, C.L., & Sandman, C. (1992). Relationship between diet and self-injurious behavior: a survey. *Journal of Developmental and Physical Disabilities* **4**, 189–94.

Newsom, C., Favell, J.E., & Rincover, A. (1983). Side effects of punishment. In S. Axelrod & J. Apsche (Eds.). *The Effects of Punishment on Human Behavior.* New York: Academic Press.

Newton, J.T., & Sturmey, P. (1991). The Motivation Assessment Scale: inter-rater reliability and internal consistency in a British sample. *Journal of Mental Deficiency Research* **35**, 472–4.

Newton, T.S., Ard, W.R., & Horner, R.H. (1993). Validating predicted activity preferences of individuals with severe disabilities. *Journal of Applied Behavior Analysis* **26**, 239–45.

Nissen, J.M.J.F., & Haveman, M.J. (1997). Mortality and avoidable death in people with severe self-injurious behaviour: results of a Dutch study. *Journal of Intellectual Disability Research* **41**, 252–7.

Nordquist, V.M., Twardosz, S., & McEvoy, M.A. (1991). Effects of environmental reorganization in classrooms for children with autism. *Journal of Early Intervention* **15**, 135–52.

Northup, J., Wacker, D.P., Berg, W., Kelly, L., Sasso, G., & DeRaad, A. (1994). The treatment of severe behavior problems in school settings using a technical assistance model. *Journal of Applied Behavior Analysis* **27**, 33–47.

Northup, J., Wacker, D.P., Sasso, G. et al. (1991). A brief functional analysis of aggressive and alternative behavior in an out-clinic setting. *Journal of Applied Behavior Analysis* **24**, 509–22.

Nyhan, W.L. (1994). The Lesch–Nyhan disease. In T. Thompson & D.B. Gray (Eds.). *Destructive Behavior in Developmental Disabilities: Diagnosis and Treatment*, pp. 181–97. Thousand Oaks: Sage.

O'Brien, J. (1991). Against pain as a tool in professional work on people with severe disabilities. *Disability, Handicap and Society* **6**, 81–90.

O'Brien, S., & Repp, A.C. (1990). Reinforcement-based reductive procedures: a review of 20 years of their use with persons with severe or profound mental retardation. *Journal of the Association for Persons with Severe Handicaps* **15**, 148–59.

O'Neill, R.E., Horner, R.H., Albin, R.W., Storey, K., Sprague, J.R. (1997). *Functional Analysis and Program Development For Problem Behavior.* Pacific Grove, CA: Brooks/Cole.

O'Reilly, M.F. (1995). Functional analysis and treatment of escape-maintained aggression correlated with sleep deprivation. *Journal of Applied Behavior Analysis* **28**, 225–6.

O'Reilly, M.F. (1996). Assessment and treatment of episodic self-injury: a case study. *Research in Developmental Disabilities* **17**, 349–61.

O'Reilly, M.F. (1997). Functional analysis of episodic self-injury correlated with recurrent otitis media. *Journal of Applied Behavior Analysis* 30, 165–7.

O'Reilly, M.F. (1999). Effects of presession attention on the frequency of attention maintained behavior. *Journal of Applied Behavior Analysis* **32**, 371–4.

O'Reilly, M.F., & Carey, Y. (1996). A preliminary analysis of the effects of prior classroom conditions on performance under analogue analysis conditions. *Journal of Applied Behavior Analysis* **29**, 581–4.

O'Reilly, M.F., Lancioni, G., & Emerson, E. (in press). A systematic analysis of the influence of prior social context on aggression and self-injury within analogue assessments. *Behavior Modification*.

Oliver, C. (1991). The application of analogue methodology to the functional analysis of challenging behaviour. In B. Remington (Ed.). *The Challenge of Severe Mental Handicap: A Behaviour Analytic Approach*. Chichester: Wiley.

Oliver, C. (1993). Self-injurious behaviour: from response to strategy. In C. Kiernan (Ed.). *Research to Practice? Implication of Research on the Challenging Behaviour of People with Learning Disabilities*, pp. 135–88. Clevedon: British Institute of Learning Disabilities.

Oliver, C. (1995). Self-injurious behaviour in children with learning disabilities: recent advances in assessment and intervention. *Journal of Child Psychology and Psychiatry* **30**, 909–27.

Oliver, C., Hall, S., Hales, J., & Head, D. (1996). Self-injurious behaviour and people with intellectual disabilities: assessing the behavioural knowledge and causal explanations of care staff. *Journal of Applied Research in Intellectual Disabilities* **9**, 229–39.

Oliver, C., Murphy, G.H., & Corbett, J.A. (1987). Self-injurious behaviour in people with mental handicap: a total population survey. *Journal of Mental Deficiency Research* **31**, 147–62.

Overskeid, G. (1992). Is any human behavior schedule-induced? *Psychological Record* **42**, 323–40.

Pace, G.M., Ivancic, M.T., Edwards, G.L., Iwata, B.A., & Page, T.J. (1985). Assessment of stimulus preference and reinforcer value with profoundly retarded individuals. *Journal of Applied Behavior Analysis* **18**, 249–55.

Pace, G.M., Iwata, B.A., Cowdery, G.E., Andree, P.J., & McIntyre, T. (1993). Stimulus (instructional) fading during extinction of self-injurious behavior. *Journal of Applied Behavior Analysis* **26**, 205–12.

Paisey, T.J.H., Whitney, R.B., & Hislop, P.M. (1991). Non-intrusive operant analysis of aggressive behavior in persons with mental retardation. *Behavioral Residential Treatment* **6**, 51–64.

Paisey, T.J.H., Whitney, R.B., & Moore, J. (1989). Person-treatment interactions across nonaversive response-deceleration procedures for self-injury: A case study of effects and side effects. *Behavioral Residential Treatment* **4**, 69–88.

Parrish, J.M., Cataldo, M.F., Kolko, D.J., Neef, N.A., & Egel, A.L. (1986). Experimental analysis of response covariation among compliant and inappropriate behaviors. *Journal of Applied Behavior Analysis* **19**, 241–54.

Parrish, J.M., & Roberts, M.L. (1993). Interventions based on covariation of desired and inappropriate behavior. In J. Reichle & D.P. Wacker (Eds.). *Communicative Alternatives to Challenging Behavior*. Baltimore: Paul H. Brookes.

Parsons, M.B., Reid, D.H., & Green, C.W. (1993). Preparing direct-care staff to teach people with severe disabilities: a comprehensive evaluation of an effective and acceptable training programme. *Behavioral Residential Treatment* **8**, 163–85.

Parsons, M.B., Reid, D.H., Reynolds, J. & Bumgarner, M. (1990). Effects of chosen versus assigned jobs on the work performance of persons with severe handicaps. *Journal of Applied Behavior Analysis* **23**, 253–8.

Peck, S.M., Wacker, D.P., Berg, W.K. et al. (1996). Choice-making treatment of young children's severe behavior problems. *Journal of Applied Behavior Analysis* **29**, 263–90.

Peine, H.A., Darvish, R., Adams, K., Blalelock, H., Jenson, W., & Osborne, J.G. (1995). Medical problems, maladaptive behaviors and the developmentally disabled. *Behavioral Interventions* **10**, 149–60.

Pelios, L., Morren, J., Tesch, D., & Axelrod, S. (1999). The impact of functional analysis methodology on treatment choice for self-injurious and aggressive behavior. *Journal of Applied Behavior Analysis* **32**, 185–95.

Piazza, C.C., Contrucci, S.A., Hanley, G.P., & Fisher, W.W. (1997b). Nondirective prompting and noncontingent reinforcement in the treatment of destructive behavior during hygiene routines. *Journal of Applied Behavior Analysis* **30**, 705–8.

Piazza, C.C., Fisher, W.W., Hanley, G.P., LeBlanc, L.A., Worsdell, A.S., Lindauer, S.E., & Keeney, K.M. (1998a). Treatment of pica through multiple analyses of its reinforcing functions. *Journal of Applied Behavior Analysis* **31**, 165–89.

Piazza, C.C., Fisher, W.W., Hanley, G.P., Remick, M.L., Contrucci, S.A., & Aitken, T.L. (1997c). The use of positive and negative reinforcement in the treatment of escape-maintained destructive behavior. *Journal of Applied Behavior Analysis* **30**, 279–98.

Piazza, C.C., Fisher, W.W., Hagopian, L.P., Bowman, L.G., & Toole, L. (1996). Using a choice assessment to predict reinforcer effectiveness. *Journal of Applied Behavior Analysis* **29**, 1–9.

Piazza, C.C., Hagopian, L.P., Hughes, C.R., & Fisher, W.W. (1998b). Using chronotherapy to treat severe sleep problems: a case study. *American Journal of Mental Retardation* **102**, 358–66.

Piazza, C.C., Hanley, G.P., Bowman, L.G., Rutter, J.M., Lindauer, S.E., & Cense, D.M. (1997a). Functional analysis and treatment of elopement. *Journal of Applied Behavior Analysis* **30**, 653–72.

Piazza, C.C., Hanley, G.P., & Fisher, W.W. (1996). Functional analysis and treatment of cigarette pica. *Journal of Applied Behavior Analysis* **29**, 437–50.

Pierce, K.A., & Schreibman, L. (1994). Teaching daily living skills to children with autism in unsupervised settings through pictorial self-management. *Journal of Applied Behavior Analysis* **27**, 471–81.

Pierce, W.D., & Epling, W.F. (1980). What happened to the analysis in applied behavior analysis? *The Behavior Analyst* **3**, 1–9.

Podboy, J.W., & Mallery, W.A. (1977). Caffeine reduction and behavior change in the severely retarded. *Mental Retardation* **15**, 40.

Poindexter, A.R., Cain, N.N., Clarke, D.J., Cook, E.H., Corbett, J.A., & Levita, A. (1998). Mood stabilisers. In S. Reiss & M.G. Aman (Eds.). *Psychotropic Medication and Developmental Disabilities: The International Consensus Handbook*, pp. 215–28. Ohio: Nisonger Center, Ohio State University.

Poling, A., & Ehrhardt, K. (1999). Applied behaviour analysis, social validation, and the psychopharmacology of mental retardation. *Mental Retardation and Developmental Disabilities Research Reviews* **5**, 342–7.

Poling, A., & LeSage, M. (1995). Evaluating psychotropic drugs in people with mental retardation: where are the social validity data? *American Journal of Mental Retardation* **100**, 193–200.

Pope, S.T., & Jones, R.S.P. (1996). The therapeutic effect of reactive self-monitoring on the reduction of inappropriate social and stereotypic behaviors. *British Journal of Clinical Psychology* **35**, 585–94.

Premack, D. (1959). Toward empirical behavior laws: I. Positive reinforcement. *Science* **136**,

255–7.

Pyles, D.A.M., & Bailey, J.S. (1990). Diagnosing severe behavior problems. In A. C. Repp & N.N. Singh (Eds.). *Perspectives on the Use of Nonaversive and Aversive Interventions for Persons with Developmental Disabilities*. Sycamore, IL: Sycamore Publishing Company.

Quine, L., & Pahl, J. (1985). Examining the causes of stress in families with mentally handicapped children. *British Journal of Social Work* **15**, 501–17.

Quine, L., & Pahl, J. (1991). Stress and coping in mothers caring for a child with severe learning difficulties: a test of Lazarus's transactional model of coping. *Journal of Community and Applied Psychology* **1**, 57–70.

Qureshi, H. (1992). Young adults with learning difficulties and challenging behavior: parents' views of services in the community. *Social Work and Social Services Review* **3**, 104–23.

Qureshi, H. (1993). Prevalence of challenging behaviour in adults. In *People with Learning Disability and Severe Challenging Behaviour: New Developments in Services and Therapy* (Ed. I. Fleming & B. Stenfert Kroese). Manchester University Press: Manchester.

Qureshi, H. (1994). The size of the problem. In E. Emerson, P. McGill & J. Mansell (Eds.). *Severe Learning Disabilities and Challenging Behaviours: Designing High Quality Services*. London: Chapman & Hall.

Qureshi, H. & Alborz, A. (1992). The epidemiology of challenging behaviour. *Mental Handicap Research* **5**, 130–45.

Racusin, R., Kovner-Kline, K., & King, B.H. (1999). Selective serotonin reuptake inhibitors in intellectual disability. *Mental Retardation and Developmental Disabilities Research Reviews* **5**, 264–9.

Rast, J., Johnston, J.M., & Drum, C. (1984). A parametric analysis of the relationship between food quantity and rumination. *Journal of the Experimental Analysis of Behavior* **41**, 125–34.

Rast, J., Johnston, J.M., Drum, C., & Conrin, J. (1981). The relation of food quantity to rumination behavior. *Journal of Applied Behavior Analysis* **14**, 121–30.

Raynes, N.V., Wright, K., Shiell, A., & Pettipher, C. (1994). *The Cost and Quality of Community Residential Care: an Evaluation of the Services for Adults with Learning Disabilities*. London: David Fulton Publishers.

Realon, R.E., & Konarski, E.A. (1993). Using decelerative contingencies to reduce the self-injurious behavior of people with multiple handicaps: the effects of response satiation? *Research in Developmental Disabilities* **14**, 341–57.

Reese, R.M., Sherman, J.A., & Sheldon, J. (1984). Reducing agitated–disruptive behavior of mentally retarded residents of community group homes: the role of self-recording and peer prompted self-recording. *Analysis and Intervention in Developmental Disabilities* **4**, 91–107.

Reichle, J., & Wacker, D.P. (1993). *Communicative Alternatives to Challenging Behavior*. Baltimore: Paul H. Brookes.

Reid, A.H. (1982). *The Psychiatry of Mental Handicap*. Oxford: Blackwell.

Reid, A.H., & Ballinger, B.R. (1995). Behaviour symptoms among severely and profoundly mentally retarded patients. *British Journal of Psychiatry* **167**, 452–5.

Reid, A.H., Naylor, G.J., & Kay, D.S.G. (1981). A double-blind, placebo controlled crossover trial of carbamazepine in overactive severely mentally handicapped patients. *Psychological*

*Medicine* **11**, 109–13.

Reid, D.H., Everson, J.M., & Green, C.W. (1999). A systematic evaluation of preferences identified through person-centred planning for people with profound multiple disabilities. *Journal of Applied Behavior Analysis* **32**, 467–78.

Reid, D.H., & Green, C.W. (1990). Staff training. In J.L. Matson (Ed.). *Handbook of Behavior Modification with the Mentally Retarded.* New York: Plenum.

Reid, D.H., Parsons, M.B., & Green, C.W. (1989a). *Staff Management in Human Services: Behavioral Research and Application.* Springfield, IL: Charles C. Thomas.

Reid, D.H., Parsons, M.B., & Green, C.W. (1989b). Treating aberrant behavior through effective staff management: a developing technology. In Cipani, E. (Ed.). *The Treatment of Severe Behavior Disorders: Behavior Analysis Approaches.* Washington, DC: American Association on Mental Retardation.

Reiss, S. & Aman, M.G. (1998). *Psychotropic Medication and Developmental Disabilities: The International Consensus Handbook.* Ohio: Nisonger Center, Ohio State University.

Reiss, S., & Rojahn, J. (1993). Joint occurrence of depression and aggression in children and adults with mental retardation. *Journal of Intellectual Disability Research,* **37**, 287–94.

Remington, B. (1991). *The Challenge of Severe Mental Handicap: A Behaviour Analytic Approach.* Chichester: Wiley.

Repp, A.C., Felce, D., & Barton, L.E. (1988). Basing the treatment of stereotypic and self-injurious behaviors on hypotheses of their causes. *Journal of Applied Behavior Analysis* **21**, 281–9.

Repp, A.C., & Singh, N.N. (1990). *Perspectives on the Use of Nonaversive and Aversive Interventions for Persons with Developmental Disabilities.* Sycamore, IL: Sycamore Publishing Company.

Richman, D.M., & Hagopian, L.P. (1999). On the effects of 'quality' of attention in the functional analysis of destructive behavior. *Research in Developmental Disabilities* **20**, 51–62.

Richman, D.M., Wacker, D.P., Asmus, J.M., & Casey, S.D. (1998). Functional analysis and extinction of different behavior problems exhibited by the same individual. *Journal of Applied Behavior Analysis* **31**, 475–8.

Richman, D.M., Wacker, D.P., Asmus, J.M., Casey, S.D., & Andelman, M. (1999). Further analysis of problem behavior in response class hierarchies. *Journal of Applied Behavior Analysis* **32**, 269–83.

Richmond, G., Schroeder, S.R., & Bickel, W. (1986). Tertiary prevention of attrition related to self-injurious behaviors. In K.D. Gadow (Ed.). *Advances in Learning and Behavioral Disabilities,* Volume 5. London: JAI Press.

Ricketts, R.W., Goza, A.B., & Matese, M. (1992). Case study: effects of naltrexone and SIBIS on self-injury. *Behavioral Residential Treatment* **7**, 315–26.

Rinck, C. (1998). Epidemiology and psychoactive medication. In S. Reiss & M.G. Aman (Eds.). *Psychotropic Medication and Developmental Disabilities: The International Consensus Handbook,* pp. 31–44. Ohio: Nisonger Center, Ohio State University.

Rincover, A., Cook, A., Peoples, A., & Packard, D. (1979). Sensory extinction and sensory reinforcement principles for programming multiple adaptive behavior change. *Journal of*

*Applied Behavior Analysis* **12**, 221–33.

Rincover, A., & Devany, J. (1982). The application of sensory extinction procedures to self-injury. *Analysis and Intervention in Developmental Disabilities* **2**, 67–81.

Rincover, A., Newsom, C.D., & Carr, E.G. (1979). Use of sensory extinction procedures in the treatment of compulsive-like behavior of developmentally disabled children. *Journal of Consulting and Clinical Psychology* **47**, 695–701.

Ringdahl, J.E., Vollmer, T.R., Marcus, B.A., & Roane, H.S. (1997). An analogue evaluation of environmental enrichment: the role of stimulus preference. *Journal of Applied Behavior Analysis* **30**, 203–16.

Risley, T. (1996). Get a life! Positive behavioral intervention for challenging behavior through life arrangement and life coaching. In L.K. Koegel, R.L. Koegel & G. Dunlap (Eds.). *Positive Behavioral Support: Including People With Difficult Behavior in the Community*, pp. 425–38. Baltimore: Paul H. Brookes.

Roane, H.S., Lerman, D.C., Kelley, M.E., & Van Camp, C.M. (1999). Within-session patterns of responding during functional analyses: the role of establishing operations in clarifying behavioral function. *Research in Developmental Disabilities* **20**, 73–89.

Roane, H., Vollmer, T.R., Ringdahl, J.E., & Marcus, B.A. (1998). Evaluation of a brief stimulus preference assessment. *Journal of Applied Behavior Analysis* **31**, 605–20.

Robertson, J., Emerson, E., Gregory, N., Hatton, C., & Kessissoglou, S. (in press a). Receipt of psychotropic medication by people with intellectual disabilities in residential settings. *Journal of Intellectual Disability Research*

Robertson, J., Emerson, E., Gregory, N. et al. (in press b). Social networks of people with intellectual disabilities in residential settings. *Mental Retardation.*

Robertson, J., Emerson, E., Hatton, C. et al. (in press c). Environmental opportunities for exercising self-determination in residential settings. *Journal of the Association for Persons with Severe Handicaps.*

Rojahn, J. (1986). Self-injurious and stereotypic behavior of noninstitutionalized mentally retarded people: prevalence and classification. *American Journal of Mental Deficiency* **91**, 268–76.

Rojahn, J. (1994). Epidemiology and topographic taxonomy of self-injurious behavior. In T. Thompson & D.B. Gray (Eds.). *Destructive Behavior in Developmental Disabilities: Diagnosis and Treatment*, pp. 49–67. Thousand Oaks: Sage.

Rojahn, J., & Marshburn, E.C. (1992). Facial screening and visual occlusion. In J.K. Luiselli, J.K. Matson & N.N. Singh (Eds.). *Self-Injurious Behavior: Analysis, Assessment and Treatment.* New York: Springer-Verlag.

Rolider, A., & Van Houten, R. (1990). The role of reinforcement in reducing inappropriate behavior: some myths and misconceptions. In A. C. Repp & N.N. Singh (Eds.). *Perspectives on the Use of Nonaversive and Aversive Interventions for Persons with Developmental Disabilities.* Sycamore, IL: Sycamore.

Romanczyk, R.G. (1986). Self-injurious behavior: conceptualization, assessment, and treatment. In K.D. Gadow (Ed.). *Advances in Learning and Behavioral Disabilities*, Volume 5. London: JAI Press.

Romanczyk, R.G., Lockshin, S., & O'Connor, J. (1992). Psychophysiology and issues of anxiety and arousal. In J.K. Luiselli, J.L. Matson & N.N. Singh (Eds.). *Self-Injurious Behavior: Analysis, Assessment and Treatment*, pp. 93–121. New York: Springer-Verlag.

Romanczyk, R.G., & Matthews, A.J. (1998). Physiological state as antecedent: utilization in functional analysis. In J.K. Luiselli & M.J. Cameron (Eds.). *Antecedent Control: Innovative Approaches to Behavioral Support*, pp. 115–38. Baltimore: Paul H. Brookes.

Rosales-Ruiz, J., & Baer, D.M. (1997). Behavioral cusps: a developmental and pragmatic concept for behavior analysis. *Journal of Applied Behavior Analysis* **30**, 533–44.

Roscoe, E.M., Iwata, B.A., & Goh, H-L. (1998). A comparison of noncontingent reinforcement and sensory extinction as treatments for self-injurious behavior. *Journal of Applied Behavior Analysis* **31**, 635–46.

Rose, J. (1996). Anger management: a group treatment for people with mental retardation. *Journal of Developmental and Physical Disabilities* **8**, 133–49.

Rose, J., & West, C. (in press). Assessment of anger in people with intellectual disabilities. *Journal of Applied Research in Intellectual Disabilities*

Rose, J., West, C., & Clifford, D. (in press). Group interventions for anger in people with intellectual disabilities. *Research in Developmental Disabilities*

Rosine, L.P.C., & Martin, G.L. (1983). Self-management training to decrease undesirable behavior of mentally handicapped adults. *Rehabilitation Psychology* **28**, 195–205.

Rudolph, C., Lakin, K.C., Oslund, J.M., & Larson, W. (1998). Evaluation of outcomes and cost-effectiveness of a community behavioral support and crisis response demonstration project. *Mental Retardation* **36**, 187–97.

Rudrud, E.H., Ziarnik, J.P., & Coleman, G. (1984). Reduction of tongue protrusion of a 24-year-old woman with Downs Syndrome through self-monitoring. *American Journal of Mental Deficiency* **88**, 647–52.

Ruedrich, S., & Erhardt, L. (1999). Beta-adrenergic blockers in mental retardation and developmental disabilities. *Mental Retardation and Developmental Disabilities Research Reviews* **5**, 290–8.

Rush, A.J. & Frances, A. (2000). Treatment of psychiatric and behavioral problems in mental retardation. *American Journal on Mental Retardation* **105**, 158–228.

Rusch, R.G., Hall, J.C., & Griffin, H.C. (1986). Abuse provoking characteristics of institutionalized mentally retarded individuals. *American Journal of Mental Deficiency* **90**, 618–24.

Russo, D.C., Cataldo, M.F., & Cushing, P.J. (1981). Compliance training and behavioral covariation in the treatment of multiple behavior problems. *Journal of Applied Behavior Analysis* **14**, 209–22.

Ryan, E.P., Helsel, W.J., Lubetsky, M.J., Miewald, B.K., Hersen, M., & Bridge, J. (1989). Use of naltrexone in reducing self-injurious behavior: a single case analysis. *Journal of the Multihandicapped Person* **2**, 295–309.

Sackett, G.P. (1979). The lag sequential analysis of contingency and cyclicity in behavioral interaction research. In J.D. Osofsky (Ed.). *Handbook of Infant Development*. New York: Wiley.

Sackett, G.P. (1987). Analysis of sequential social interaction data: some issues, recent developments, and a causal inference model. In J.D. Osofsky (Ed.). *Handbook of Infant Development* (2nd Edition). New York: Wiley.

Sandman, C.A. (1990/1991). The opiate hypothesis in autism and self-injury. *Journal of Child and Adolescent Psychopharmacology* **1**, 237–48.

Sandman, C., & Barron, J.L. (1992). Paradoxical response to sedative/hypnotics in patients with self-injurious behavior and stereotypy. *Journal of Developmental and Physical Disabilities* **4**, 307–16.

Sandman, C.A., Barron, J.L., Chicz-DeMet, A., & DeMet, E.M. (1990a). Plasma β-endorphin levels in patients with self-injurious behavior and stereotypy. *American Journal on Mental Retardation* **95**, 84–92.

Sandman, C.A., Barron, J.L., & Colman, H. (1990b). An orally administered opiate blocker, naltrexone, attenuates self-injurious behavior. *American Journal on Mental Retardation* **95**, 93–102.

Sandman, C.A., & Hetrick, W.P. (1995). Opiate mechanisms in self-injury. *Mental Retardation and Developmental Disabilities Research Reviews* **1**, 130–6.

Sandman, C.A., Hetrick, W.P., Taylor, D.V., & Chicz-DeMet, A. (1997). Dissociation of POMC peptides after self-injury predicts responses to centrally acting opiate blocker. *American Journal of Mental Retardation* **102**, 182–99.

Sandman, C.A., Spence, M.A., & Smith, M. (1999). Proopiomelanocortin (POMC) disregulation and response to opiate blockers. *Mental Retardation and Developmental Disabilities Research Reviews* **5**, 314–21.

Sandman, C.A., Thompson, T., Barrett, R.P. et al. (1998). Opiate blockers. In S. Reiss & M.G. Aman (Eds.). *Psychotropic Medication and Developmental Disabilities: The International Consensus Handbook*, pp. 291–302. Ohio: Nisonger Center, Ohio State University.

Sasso, G.M., Reimers, T.M., Cooper, L.J. et al. (1992). Use of descriptive and experimental analyses to identify the functional properties of aberrant behavior in school settings. *Journal of Applied Behavior Analysis* **25**, 809–21.

Saunders, R.R., & Saunders, M.D. (1998). Supported routines. In J.K. Luiselli & M.J. Cameron (Eds.). *Antecedent Control: Innovative Approaches to Behavioral Support*, pp. 245–72. Baltimore: Paul H. Brookes.

Saunders, R.R., Saunders, M.D., Brewer, A., & Roach, T. (1996). The reduction of self-injury in two adolescents with profound retardation by the establishment of a supported routine. *Behavioral Interventions* **11**, 59–86.

Saunders, R.R., & Spradlin, J.E. (1991). A supported routines approach to active treatment for enhancing independence, competence and self-worth. *Behavioral Residential Treatment* **6**, 11–37.

Saxby, H., & Morgan, H. (1993). Behaviour problems in children with learning disabilities: to what extent do they exist and are they a problem? *Child: Care, Health & Development* **19**, 149–57.

Schalock, R.L. (1996). *Quality of Life: Volume 1 – Conceptualization and Measurement*. Washington, DC: American Association on Mental Retardation.

Schalock, R.L. (1999). *Adaptive Behavior and Its Measurement*. Washington: American Association on Mental Retardation.

Schalock, R.L., Harper, R.S., & Genung, T. (1981). Community integration of mentally retarded adults: community placement and program success. *American Journal of Mental Deficiency*

**85**, 478–88.

Schlosser, R.W., & Goetze, H. (1992). Effectiveness and treatment validity of interventions addressing self-injurious behavior: from narrative reviews to meta-analyses. *Advances in Learning and Behavioral Disabilities* **7**, 135–76.

Schneider, M.J., Bijam-Schulte, A.M., Janssen, C.G.C., & Stolk, J. (1995). The origin of self-injurious behaviour of children with mental retardation. *British Journal of Developmental Disabilities* **42**, 136–48.

Schreibman, L., Stahmer, A.C., & Pierce, K.L. (1996). Alternative applications of pivotal response training. In L.K. Koegel, R.L. Koegel & G. Dunlap (Eds.). *Positive Behavioral Support: Including People With Difficult Behavior in the Community*, pp. 403–24. Baltimore: Paul H. Brookes.

Schroeder, S.R. (1991). Self-injury and stereotypy. In J.L. Matson & J.A. Mulick (Eds.). *Handbook of Mental Retardation.* New York: Pergamon.

Schroeder, S.R. (1999). Psychopharmacotherapy in developmental disabilities. *Mental Retardation and Developmental Disabilities Research Reviews* **5**, 251–369.

Schroeder, S.R., Bickel, W.K., & Richmond, G. (1986). Primary and secondary prevention of self-injurious behaviors: a life-long problem. In K.D. Gadow (Eds.). *Advances in Learning and Behavioral Disabilities* (Volume 5). Little, Brown & Co.: Boston.

Schroeder, S.R., Hammock, R.G., Mulick, J.A. et al. (1995). Clinical trials of D1 and D2 dopamine modulating drugs and self-injury in mental retardation and developmental disability. *Mental Retardation and Developmental Disabilities Research Reviews* **1**, 1120–9.

Schroeder, S.R., Kanoy, R.C., Mulick, J.A. et al. (1982). Environmental antecedents which affect management and maintenance of programs for self-injurious behavior. In J.H. Hollis & C.E. Meyers (Eds.). *Life-Threatening Behavior: Analysis and Intervention.* Washington, DC: American Association on Mental Deficiency.

Schroeder, S.R., & MacLean, W. (1987). If it isn't one thing it's another: experimental analysis of covariation in behavior management data of severe behavior disturbances. In S. Landesman & P. Vietze (Eds.). *Living Environments and Mental Retardation.* Washington, DC: American Association on Mental Retardation.

Schroeder, S.R., Rojahn, J., & Oldenquist, A. (1991). Treatment of destructive behaviors among people with mental retardation and developmental disabilities: overview of the problem. In National Institute of Health (Ed.). *Treatment of Destructive Behaviors in Persons with Developmental Disabilities.* Washington, DC: US Department of Health and Human Services.

Schroeder, S.R., Schroeder, C.S., Smith, B., & Dalldorf, J. (1978). Prevalence of self-injurious behaviors in a large state facility for the retarded: a three year follow-up. *Journal of Autism and Childhood Schizophrenia* **8**, 261–9.

Schroeder, S.R., & Tessel, R. (1994). Dopaminergic and serotonergic mechanisms in self-injury and aggression. In T. Thompson & D.B. Gray (Eds.). *Destructive Behavior in Developmental Disabilities: Diagnosis and Treatment.* Thousand Oaks: Sage.

Schwartz, I.S., & Baer, D.M. (1991). Social validity assessments: is current practice state of the art? *Journal of Applied Behavior Analysis* **24**, 189–204.

Scorer, S., Cale, T., Wilkinson, L., Pollock, P., & Hargan, J. (1993). Challenging behaviour project team: a six month pilot project evaluation. *Mental Handicap* **21**, 49–53.

Scotti, J.R., Evans, I., Meyer, L., & DiBenedetto, A. (1991a). Individual repertoires as behavioural systems: implications for program design and evaluation. In B. Remington (Ed.) *The Challenge of Severe Mental Handicap: A Behaviour Analytic Approach.* Chichester: Wiley.

Scotti, J.R., Evans, I.M., Meyer, L.H., & Walker, P. (1991b). A meta-analysis of behavioral research with problem behavior: treatment validity and standards of practice. *American Journal of Mental Retardation* **93**, 233–56.

Scotti, J.R., & Meyer, L.H. (1999). *Behavioral Intervention.* Baltimore: Brookes.

Scotti, J.R., Ujcich, K.J., Weigle, K.A., Holland, C.M., & Kirk, K.S. (1996). Interventions with challenging behavior of persons with developmental disabilities: a review of current research practices. *Journal of the Association For Persons With Severe Handicaps* **21**, 123–34.

Severence, L.J., & Gastrom, L.L. (1977). Effects of the label 'mentally retarded' on causal explanations for success and failure outcomes. *American Journal on Mental Deficiency* **81**, 547–55.

Seys, D., & Duker, P. (1988). Effects of staff management on the quality of residential care for mentally retarded individuals. *American Journal on Mental Retardation* **93**, 290–9.

Shirley, M.J., Iwata, B.A., & Kahng, S.W. (1999). False-positive maintenance of self-injurious behavior by access to tangible reinforcers. *Journal of Applied Behavior Analysis* **32**, 201–4.

Shirley, M.L., Iwata, B.A., Kahng, S.W., Mazaleski, J.L., & Lerman, D.C. (1997). Does functional communication training compete with ongoing contingencies of reinforcement? An analysis during response acquisition and maintenance. *Journal of Applied Behavior Analysis* **30**, 93–104.

Shoham-Vardi, I., Davidson, P.W., Cain, N.N. et al. (1996). Factors predicting re-referral following crisis intervention for community-based persons with developmental disabilities and behavioral and psychiatric disorders. *American Journal of Mental Retardation* **101**, 109–17.

Shore, B.A., Iwata, B.A., Vollmer, T.R., Lerman, D.C., & Zarcone, J.R. (1995). Pyramidal staff training in the extension of treatment for severe behavior disorders. *Journal of Applied Behavior Analysis* **28**, 323–32.

Shukla, S., & Albin, R.W. (1996). Effects of extinction alone and extinction plus functional communication training on covariation of problem behavior. *Journal of Applied Behavior Analysis* **29**, 565–8.

Sidman, M. (1986). Functional analysis of emergent verbal classes. In T. Thompson & M.D. Zeilor (Eds.). *Analysis and Integration of Behavioral Units.* Hillsdale, NJ: Lawrence Erlbaum Associates.

Sidman, M. (1989). *Coercion and its Fallout.* Boston: Authors' Cooperative.

Sigafoos, J. (1998). Choice making and personal selection strategies. In J.K. Luiselli & M.J. Cameron (Eds.). *Antecedent Control: Innovative Approaches to Behavioral Support*, pp. 187–222. Baltimore: Paul H. Brookes.

Sigafoos, J. (in press). Communication development and aberrant behavior in children with developmental disabilities. *Education and Training in Mental Retardation and Developmental Disabilities.*

Sigafoos, J., & Dempsey, R. (1992). Assessing choice making among children with multiple disabilities. *Journal of Applied Behavior Analysis* **25**, 747–55.

Sigafoos, J, & Kerr, M. (1994). Provision of leisure activities for the reduction of challenging behavior. *Behavioral Interventions* **9**, 43–53.

Sigafoos, J., Kerr, M., & Roberts, D. (1994). Interrater reliability of the Motivation Assessment Scale: failure to replicate with aggressive behavior. *Research in Developmental Disabilities* **15**, 333–42.

Sigafoos, J., & Tucker, M. (in press). Brief assessment and treatment of multiple challenging behaviors. *Behavioral Interventions*

Singer, G.H.S., Singer, J., & Horner, R.H. (1987). Using pretask requests to increase the probability of compliance for students with severe disabilities. *Journal of the Association for Persons with Severe Handicaps* **12**, 287–91.

Singh, A.N., Kleynhans, D., & Barton, G. (1998). Selective serotonin re-uptake inhibitors in the treatment of self-injurious behaviour in adults with mental retardation. *Human Psychopharmacology–Clinical and Experimental* **13**, 267–70.

Singh, N.N. (1997) (Ed.) *Prevention and Treatment of Severe Behavior Problems: Models and Methods in Developmental Disabilities.* Baltimore: Paul H. Brookes.

Singh, N.N., Donatelli, L.S., Best, A. et al. (1993a). Factor structure of the Motivation Assessment Schedule. *Journal of Intellectual Disability Research* **37**, 65–74.

Singh, N.N., & Repp, A.C. (1989). The behavioural and pharmacological management of problem behaviours in people with mental retardation. *Irish Journal of Psychology* **9**, 264–85.

Singh, Y.N., Ricketts, R.W., Ellis, C.R., & Singh, N.N. (1993b). Opioid antagonists I: pharmacology and rationale for use in treating self-injury. *Journal of Developmental and Physical Disabilities* **5**, 5–16.

Singh, N.N., Singh, Y.N., & Ellis, C.R. (1992). Psychopharmacology of self-injury. In *Self-Injurious Behavior: Analysis, Assessment and Treatment*, pp. 307–51 (Eds. J.K. Luiselli, J.L. Matson & N.N. Singh). Springer-Verlag: New York.

Singh, N.N, Watson, J.E., & Winton, A.S.W. (1986). Treating self-injury: water mist spray versus facial screening or forced arm exercise. *Journal of Applied Behavior Analysis* **19**, 403–10.

Singh, N.N., Winton, A.S.W., & Dawson, M.J. (1982). Suppression of anti-social behavior by facial screening using multiple baseline and alternating treatments designs. *Behavior Therapy* **13**, 511–20.

Skinner, B.F. (1953). *Science and Human Behavior.* New York: MacMillan.

Skinner, B.F. (1966). An operant analysis of problem solving. In B. Klienmuntz (Ed.). *Problem Solving: Research, Methods and Theory.* New York: Wiley.

Skinner, B.F. (1971). *Beyond Freedom and Dignity.* New York: Knopf.

Slifer, K.J., Ivancic, M.T., Parrish, J.M., Page, T.J., & Burgio, L. (1986). Assessment and treatment of multiple behavior problems exhibited by a profoundly retarded adolescent. *Journal of Behavior Therapy and Experimental Psychiatry* **17**, 203–13.

Sloper, P., Knussen, C., Turner, S., & Cunningham, C. (1991). Factors relating to stress and satisfaction with life in families of children with Down's syndrome. *Journal of Child Psychology and Psychiatry* **32**, 655–76.

Smith, M.D. (1985). Managing the aggressive and self-injurious behavior of adults disabled by autism. *Journal of the Association for Persons with Severe Handicaps* **10**, 228–32.

Smith, M.D., & Coleman, D. (1986). Managing the behavior of adults with autism in the job setting. *Journal of Autism and Developmental Disorders* **16**, 145–54.

Smith, R.G., & Iwata, B.A. (1997). Antecedent influences on behavior disorders. *Journal of Applied Behavior Analysis* **30**, 343–75.

Smith, R.G., Iwata, B.A., Goh, H-L., & Shore, B.A. (1995a). Analysis of establishing operations for self-injury maintained by escape. *Journal of Applied Behavior Analysis* **28**, 515–35.

Smith, R.G., Iwata, B.A., & Shore, B.A. (1995b). Effects of subject- versus experimenter-selected reinforcers on the behavior of individuals with profound developmental disabilities. *Journal of Applied Behavior Analysis* **28**, 61–71.

Smith, R.G., Iwata, B.A., Vollmer, T.R., & Zarcone, J.R. (1993a). Experimental analysis and treatment of multiply controlled self-injury. *Journal of Applied Behavior Analysis* **26**, 183–96.

Smith, T., Eikeseth, S., Klevstrand, M., & Lovaas, O.I. (1997). Intensive behavioral treatment for preschoolers with severe mental retardation and pervasive developmental disorder. *American Journal of Mental Retardation* **102**, 238–49.

Smith, T., McEachin, J.J., & Lovaas, O.I. (1993b). Comments on replication and evaluation of outcome. *American Journal on Mental Retardation* **97**, 385–91.

Solnick, J.V., Rincover, A., & Peterson, C.R. (1977). Some determinants of the reinforcing and punishing effects of timeout. *Journal of Applied Behavior Analysis* **10**, 415–24.

Sovner, R., Fox, C.J., Lowry, M.J., & Lowry, M.A. (1993). Fluoxetine treatment of depression and associated self-injury in two adults with mental retardation. *Journal of Intellectual Disability Research* **37**, 301–11.

Sovner, R., & Hurley, D.A. (1983). Do the mentally retarded suffer from affective illness? *Archives of General Psychiatry* **40**, 61–7.

Sovner, R., Pary, R.J., Dosen, A. et al. (1998). Antidepressants. In S. Reiss & M.G. Aman (Eds.). *Psychotropic Medication and Developmental Disabilities: The International Consensus Handbook*, pp. 179–200. Ohio: Nisonger Center, Ohio State University.

Sprague, J.R., & Horner, R.H. (1992). Covariation within functional response classes: implications for treatment of severe problem behavior. *Journal of Applied Behavior Analysis* **25**, 735–45.

Sprague, R.L., & Werry, J.S. (1971). Methodology of psychopharmacological studies with the retarded. In N. Ellis (Ed.). *International Review of Research in Mental Retardation* (Volume 5). New York: Academic Press.

Spreat, S., & Connelly, L. (1996). Reliability analysis of the Motivation Assessment Scale. *American Journal of Mental Retardation* **100**, 528–32.

Spreat, S., Lipinski, D., Hill, J., & Halpin, M.E. (1986). Safety indices associated with the use of contingent restraint procedures. *Applied Research in Mental Retardation* **7**, 475–81.

Staddon, J.E.R. (1977). Schedule-induced behavior. In W.K. Honig & J.E.R. Staddon (Eds.). *Handbook of Operant Behavior*. Englewood Cliffs, NJ: Prentice Hall.

Stahmer, A., & Schreibman, L. (1992). Teaching children with autism appropriate play in unsupervised settings using a self-management treatment package. *Journal of Applied Behavior Analysis* **25**, 447–59.

Stancliffe, R.J., Hayden, M.F., & Lakin, K.C. (1999). Interventions for challenging behavior in residential settings. *American Journal of Mental Retardation* **104**, 364–75.

Steege, M.W., Wacker, D.P., Berg, W.K., Cigrand, K.K., & Cooper, L.J. (1989). The use of behavioral assessment to prescribe and evaluate treatments for severely handicapped children. *Journal of Applied Behavior Analysis* **22**, 23–33.

Steege, M.W., Wacker, D.P., Cigrand, K.C. et al. (1990). Use of negative reinforcement in the treatment of self-injurious behavior. *Journal of Applied Behavior Analysis* **23**, 459–67.

Steen, P.L., & Zuriff, G.E. (1977). The use of relaxation in the treatment of self-injurious behavior. *Journal of Behavior Therapy and Experimental Psychiatry* **8**, 447–8.

Stenfert Kroese, B., & Fleming, I. (1993). Prevalence and persistency of challenging behaviour in children. In I. Fleming & B. Stenfert Kroese (Eds.). *People with Learning Disability and Severe Challenging Behaviour: New Developments in Services and Therapy.* Manchester: Manchester University Press.

Stolz, S. (1981). Adoption of innovations from applied behavioral research: 'Does anybody care?'. *Journal of Applied Behavior Analysis* **14**, 491–505.

Stores, R., Stores, G., Fellows, B., & Buckley, S. (1998). Daytime behaviour problems and maternal stress in children with Down's syndrome, their siblings, and non-intellectually disabled and other intellectually disabled peers. *Journal of Intellectual Disability Research* **42**, 228–37.

Stromer, R., Mackay, H.A., & Remington, B. (1996). Naming, the formation of stimulus classes, and applied behavior analysis. *Journal of Applied Behavior Analysis* **29**, 409–31.

Sturmey, P. (1995). Analog baselines: a critical review of the methodology. *Research in Developmental Disabilities* **16**, 269–84.

Sturmey, P., Carlsen, A., Crisp, A.G., & Newton, J.T. (1988). A functional analysis of multiple aberrant responses: a refinement and extension of Iwata et al's methodology. *Journal of Mental Deficiency Research* **32**, 31–46.

Suen, H.K., & Ary, D. (1989). *Analyzing Quantitative Behavioral Observation Data.* Hillsdale, NJ: Lawrence Erlbaum Associates.

Symons, F.J., Butler, M.G., Sanders, M.D., Feurer, I.D., & Thompson, T. (1999b). Self-injurious behavior and Prader–Willi syndrome: behavioural forms and body locations. *American Journal of Mental Retardation* **104**, 260–9.

Symons, F.J., Fox, N.D., & Thompson, T. (1998). Functional communication training and naltrexone treatment of self-injurious behaviour: an experimental case study. *Journal of Applied Research in Intellectual Disabilities* **11**, 273–92.

Symons, F.J., Koppekin, A., & Wehby, J.H. (1999a). Treatment of self-injurious behavior and quality of life for persons with mental retardation. *Mental Retardation* **37**, 297–307.

Symons, F.J., & MacLean, W.E. (2000). Analyzing and treating severe behavior problems in people with developmental disabilities: observational methods using computer-assisted technology. In T. Thompson, D. Felce & F. Symons (Eds.). *Computer Assisted Behavioral Observation Methods for Developmental Disabilities.* Baltimore: Paul H. Brookes.

Symons, F.J., & Thompson, T. (1997). Self-injurious behaviour and body site preference. *Journal of Intellectual Disability Research* **41**, 456–68.

Talkington, L., & Riley, J. (1971). Reduction diets and aggression in institutionalized mentally retarded patients. *American Journal of Mental Deficiency* **76**, 370–2.

Tate, B.G., & Baroff, G.S. (1966). Aversive control of self-injurious behavior in a psychotic boy.

*Behaviour Research and Therapy* **4**, 281–7.

Tausig, M. (1985). Factors in family decision making about placement for developmentally disabled adults. *American Journal of Mental Deficiency* **89**, 352–61.

Taylor, D.V., Rush, D., Hetrick, W.P., & Sandman, C. (1993a). Self-injurious behavior within the menstrual cycle of women with mental retardation. *American Journal on Mental Retardation* **97**, 659–64.

Taylor, D.V., Hetrick, W.P., Neri, C.L., Touchette, P., Barron, J.L., & Sandman, C.A. (1991). Effect of naltrexone on self-injurious behavior, learning and activity: a case study. *Pharmacology Biochemistry and Behavior* **40**, 79–82.

Taylor, D.V., Sandman, C.A., Touchette, P., Hetrick, W.P., & Barron, J.L. (1993b). Naltrexone improves learning and attention in self-injurious individuals with developmental disabilities. *Journal of Developmental and Physical Disabilities* **5**, 29–42.

Taylor, I., & O'Reilly, M.F. (1997). Toward a functional analysis of private verbal self-regulation. *Journal of Applied Behavior Analysis* **30**, 43–58.

Taylor, J.C., & Carr, E.G. (1993). Reciprocal social influences in the analysis and intervention of severe challenging behavior. In J. Reichle & D.P. Wacker (Eds.). *Communicative Alternatives to Challenging Behavior*, pp. 63–82. Baltimore: Paul H. Brookes.

Taylor, J.C., & Carr, E.G. (1994). Severe problem behaviors of children with developmental disabilities: reciprocal social influences. In T. Thompson & D.B. Gray (Eds.). *Destructive Behavior in Developmental Disabilities*, pp. 274–91. Thousand Oaks: Sage.

Taylor, J.C., & Romanczyk, R.G. (1994). Generating hypotheses about the function of student problem behavior by observing teacher behavior. *Journal of Applied Behavior Analysis* **27**, 251–65.

Tessel, R.E., Schroeder, S.R., Stodgell, C.J., & Loupe, P.S. (1995). Rodent models of mental retardation: self-injury, aberrant behavior and stress. *Mental Retardation and Developmental Disabilities Research Reviews* **1**, 99–103.

Thompson, R.H., Fisher, W.W., Piazza, C.C., & Kuhn, D.E. (1998). The evaluation and treatment of aggression maintained by attention and automatic reinforcement. *Journal of Applied Behavior Analysis* **31**, 103–16.

Thompson, S., & Emerson, E. (1995). Inter-observer agreement on the Motivation Assessment Scale: another failure to replicate. *Mental Handicap Research* **8**, 203–8.

Thompson, T., Egli, M., Symons, F., & Delaney, D. (1994a). Neurobehavioral mechanisms of drug action in developmental disabilities. In T. Thompson & D.B. Gray (Eds.). *Destructive Behavior in Developmental Disabilities: Diagnosis and Treatment*, pp. 133–80. Thousand Oaks: Sage.

Thompson, T., Felce, D. & Symons, F. (2000). *Computer Assisted Behavioral Observation Methods for Developmental Disabilities*. Baltimore: Paul H. Brookes.

Thompson, T., Hackenberg, T., Cerutti, D., Baker, D., & Axtell, S. (1994b). Opioid antagonist effects on self-injury in adults with mental retardation: response form and location as determinants of medication effects. *American Journal of Mental Retardation* **99**, 85–102.

Thompson, T., Hackenberg, T., & Schaal, D. (1991). Pharmacological treatments for behavior problems in developmental disabilities. In U.S. Department of Health and Human Services (Ed.). *Treatment of Destructive Behaviors in Persons with Developmental Disabilities*, pp. 343–445. Bethesda, MD: National Institutes of Health.

Thompson, T., Symons, F.J., Delaney, D., & England, C. (1995). Self-injurious behavior as endogenous neurochemical self-administration. *Mental Retardation and Developmental Disabilities Research Reviews* **1**, 137–48.

Timberlake, W. (1980). A molar equilibrium theory of learned performance. In G. Bower (Ed.). *The Psychology of Learning and Motivation* (Volume 14), pp. 1–58. New York: Academic Press.

Tincani, M.J., Castrogiavanni, A., & Axelrod, S. (1999). A comparison of the effectiveness of brief versus traditional functional analyses. *Research in Developmental Disabilities* **20**, 327–38.

Tomporowski, P., & Ellis, N.R. (1984). Effects of exercise on the physical fitness, intelligence and adaptive behavior of institutionalized mentally retarded adults. *Applied Research in Mental Retardation* **5**, 329–37.

Tomporowski, P., & Ellis, N. (1985). The effects of exercise on the health, intelligence, and adaptive behavior of institutionalized severely and profoundly mentally retarded adults. *Applied Research in Mental Retardation* **6**, 465–73.

Toogood, S., Bell, A., Jacques, H., Lewis, S., Sinclair, C., & Wright, L. (1994). Meeting the challenge in Clwyd: the Intensive Support Team. *British Journal of Learning Disabilities* **22**, 46–52.

Toogood, S., & Timlin, K. (1996). The functional assessment of challenging behaviour. *Journal of Applied Research in Intellectual Disabilities* **9**, 206–22.

Touchette, P.E., McDonald, R.F., & Langer, S.N. (1985). A scatter plot for identifying stimulus control of problem behavior. *Journal of Applied Behavior Analysis* **18**, 343–51.

Tracey, E.M., & Whittaker, J.K. (1990). The Social Network Map: assessing social support in clinical practice. *Families in Society* **71**, 461–70.

Tröster, H. (1994). Prevalence and functions of stereotyped behaviors in non-handicapped children in residential care. *Journal of Abnormal Child Psychology* **22**, 79–97.

Turk, J. (1998). Fragile X syndrome and attentional deficits. *Journal of Applied Research in Intellectual Disabilities* **11**, 175–91.

Turner, S., & Sloper, P. (1996). Behaviour problems among children with Down's syndrome: prevalence, persistence and parental appraisal. *Journal of Applied Research in Intellectual Disabilities* **9**, 129–44.

Ullman, L., & Krasner, L. (Eds.) (1965). *Case Studies in Behavior Modification.* New York: Holt, Rinehart and Winston.

Van Houten, R., Axelrod, S., Bailey, J.S. et al. (1988). The right to effective behavioral treatment. *Journal of Applied Behavior Analysis* **21**, 381–4.

Van Houten, R., Rolider, A., & Houlihan, M. (1992). Treatments of self-injury based on teaching compliance and/or brief physical restraint. In J.K. Luiselli, J.L. Matson & N.N. Singh (Eds.). *Self-Injurious Behavior: Analysis, Assessment and Treatment.* New York: Springer-Verlag.

Vaughn, B.J., Dunlap, G., Fox, L., Clarke, S., & Bucy, M. (1997). Parent–professional partnership in behavioral support: a case study of community-based intervention. *Journal of the Association For Persons With Severe Handicaps* **22**, 186–97.

Vaughn, B.J., & Horner, R.H. (1995). Effects of concrete versus verbal choice systems on problem behavior. *AAC: Augmentative and Alternative Communication* **11**, 89–92.

Vaughn, B.J., & Horner, R.H. (1997). Identifying instructional tasks that occasion problem behaviors and assessing the effects of student versus teacher choice among these tasks. *Journal of Applied Behavior Analysis* **30**, 299–312.

Verhoeven, W.M.A., & Tuinier, S. (1999). The psychopharmacology of challenging behaviours in developmental disabilities. In N. Bouras (Ed.). *Psychiatric and Behavioural Disorders in Developmental Disabilities and Mental Retardation*, pp. 295–318. Cambridge: Cambridge University Press.

Verhoeven, W.M.A., Tuinier, S., van den Berg, Y.W.M.M. et al. (1999). Stress self-injurious behaviour, hormonal and serotonergic parameters in mentally retarded subjects. *Pharmaco-psychiatry* **32**, 13–20.

Voeltz, L.M., & Evans, I.M. (1982). Behavioral interrelationships in child behavior therapy. *Behavioral Assessment* **4**, 131–65.

Vollmer, T.R. (1994). The concept of automatic reinforcement: implications for behavioral research in developmental disabilities. *Research in Developmental Disabilities* **15**, 187–207.

Vollmer, T.R., & Iwata, B.A. (1992). Differential reinforcement as treatment for behavior disorders: procedural and functional variations. *Research in Developmental Disabilities* **13**, 393–417.

Vollmer, T.R., Iwata, B.A., Zarcone, J.R., Smith, R.G., & Mazaleski, J.L. (1993). The role of attention in the treatment of attention-maintained self-injurious behavior: noncontingent reinforcement and differential reinforcement of other behavior. *Journal of Applied Behavior Analysis* **26**, 9–21.

Vollmer, T.R., Marcus, B.A., & LeBlanc, L. (1994). Treatment of self-injury and hand mouthing following inconclusive functional analysis. *Journal of Applied Behavior Analysis* **27**, 331–44.

Vollmer, T.R., Marcus, B.A., & Ringdahl, J.E. (1995a). Noncontingent escape as a treatment for self-injurious behavior maintained by negative reinforcement. *Journal of Applied Behavior Analysis* **28**, 15–26.

Vollmer, T.R., Marcus, B.A., Ringdahl, J.E., & Roane, H.S. (1995b). Progressing from brief assessments to extended experimental analyses in the evaluation of aberrant behavior. *Journal of Applied Behavior Analysis* **28**, 561–76.

Vollmer, T.R., Progar, P.R., Lalli, J.S. et al. (1998). Fixed time schedules attenuate extinction-induced phenomena in the treatment of severe aberrant behavior. *Journal of Applied Behavior Analysis* **31**, 529–42.

Vollmer, T.R., Ringdahl, J.E., Roane, H.S., & Marcus, B.A. (1997). Negative side effects of noncontingent reinforcement. *Journal of Applied Behavior Analysis* **30**, 161–4.

Vollmer, T.R., & Van Camp, C.M. (1998). Experimental designs to evaluate antecedent control. In J.K. Luiselli & M.J. Cameron (Eds.). *Antecedent Control: Innovative Approaches to Behavioral Support*, pp. 87–114. Baltimore: Paul H. Brookes.

Vollmer, T.R., & Vorndran, C.M. (1998). Assessment of self-injurious behavior maintained by access to self-restraint materials. *Journal of Applied Behavior Analysis* **31**, 647–50.

Wacker, D.P., Berg, W.K., Asmus, J.M., Harding, J.W., & Cooper, L.J. (1998). Experimental analysis of antecedent influences on challenging behaviors. In J.K. Luiselli & M.J. Cameron (Eds.). *Antecedent Control: Innovative Approaches to Behavioral Support*, pp. 67–86. Baltimore: Paul H. Brookes.

Wacker, D.P., Berg, W.K., Wiggins, B., Muldoon, M., & Cavanaugh, J. (1985). Evaluation of reinforcer preferences for profoundly handicapped students. *Journal of Applied Behavior Analysis* **18**, 173–8.

Wacker, D.P., Harding, J., Cooper, L.J. et al. (1996a). The effects of meal scheduling and quantity on problematic behavior. *Journal of Applied Behavior Analysis* **29**, 79–87.

Wacker, D., McMahon, C., Steege, M., Berg, W., Sasso, G., & Melloy, K. (1990a). Applications of sequential alternating treatments design. *Journal of Applied Behavior Analysis* **23**, 333–9.

Wacker, D.P., Peck, S.P., Derby, M., Berg, W., & Harding, J. (1996b). Developing long-term reciprocal interactions between parents and their young children with problematic behavior. In L.K. Koegel, R.L. Koegel & G. Dunlap (Eds.). *Positive Behavioral Support: Including People With Difficult Behavior in the Community*, pp. 51–80. Baltimore: Paul H. Brookes.

Wacker, D.P., Steege, J.N., Sasso, G. et al. (1990b). A component analysis of functional communication training across three topographies of severe behavior problems. *Journal of Applied Behavior Analysis* **23**, 417–29.

Wacker, D.P., Wiggins, B., Fowler, M. & Berg, W.K. (1988). Training students with profound or multiple handicaps to make requests via microswitches. *Journal of Applied Behavior Analysis* **21**, 331–43.

Wahler, R.G. (1975). Some structural aspects of deviant child behavior. *Journal of Applied Behavior Analysis* **8**, 27–42.

Wahler, R.G. (1980). The insular mother: her problems in parent–child treatment. *Journal of Applied Behavior Analysis* **13**, 207–17.

Wahler, R.G., & Fox, J.J. (1981). Setting events in applied behavior analysis: toward a conceptual and methodological expansion. *Journal of Applied Behavior Analysis* **14**, 327–38.

Wahler, R.G., & Graves, M.G. (1983). Setting events in social networks: ally or enemy in child behavior therapy? *Behavior Therapy* 14, 19–36.

Wallace, M.D., & Iwata, B.A. (1999). Effects of session duration on functional analysis outcomes. *Journal of Applied Behavior Analysis* **32**, 175–83.

Walters, A.S., Barrett, R.P., Feinstein, C., Mercurio, A., & Hole, W.T. (1990). A case report of naltrexone treatment of self-injury and social withdrawal in autism. *Journal of Autism and Developmental Disorders* **20**, 169–76.

Watts, M.J., Reed, T.R., & Hastings, R.P. (1997). Staff strategies and explanations for intervening with challenging behaviour: a replication in a community sample. *Journal of Intellectual Disability Research* **41**, 258–63.

Weiss, N.R. (1992). *The Application of Aversive Procedures to Individuals with Developmental Disabilities: A Call to Action*. Baltimore: Weiss.

Weiss, C.H. (1979). The many meanings of research utilization. *Public Administration Review* **39**, 426–31.

Weiss, C.H., & Bucuvalas, M. (1980). *Social Science Research and Decision Making*. New York: Columbia University Press.

Werry, J.S. (1998). Anxiolytics. In S. Reiss & M.G. Aman (Eds.). *Psychotropic Medication and*

*Developmental Disabilities: The International Consensus Handbook*, pp. 133–50. Ohio: Nisonger Center, Ohio State University.

Werry, J.S. (1999). Anxiolytics in MRDD. *Mental Retardation and Developmental Disabilities Research Reviews* **5**, 299–304.

Werry, J.S., Carlielle, J., & Fitzpatrick, J. (1983). Rhythmic motor activities (stereotypies) in children under five: etiology and prevalence. *Journal of the American Academy of Child Psychiatry* **22**, 329–36.

Westlake, C.R., & Kaiser, A.P. (1991). Early childhood services for children with severe disabilities: research, values, policy and practice. In L.H. Meyer, C.A. Peck, & L. Brown (Eds.). *Critical Issues in the Lives of People with Severe Disabilities.* Baltimore: Paul H. Brookes.

Whitaker, S. (1996). A review of DRO: the influence of the degree of intellectual disability and the frequency of the target behaviour. *Journal of Applied Research in Intellectual Disabilities* **9**, 61–79.

Whitman, T.L. (1990). Self-regulation and mental retardation. *American Journal on Mental Retardation* **94**, 347–62.

Wieseler, N.A., Hanson, R.H., Chamberlain, T.P., & Thompson, T. (1985). Functional taxonomy of stereotypic and self-injurious behavior. *Mental Retardation* **23**, 230–4.

Wieseler, N.A., Hanson, R.H., & Nord, G. (1995). Investigation of mortality and morbidity associated with severe self-injurious behavior. *American Journal of Mental Retardation* **100**, 1–5.

Willems, E.P. (1974). Behavioral technology and behavioral ecology. *Journal of Applied Behavior Analysis* **7**, 151–65.

Willemsen-Swinkles, S.H.N., Buitelaar, J.K., Nijhof, G.J., & van Engeland, H. (1995). Failure of naltrexone hydrochloride to reduce self-injurious and autistic behavior in mentally retarded adults. *Archives of General Psychiatry* **52**, 766–73.

Williams, D.E., Kirkpatrick-Sanchez, S., & Iwata, B.A. (1993). A comparison of shock intensity in the treatment of longstanding and severe self-injurious behavior. *Research in Developmental Disabilities* **14**, 207–19.

Williams, L., Ellis, C.R., Ickowicz, A., Singh, N.N., & Singh, Y.N. (1993). Pharmacotherapy of aggressive behavior in individuals with mental retardation and mental illness. *Journal of Developmental and Physical Disabilities* **5**, 87–94.

Windahl, S.I. (1988). Self-injurious behavior in a time perspective. *8th Congress of the International Association for the Scientific Study of Mental Deficiency*, Dublin.

Windsor, J., Piche, L.M., & Locke, P.A. (1994). Preference testing: a comparison of two presentation methods. *Research in Developmental Disabilities* **15**, 439–55.

Winnett, R.A., & Winkler, R.C. (1972). Current behavior modification in the classroom: be still, be quiet, be docile. *Journal of Applied Behavior Analysis* **5**, 499–504.

Winterling, V., Dunlap, G., & O'Neill, R.E. (1987). The influence of task variation on the aberrant behaviors of autistic students. *Education and Treatment of Children* **10**, 105–19.

Wise, R.A. (1982). Neuroleptics and operant behavior: the ahedonia hypothesis. *Behavioral and Brain Sciences* **5**, 39–53.

Wolery, M., & Winterling, V. (1997). Curricular approaches to controlling severe behavior problems. In N.N. Singh (Ed.). *Prevention and Treatment of Severe Behavior Problems: Models and Methods in Developmental Disabilities*, pp. 87–120. Pacific Grove: Brooks/Cole.

Wolf, M.M. (1978). Social validity: the case for subjective measurement, or how applied behavior analysis is finding its heart. *Journal of Applied Behavior Analysis* **11**, 203–14.

Wolf, M.M., Risley, T.R., & Mees, H.L. (1964). Application of operant conditioning procedures to the behavior problems of an autistic child. *Behaviour Research and Therapy* **1**, 305–12.

Wolfensberger, W. (1972). *The Principle of Normalization in Human Services.* Toronto: National Institute on Mental Retardation.

Wolfensberger, W. (1975). *The Origin and Nature of Our Institutional Models.* Human Policy Press: Syracuse.

Young, I., Sigafoos, J., Suttie, J., Ashman, A., & Grevell, P. (1998). Deinstitutionalisation of persons with intellectual disabilities: a review of Australian studies. *Journal of Intellectual and Developmental Disabilities* **23**, 155–70.

Zarcone, J.R., Iwata, B.A., Smith, R.G., Mazaleski, J.L., & Lerman, D.C. (1994). Reemergence and extinction of self-injurious escape behavior during stimulus (instructional) fading. *Journal of Applied Behavior Analysis* **27**, 307–16.

Zarcone, J.R., Iwata, B.A., Vollmer, T.R., Jagtiani, S., Smith, R.G., & Mazaleski, J.L. (1993). Extinction of self-injurious escape behavior with and without instructional fading. *Journal of Applied Behavior Analysis* **26**, 353–60.

Zarcone, J.R., Rodgers, T.A., Iwata, B.A., Rourke, D.A., & Dorsey, M.F. (1991). Reliability analysis of the Motivation Assessment Scale: a failure to replicate. *Research in Developmental Disabilities* **12**, 349–60.

Zarkowska, E., & Clements, J. (1994). *Severe Problem Behaviour: The STAR Approach.* London: Chapman & Hall.

Zeigob, L., Klukas, N., & Junginger, J. (1978). Reactivity of self-monitoring procedures with retarded adolescents. *American Journal of Mental Deficiency* **83**, 156–63.

Zingarelli, G., Ellman, G., Hom, A., Wymore, M., Heidorn, S., & Chicz-DeMet, A. (1992). Clinical effects of naltrexone on autistic behavior. *American Journal on Mental Retardation* **97**, 57–63.

# Index

Note: *c.b.s* = *challenging behaviours*; page numbers in bold denote illustrations; those in italics, tables.